Corporate Governance
Best Practices

Also by Frederick D. Lipman:

Valuing Your Business: Strategies to Maximize the Sale Price
Audit Committees
The Complete Guide to Employee Stock Options
The Complete Guide to Valuing and Selling Your Business
The Complete Going Public Handbook
Financing Your Business with Venture Capital
How Much Is Your Business Worth?
Going Public
Venture Capital and Junk Bond Financing

CORPORATE GOVERNANCE BEST PRACTICES

Strategies for Public, Private, and
Not-for-Profit Organizations

FREDERICK D. LIPMAN

with

L. KEITH LIPMAN
on
Information Technology

WILEY

John Wiley & Sons, Inc.

For general information on our other products and services, or technical support, please
contact our Customer Care Department within the United States at 800-762-2974, outside
the United States at 317-572-3993 or fax 317-572-4002.

Wiley also publishes its books in a variety of electronic formats. Some content that
appears in print may not be available in electronic books.

For more information about Wiley products, visit our Web site at www.wiley.com.

Library of Congress Cataloging in Publication Data:

Lipman, Frederick D.
    Corporate governance best practices : strategies for public, private and not-for-profit
organizations / Frederick Lipman, L. Keith Lipman.
        p.   cm.
    Includes index.
    ISBN-13: 978-0-470-04379-0 (cloth)
    ISBN-10: 0-470-04379-2 (cloth)
    1. Corporate governance.   I. Lipman, L. Keith, 1967–   II. Title.
HD2741.L5323 2006
658.4—dc22

2006008675

Printed in the United States of America

10 9 8 7 6 5 4 3 2 1

To Gail and Kimberly

Contents

PART III

THE PUBLIC COMPANY AUDIT COMMITTEE   135

PART IV

PRIVATE AND NOT-FOR-PROFIT ORGANIZATIONS   213

PART V

APPENDIXES   235

Preface

This book is intended to be a practical guide to best corporate governance practices for public, private (including family-owned businesses), and nonprofit organizations, using concrete real-life examples. Good corporate governance is important to private companies that wish to attract bank and other institutional financing and equity investors. Private family-owned businesses need good corporate governance to establish dispute resolution mechanisms to prevent family quarrels from harming the business, particularly after the founder has died or retired. Not-for-profit organizations need to practice good corporate governance in order to assure their contributors that their gifts will be well spent.

The Sarbanes-Oxley Act of 2002 and accompanying Securities and Exchange Commission (SEC) and listing rules legally mandate minimum corporate governance practices for most public companies. This book will be helpful to boards of directors and management of public companies that want to engage in the best practices, not just minimum legal requirements. Public companies that engage in best practices will generally be more attractive to investors and will receive higher corporate governance ratings.

This book proceeds on the assumption that a "best practice" is one in which the benefits to the organization substantially exceed the cost of implementation. This book discusses current best practices, with the understanding that best practices tend to evolve over time. What is a best practice today may not be a best practice in the future. Although the book is addressed primarily to U.S.-based organizations, the general principles are applicable to foreign entities as well, although modifications must be made to account for legal and cultural differences.

Part I of this book (Chapters 1 through 8) describes best practices and provides practical guidance to the boards of directors and management of all organizations, whether public, private, or not-for-profit. Chapter 1 describes the benefits to all organizations of good corporate governance, how to make the benefits exceed the cost, and why exclusive reliance on outside auditors does not work. The assumption that only public companies need to follow best practices is disputed in Chapter 1.

Chapter 2 summarizes best practices in general for all organizations and discusses internal investigations and the fiduciary duties of directors, using concrete examples. Chapter 3 deals with the best practices to monitor risk in different organizational departments, such as human resources, sales, purchasing, insurance, tax, legal, and corporate development, whether these services are provided in-house or are outsourced. Chapter 4 focuses on the important issue of corporate culture and provides examples of best practices to monitor and change the corporate culture. Chapter 5 discusses the internal audit function, which is extremely important to good corporate governance, and suggests best practices for internal audit. Chapters 6 and 7 describe best practices for the compensation and other committees.

The formation and operation of independent director committees (also called special committees) is covered by Chapter 8.

Part II of this book (Chapters 9 and 10) covers best corporate governance practices for information technology (IT) content and security. Part II is also applicable to all organizations, since all organizations use IT to some degree. Chapter 9 deals with IT content best practices, and Chapter 10 deals with IT security best practices.

Part III of this book (Chapters 11 through 16) focuses on the particular corporate governance issues of public company audit committees. Chapter 11 deals with the qualifications for a public company audit committee. Chapter 12 discusses the personal liability of audit committee members. The minimum responsibility and other functions of public company audit committees are covered in Chapters 13 and 14.

Chapter 15 discusses 30 issues of importance to public company audit committees and provides best practice advice on each issue. Specific warning events to the audit committee are described (such as insider stock sales, a significant short position in the stock, a chief executive officer with an extravagant lifestyle), which should trigger more intensive audits. Chapter 16 deals with the important topic of when an auditor can be considered "independent" and focuses on the serious consequences to public companies whose auditors flunk the independence test.

Not-for-profit and private companies should review carefully the best practices for public companies discussed in Part III; they may wish to adopt many of these same practices.

Part IV of this book (Chapters 17 and 18) deals with the special issues of nonprofit and private organizations (including family-owned businesses), many of which wish to adopt good corporate governance but do not wish to be bound by all of the costly procedures applicable to public companies.

Part V of this book contains Appendixes A through D, which include a short summary of the Sarbanes-Oxley Act of 2002 (Appendix A), a Risk Assessment Chart describing a risk rating system for financial statement accounts (Appendix B), an interesting article, entitled "Uncooking the Books: How Three Unlikely Sleuths Discovered Fraud at WorldCom" on how the internal auditor discovered the WorldCom fraud (Appendix C), and a few suggested corporate governance Web site resources (Appendix D).

Acknowledgments

The authors wish to acknowledge the assistance of these attorneys at Blank Rome LLP in preparing this book: Jane Storero, Esq., Jeffrey Myers, Esq., Jennifer Hale Eagland, Esq., Jonathan Goldstein, Esq., Kevin Cronin, Esq., Yelena Barychev, Esq., Jay Reynolds, Esq., and Stephen Luongo, Esq. We would also like to acknowledge the contributions of Alexander D. Bono, Esq., former partner of Blank Rome LLP and currently General Counsel of Commerce Bancorp, Inc., particularly to Chapter 12. Kara Popovich, a Blank Rome LLP paralegal, was kind enough to proofread different versions of the manuscript.

Barbara Helverson, my secretary, showed great patience in assisting me in typing, retyping, and further retyping the manuscript for this book.

Part I

Best Practices for All Organizations

Chapter 1

Why Is Corporate Governance Important?

Good corporate governance helps to prevent corporate scandals, fraud, and potential civil and criminal liability of the organization. It is also good business. A good corporate governance image enhances the reputation of the organization and makes it more attractive to customers, investors, suppliers and, in the case of nonprofit organizations, contributors.

There is some evidence that good corporate governance produces direct economic benefit to the organization. One study, conducted at Georgia State University and published in December 2004, found that public companies with independent boards of directors have higher returns on equity, higher profit margins, larger dividend yields, and larger stock repurchases.[1] This study was consistent with another study of 250 companies by the MIT Sloan School of Management which concluded that, on average, businesses with superior information technology (IT) governance practices generate 25 percent greater profits than firms with poor governance, given the same strategic objectives.[2]

Although the Sarbanes-Oxley Act of 2002 (summarized in Appendix A) applies almost exclusively to publicly held companies, the corporate scandals that gave rise to that legislation have increased pressure on all organizations (including family-owned businesses and not-for-profit organizations) to have better corporate governance. Private and not-for-profit organizations may feel pressure from lenders, insurance underwriters, regulators, venture capitalists, vendors, customers, and contributors to be Sarbanes-Oxley compliant. In addition, some courts and state legislatures may by analogy apply the enhanced corporate governance practices developed under Sarbanes-Oxley to private and not-for-profit organizations. Finally, a few provisions of Sarbanes-Oxley do affect private and not-for-profit organizations, such as the provisions relating to criminal liability for document destruction and for retaliation against whistleblowers.

Nonprofit organizations are not immune from scandal. Even before there was an Enron, there was the scandalous bankruptcy of AHERF (the Allegheny Health, Education and Research Foundation), a nonprofit organization. The scandals involving The Nature Conservancy, the United Way of the National Capital Area, and PipeVine, Inc., attest to the need for not-for-profit organizations to have at least the perception of good corporate governance. On August 16, 2005, it was reported in *The Wall Street Journal* that Cornell University Medical School agreed to pay $4.4 million in connection with fraudulent U.S. Government claims that allegedly occurred as a result of Cornell's failure to pay attention to a whistleblower who was a member of the Cornell faculty.

3

Private companies that intend to seek capital from financial institutions and institutional investors should also be sensitive to their corporate governance image, since this image is an important factor in the ultimate decision to provide capital to the organization. Family-owned private companies benefit from good corporate governance by avoiding the devastating effects of sibling rivalry and expensive litigation between family members who have different views concerning the business.

IS PERCEPTION IMPORTANT?

The *perception* of good corporate governance is an important ingredient of the image of an organization, whether public, private, or nonprofit.

For example, when The Nature Conservancy, a not-for-profit organization, was perceived to have poor corporate governance, the public contributions to this organization were substantially reduced[3] (see Chapter 18). Private, including family-owned, companies that have a poor reputation for corporate governance are less likely to be welcomed at financial institutions and will appear less attractive to venture capitalists and private equity funds. Some investment and private equity funds will not purchase the securities of public companies that have low corporate governance ratings.

A perception of unethical conduct by an organization can be very costly in legal cases. For example, a Texas jury rendered a $253 million verdict against Merck & Co. in August 2005 in the first Vioxx case. A factor in the jury verdict was an in-house training game for Vioxx sales representatives called "Dodge Ball." The plaintiff's attorney was able to create the impression that this was a game that encouraged Merck sales representatives to dodge questions from doctors about the safety of Vioxx, despite the denials by Merck's witness.[4]

PRACTICAL CORPORATE GOVERNANCE

Practical corporate governance is the process of developing cost-efficient corporate governance structures for an organization and instituting "best practices" by weighing costs against benefits. This is accomplished by analyzing specific risks of the organization, making cost-benefit judgments, and utilizing the lessons of past corporate scandals. It rejects the mindless "check-the box" mentality of corporate governance rating groups and some major accounting firms. Rather, the focus is on specific risk analysis, a cost-benefit analysis, and learning from the past.

The implementation of Section 404 of the Sarbanes-Oxley Act of 2002 is a classic example of "impractical" corporate governance. Section 404 requires (among other things) that independent auditors attest to the internal controls of public companies. This requirement imposed a huge cost burden on public companies because it spawned an expensive "check-the-box" mentality among major auditing firms. A Securities and Exchange Commission (SEC) commissioner reported that one auditing firm found 60,000 "key" internal controls at a single company![5]

As initially interpreted, Section 404 was not tailored to specific organizational risks and did not require a cost-benefit analysis. Public companies were forced to incur inordinate expense in complying with Section 404 and had to divert their internal audit efforts into compliance with mind-numbing documentation requirements that were intended to prevent low-level management frauds, even though the major frauds that forced the adoption of this requirement were the result of top management manipulations. Moreover, Section 404 created a monopoly for major auditing firms since only independent auditors could attest to the internal controls. This tie-in of auditing and attestation services permitted monopoly pricing by major auditing firms; a public company was in effect forced to change independent auditors in order to obtain competition in the pricing of the Section 404 attestation services, and many companies were reluctant to do so.

In May 2005 (and again in November 2005), the SEC and the Public Company Accounting Oversight Board (PCAOB), to their credit, recognized some of the problems engendered by their own rules and permitted a top-down, risk-based approach to internal controls, rejecting the "check-the-box" analysis.[6] As a result of this regrettable episode, corporate governance unfortunately received an undeserved bad reputation as being synonymous with huge costs and little corporate benefit.

IS CORPORATE GOVERNANCE COSTLY?

Good corporate governance can be performed in a cost-efficient manner by focusing efforts on the significant risks facing the organization rather than attempting to cover any possible theoretical risk, and by installing the best cost-efficient practices within the organization. Resources must be concentrated in areas that have the greatest potential benefit, such as improving the corporate culture and establishing an effective internal audit function (see Chapters 4 and 5). Creating an ethical, law-abiding culture provides the greatest benefit for the organization compared to the relatively minimal cost of establishing such a culture. The benefits of good corporate governance, by avoiding governmental investigations, lawsuits, and damage to the reputation to the organization, should significantly outweigh the cost of good corporate governance.

The benefits of good corporate governance are longer term, whereas the costs of good corporate governance are incurred in the short term. Executives who are focused on short-term results may see only the costs and not the benefits. Consequently, management tends to be skeptical of incurring these costs and tends to do no more than is legally required.

Boards of directors must be sensitive to management's skepticism of good corporate governance. Incentives must be provided to management for accomplishing specific corporate governance goals. These goals should include, at a minimum, the creation of an ethical, law- abiding corporate culture and the establishment of an effective internal audit function that monitors management on financial issues as well as operational issues. If the board's compensation incentives to top management are focused solely on "hitting the numbers," the board must share the blame with management for any subsequent scandals involving cooking the books.

Directors should also weigh the costs of good corporate governance against their own personal liability. In January 2005, 10 former directors of WorldCom agreed to contribute $18 million of their personal funds, which amounted to 20 percent of their combined net worth, as part of a $54 million settlement with the bankrupt corporation's shareholders.[7] Similarly, 10 former Enron directors agreed to pay $13 million of their own funds, roughly 10 percent of their profits from selling Enron stock, toward the total $168 million settlement of shareholder claims.[8] In 2004, a former chairman of Global Crossing personally contributed $30 million to a securities/ERISA (Employee Retirement Income Security Act) class action settlement.[9]

CAN YOU RELY ON THE OUTSIDE AUDITOR?

Many audit committees rely almost exclusively on the outside auditor in performing their task of monitoring management and providing good corporate governance. Unfortunately, there is a serious disconnect between what directors believe the outside auditor is responsible for and what the outside auditor believes. Given the large number of corporate scandals that have occurred at organizations audited by a "Big Four" auditor, it is difficult to understand how any board of directors can place exclusive reliance on its auditor.

Excerpts from the statement of Mel Dick, the engagement partner responsible for Arthur Andersen's audit of WorldCom, to the Committee on Financial Services of the U.S. House of Representatives, follow. These excerpts should cause all boards of directors and their audit committees to reexamine their exclusive reliance on the outside auditor.

Chairman Oxley, Congressman LaFalce, Members of the Committee:

"I am Mel Dick. I am a graduate of the University of South Dakota. Upon graduation in 1975, I joined Arthur Andersen as a staff auditor. I was a partner at Andersen until I left Andersen on June 1 of this year. I have spent the majority of my career working with diverse telecommunications companies.

The Chairman's letter of invitation, faxed to my attorney on the night of July 3, states:—This hearing will focus on the recent announcement that WorldCom overstated profits and understated liabilities in the amount of $3.9 billion.

The Chairman's letter refers to the disclosure by WorldCom on June 25 that approximately $3.1 billion in expenses were improperly booked as capital expenditures in 2001 and an additional $797 million of expenses were improperly booked as capital expenditures in first quarter of 2002. The newspaper reports that I have read allege that senior financial management at WorldCom improperly transferred line costs expenses to capital accounts in the company's accounting records.

Let me state clearly and without any qualification that, prior to June 21, 2002, when Andersen was first contacted about this matter, neither I, nor to my knowledge, any member of the Andersen team had any inkling that these transfers had been made.

In fact, in connection with our quarterly reviews for March 31, June 30 and September 30, 2001, our year end audit at December 31, 2001 and our quarterly review for March 30, 2002, the Andersen audit team specifically asked WorldCom senior financial management whether there were any significant top side entries. On each occasion, management represented to Andersen that there were no such entries.

The fundamental premise of financial reporting is that the financial statements of a company—in this case WorldCom—are the responsibility of the company's management, not its outside auditors. WorldCom management is responsible for managing its business, supervising its operational and accounting personnel, and preparing accurate financial statements. It is the responsibility of management to keep track of capital projects and expenditures under its supervision. The role of an outside auditor is to review the financial statements to determine if they are prepared in accordance with Generally Accepted Accounting Principles and to conduct its audit in accordance with Generally Accepted Auditing Standards, which require that auditors plan and perform the audit to obtain reasonable assurance about whether the financial statements are free of material misstatement. [Emphasis added.]

Our audit and our reviews of WorldCom were performed by experienced audit professionals. Our audit plan was the product of a deliberative and diligent evaluation of a global telecommunications company with over $100 billion in assets.

As with any audit, we planned our audit of WorldCom in general reliance on the honesty and integrity of management of the company. One of the key elements of evidence all auditors rely upon are management's representations. As all auditors do, we also tested and, based on our tests, concluded that we could rely on the company's management processes and internal controls, including the internal audit function. We relied on the results of our testing and the effectiveness of these systems in planning and performing our audit. At the same time, we approached our work with a degree of professional skepticism, alert for potential misapplication of accounting principles. [Emphasis added.]

Additionally, we performed numerous analytical procedures of the various financial statement line items, including line costs, revenues, and plant and service in order to determine if there were any significant variations that required additional work. We also utilized sophisticated auditing software to study WorldCom's financial statement line items, which did not trigger any indication that there was a need for additional work.

In performing our work, we relied on the integrity and professionalism of WorldCom's senior management, including Scott Sullivan, WorldCom CFO and David Myers, WorldCom Controller, and their staff. [Emphasis added.]

If the reports are true that Mr. Sullivan and others at WorldCom improperly transferred line cost expenses to capital accounts so as to misstate the company's actual performance, I am deeply troubled by this conduct. In addition, if reports are true that WorldCom's internal auditors discovered these entries, I would be very interested to know how and when they discovered these entries.

I do not know the specifics of what Mr. Sullivan did or directed others at WorldCom to do, and I have not had the opportunity to review the entries that are at issue here. I understand that Mr. Sullivan has acknowledged that he never told Andersen about the accounting he is said to have employed.

At this point, however, while I can explain our general approach to the WorldCom audit and explain generally the work that we did, I do not have enough information to comment on the entries that WorldCom senior financial management are said to have made, or how they were hidden from the Andersen auditors . . ."[10]

Although the Auditing Standards Board has, since WorldCom, enhanced the duties of the auditor to detect fraud in Statement of Accounting Standards (SAS) No. 99 (effective for audits beginning after December 15, 2002), it is not clear that auditors no longer have the right to assume that management is honest. SAS No. 99 does state in Paragraph .13:

> The auditor should conduct the engagement with a mindset that recognizes the possibility that a material misstatement due to fraud could be present, regardless of any past experience with the entity and regardless of the auditor's belief about management's honesty and integrity. Furthermore, professional skepticism requires an ongoing questioning of whether the information and evidence obtained suggests that a material misstatement due to fraud has occurred. In exercising professional skepticism in gathering and evaluating evidence, the auditor should not be satisfied with less-than-persuasive evidence because of a belief that management is honest.[11]

The quoted language from SAS No. 99 does not specifically state that the auditor has no right to assume that management is honest. While the quoted language does not completely repudiate the position stated by Mel Dick, it is helpful in enhancing the responsibilities of the auditors to detect fraud.

ENDNOTES

1. Lawrence D. Brown and Marcus L. Caylor, "Corporate Governance and Firm Performance," Georgia State University, December 7, 2004, http://papers.ssrn.com/sol3/papers.cfm?abstract_id=586423.
2. Weill, *IT Governance: How Top Performers Manage IT Decision Rights for Superior Results.* (Boston: Harvard Business School Press, 2004).
3. Stephens et al., "Senators Question Conservancy's Practices," *Washington Post*, June 8, 2005.
4. Berenson, "Some Pointed Questioning at the Vioxx Trial in Texas," *New York Times*, July 19, 2005.
5. Speech by SEC Commissioner Paul Atkins before the Securities Regulation Institute in San Diego, California, January 19, 2006, www.sec.gov/news/speech/spch011906psa.htm.
6. "Commission Statement on Implementation of Internal Control Reporting Requirements," May 16, 2005, www.sec.gov/news/press/2005-74.htm, "Policy Statement Regarding Implementation of Auditing Standard No. 2, an Audit of Internal Control over Financial Reporting Performed in Conjunction with an Audit of Financial Statements," Public Company Accounting Oversight Board, May 16, 2005, PCAOB Re. No. 2005-009, May 16, 2005.
7. "WorldCom Execs to Pay $18 million," CBSNews.com, January 7, 2005, www.cbsnews.com/stories/2005/01/07/national/main665522.shtml?CMP=ILC-SearchStories.
8. White, "Former Directors Agree to Settle Class Actions," *Washington Post,* January 8, 2005.
9. Morgenson, "Global Crossing Settles for $325 Million," New York Times.com, March 20, 2004, http://select.nytimes.com/gst/abstract.html?res=F20D14FA3A550C738EDD AA0894DC404482.
10. Remarks of Melvin Dick, United States House of Representatives, Committee on Financial Services, July 8, 2002, financial services.house.gov/media/pdf/070802md.pdf.
11. American Institute of Certified Public Accountants, "Statement on Auditing Standards No. 99: Considerations of Fraud in a Financial Statement Audit," (AICPA, 2002).

Chapter 2

Summary of Major Corporate Governance Principles and Best Practices

This chapter summarizes overall minimum corporate governance principles and best practices applicable to all organizations (whether public, private, or not-for-profit). These best practices are divided into:

- Structure of the board of directors
- Operation of the board of directors
- Other corporate governance practices

Each best practice is followed by a short discussion of the reason for the best practice. Following the best practices is a discussion of how boards should conduct internal investigations and the legal duties of directors, including court decisions that gave rise to the best practices. Chapter 3 discusses best practices applicable to specific departments or units of an organization.

When reviewing these summaries, readers should understand that certain organizations (such as public companies) may have greater obligations.[1]

STRUCTURE OF THE BOARD OF DIRECTORS

BEST PRACTICE

Governing bodies of all organizations (whether designated as boards of directors, boards of trustees or otherwise, hereafter called "boards of directors") should include completely independent directors and these directors should preferably constitute a majority of all directors, with the possible exception of privately held companies.

Independent directors should be included on the boards of directors of private companies and not-for-profit organizations. For private companies (especially family-owned businesses), independent directors can assist in resolving disputes involving management or family members; can assist the company in its business operations by providing dispassionate advice; and through selection of the independent auditor, can create credibility for the company's financial statements in the minds of banks, other financial institutions, and investors.

Not-for-profit organizations need independent directors to assist in their fundraising activities and to create public credibility.

Although independent directors should constitute a majority of the directors of a not-for-profit organization, it is not necessary to have a majority of independent directors for a private company. Public companies (other than controlled public companies) are generally required to have a majority of independent directors by stock market listing rules.

Small private companies (especially start-ups) may not be able to attract independent directors because of liability concerns. In such event, a small private company should establish a board of advisors, separate from its board of directors, which would include independent directors. The charter of the board of advisors should make it clear that it does not possess any of the powers or authority of the board of directors. The best practices to be described with regard to using independent directors on board committees do not apply to small private companies who are unable to attract independent directors to their board. Private companies and not-for-profit organizations are discussed in greater detail in Chapters 17 and 18, respectively.

BEST PRACTICE

Select independent directors who are willing and able to devote the necessary time to their director duties and preferably persons who have competencies that assist the organization and that complement the competencies of other directors.

Independent directors who sit on too many boards may not have the necessary time to devote to the organization. This should be frankly discussed with any potential director candidate. An assessment should also be made as to the potential candidate's background to determine if that background can assist the organization and complement the competencies of other directors. A diversity of backgrounds is generally helpful to the organization.

BEST PRACTICE

Directors must have their own information pipeline into the company, separate from the information provided to them by management and the independent auditors, in order to fulfill their state law fiduciary duties. An internal auditor reporting to the board of directors or its audit committee can fulfill this function.

Many of the corporate scandals occurred because the board of directors relied solely on the management and the independent auditors for their information. In order to fulfill a director's fiduciary duty to monitor management, the director must have reliable and independent sources of information. Directors cannot fulfill their duty to monitor management if all of their information comes from management. The corporate scandals indicate that independent auditors can be easily fooled by management and, therefore, cannot be the exclusive source of independent information to the board of directors. An internal auditor can assist the board of directors in obtaining the reliable and independent information they need in order to fulfill their fiduciary duties. If the organization cannot afford a full-time internal auditor, internal auditing services may be outsourced.

BEST PRACTICE

Except in the case of a private company unless there is a lead or presiding director, the chairman of the board should be an independent director and independent directors should meet separately from management directors at least once a year. If the chairman of the board is not an independent director, a lead or presiding director who is independent should be appointed.

The chairman of the board is an important position and can establish the agenda for board meetings and the nature of board discussion. Unless there is a lead or presiding director, permitting the chief executive officer (CEO) to also be the chairman of the board is a bad practice (except in private companies), since it permits the CEO to have too much power over the board of directors and undermines the board's fiduciary duty to monitor management. In situations in which the CEO or another management person is also the chairman of the board, a lead or presiding independent director should be appointed. A Spencer Stuart survey of Standard & Poor 500 companies in mid-2005 indicated that 96 percent of companies with combined chairman and CEO position had a lead or presiding director.[2]

A lead or presiding director generally advises on board meeting schedules and agendas, chairs executive sessions of the board, oversees what information is provided to the board, leads the board in emergency situations, and generally serves as an intermediary between the board and management. Lead directors generally play a more influential and strategic role than presiding directors.[3]

Separate meetings of independent directors, at least yearly, permit the independent directors to have a free and frank discussion concerning management and the organization.

BEST PRACTICE

Directors of all organizations must establish audit committees, compensation committees, and, in appropriate cases, nominating/corporate governance committees composed entirely of independent directors or, alternatively, must perform the duties of such committees acting through the whole board of directors, which should consist of a majority of completely independent directors. All important committees of the board of directors should evaluate their own activities annually.

There are many duties imposed on the board of directors of any organization, and it may be preferable to divide these duties among committees of directors. These duties include selecting and monitoring the independent auditor, establishing compensation for at least the top management of the organization, having a committee that can nominate new directors, and monitoring the corporate governance of the organization in order to establish an ethical, law-abiding culture that is necessary to avoid criminal prosecution as well as civil lawsuits (see Chapter 4). Private companies may choose not to have a nominating committee, but such a committee should be required for not-for-profit and public companies.

If the board chooses to perform these functions as a whole, it may also do so. However, in complex organization, this can be very time consuming, and it is generally preferable to use a committee structure.

Annual self-evaluation of the functions of committees of the board is a best practice and is required by New York Stock Exchange rules for audit and compensation committees.

BEST PRACTICE

The audit committee must include persons who have the ability and willingness to fully understand the organization's accounting, and they must, at a minimum, hire and determine the compensation of the independent auditor, preapprove all auditing and nonauditing services performed by the independent auditor, and assure themselves of the independence of the auditing firm. The audit committee is responsible for overseeing the organization's financial reporting process and should understand and be familiar with the organization's system of internal controls. For additional responsibilities of public company audit committees, see Chapters 11 through 16.

The audit committee of the board of directors is probably the most important board committee since it is responsible for supervising the organization's relationships with its outside auditors and overseeing the organization's financial reporting process, including reviewing the financial statements of the organization. The audit committee should be familiar with the organization's internal controls over financial reporting. The audit committee must consist of persons who have both the ability and the willingness to understand complex accounting concepts. To maintain the integrity of the audit process, the audit committee must hire and determine the compensation of the independent auditor and preapprove all auditing and nonaudit services provided by the auditor.

Some small private companies and certain not-for-profit organizations may not wish to expend the funds necessary to obtain an independent audit of their financial statements, and may only obtain so-called compilation or review reports from an auditor. This is not a good corporate governance practice. It is difficult for directors to fulfill their fiduciary duties to monitor management without audited financial statements.

Audited financial statements are essential for not-for-profit organizations that solicit contributions from the public and want to assure their potential donors that their money will be well spent.

If audited financial statements are obtained, the audit committee must determine the independence of the auditing firm. If a private company with audited financial statements is sold, it is typical for the buyer to require a representation of the independence of the auditing firm.

Best practices for public company audit committees are contained in Chapters 11 through 16. Audit committees of not-for-profit organizations and private companies should review these best practices and follow them to the extent feasible. Best practices for audit committees of not-for-profit organizations are discussed in more detail in Chapter 18.

BEST PRACTICE

All organizations (with the possible exception of small private companies) should have an internal auditor, hired and compensated by the audit committee of the board of directors and reporting directly to the board of directors. The primary responsibility of the internal auditor should be to assist the board of directors to perform its fiduciary duty to monitor management. Other operational duties may be assigned to the internal auditor by management, but these other duties should not interfere with the primary responsibility of the internal auditor. Internal auditing services may be outsourced.

The internal auditor should primarily function as the eyes and ears of the board of directors and particularly its audit and compensation committees. To make it clear to the internal auditor that he or she owes primary responsibility to the board of directors and its committees, the internal auditor should be hired by the audit committee and his or her compensation determined by the audit committee. Although internal auditors are also typically assigned operational functions by management, the audit committee must make certain that these management assigned functions do not interfere with the primary duties of the internal auditor. The audit committee should also be responsible to be certain that there is adequate funding for the internal audit function. This was one of the failures of the WorldCom audit committee (see Chapter 5).

BEST PRACTICE

The compensation committee must, at a minimum, establish the compensation of the top officers of the organization, use the internal auditor to verify that the compensation given to the top officers is consistent with what the committee authorized, and, either alone or together with a separate nominating/corporate governance committee, must determine that the compensation policies of the organization are consistent with an ethical, law-abiding culture (see Chapter 6).

The compensation committee of an organization must obtain accurate information in order to set the compensation of its top officers. According to news reports, the Tyco compensation committee never received such information. As a result, massive compensation payments were made to its top officers without proper authorization.

BEST PRACTICE

Boards of directors should be kept to a reasonable size, since large boards of directors tend to be ineffective.

As a rule of thumb, it is preferable to have not less than 4 and not more than 10 persons on the board of directors. Too many directors can make the board unwieldy and make it difficult to operate. In general, smaller is better.

Some not-for-profit organizations opt for very large boards of directors in order to increase the number of potential donors to the organization. If a not-for-profit maintains a large board of directors for this reason, all important decisions should be made by a small executive committee of the board and ultimately ratified by the full board. The executive committee would, in effect, operate as the real board of directors.

BEST PRACTICE

An organization should obtain a fairness opinion from a qualified and independent third party in the event of any material transaction involving a potential conflict of interest, such as an insider loan, purchase or sale, or a material merger or acquisition. Investment bankers and other qualified third parties rendering fairness opinions should not receive a percentage of the transaction consideration for rendering the fairness opinion.

Before approving a material transaction involving a potential conflict of interest, the board should obtain a fairness opinion from a qualified and independent third party, such as an investment banker. The fairness opinion will serve to protect the board from criticism and potential legal liability from other constituents or stakeholders of the organization, such as shareholders in the case of a public or private company or contributors in the case of a not-for-profit organization that solicits public contributions.

Many public companies use investment bankers to render fairness opinions who are entitled, as their sole compensation, to a percentage of the transaction consideration if the transaction is consummated. This practice has been properly criticized as creating a conflict of interest. Contracts for contingent compensation provide an unreasonable incentive to the investment banker to give the fairness opinion or be entitled to no compensation. At least one court in Delaware has indicated that such an arrangement may destroy the independence of the investment banker.[4]

BEST PRACTICE FOR PUBLIC COMPANIES

Public companies should establish an effective procedure for shareholders to communicate with the board or one of its committees, such as the nominating/corporate governance committee.

The Business Roundtable has recommended that the board of a public company should provide a vehicle for shareholder communication directly with the board so that it can be apprised of shareholder concerns.[5] The chair of the nominating/corporate governance committee is an appropriate person to fulfill this role.

BEST PRACTICE FOR PUBLIC COMPANIES

Board compensation should include incentives to the directors to focus on long-term shareholder value as part of director compensation, and, therefore, a meaningful portion of director compensation should be in the form of long-term equity. Directors should be required to hold a meaningful amount of the public company's stock as long as they are on the board.

To better align director interest with the interest of long-term shareholders, a significant portion of the compensation of directors should be in the form of long-term equity, such as restricted stock or stock options that vest over time. Requiring directors of public companies to be shareholders helps create confidence in shareholders that the directors have similar incentives to shareholders.

OPERATION OF THE BOARD OF DIRECTORS

BEST PRACTICE

Boards of directors should confine their activities to overseeing the management of the organization and should not engage in day-to-day management activities or in micromanagement.

The function of the board of directors is to monitor management, not to engage in normal management activities. Independent directors typically do not have the time to devote to daily management activities, nor is it their responsibility to do so. Directors can for a short period of time, or in an emergency situation, perform management duties, but these situations should be extremely limited. Some members of boards of directors misunderstand their role within the organization and undertake day-to-day management activities, typically because they are not comfortable with the competency of management. If the board does not have confidence in management, management should be replaced.

BEST PRACTICE

Although directors can engage in constructive criticism, ask tough questions of management at board meetings, and disagree with each other, the discussions should be kept collegial with a view to developing a consensus.

At board meetings, directors should avoid trying to put management or other directors down. This does not mean that directors should not ask tough questions and be prepared to disagree with both management and each other. Directors should engage in constructive criticism and should maintain a skeptical but constructive attitude. Although disagreement is acceptable, being disagreeable is not acceptable. The discussion should be kept collegial, with a goal of reaching a consensus.

BEST PRACTICE

Directors must determine what information they need from management to properly monitor management's performance.

One of the most difficult tasks of directors is to determine what information they need about the organization to assist them in overseeing the management of the organization. Directors must proactively decide what information they need and review and revise their decision from time to time, as necessary. Directors cannot passively allow management to select what information will be supplied to them.

BEST PRACTICE

Directors should develop metrics to monitor the performance of management and review such metrics from time to time to determine their efficacy.

Directors must determine the best methods of measuring management performance as part of their oversight function. There is no universal metric that is applicable to all organizations. Therefore, directors will have to select the appropriate measurement tools and review and revise them from time to time.

BEST PRACTICE

Directors must take the time to fully consider important matters to the organization and establish a record of due diligence. In transactions in which there are potential conflicts of interest, a special committee composed of completely independent directors should be formed. These special committees must establish a complete record of due diligence in order for their decisions to be respected by the courts.

Directors must take the time to fully consider important matters to the organization. For example, if the organization is considering an acquisition or sale, directors must establish a record of due diligence. The courts will tend to review directors' actions with 20/20 hindsight. In *Smith v. Van Gorkom*,[6] discussed later in this chapter, directors who gave inadequate consideration to a sale of the organization were forced to settle the claim by shareholders for $23.5 million.

The courts (particularly in Delaware) have held directors personally liable for huge amounts of damages for failing to take the time and effort to fully consider important matters and to seek appropriate independent advice.

If there is any potential for a conflict of interest with management or other directors, a special committee of completely independent directors must be established to consider the matter. For the courts to respect the decisions of the committee, it must be advised by independent advisors (see Chapter 8).

BEST PRACTICE

Directors must either directly or through committees identify the major risks of an organization, prioritize those risks, and establish internal controls and a compliance program to help ameliorate such risks. The major risk analysis should be used to develop a committee structure within the board of directors, with each committee having an oversight role with respect to each major risk.

It is important to identify and prioritize the major risks of an organization and establish internal controls to help ameliorate these risks. The board or one of its committees should, with the assistance of management, legal counsel, and independent accountants, perform such an analysis and establish appropriate internal controls. Board committee structure should be established with a view to having a committee with oversight over each major risk (see Chapter 7).

Performing this risk analysis will assist the board in demonstrating that it has complied with its fiduciary duties, discussed later in this chapter. The Delaware

Chancery Court has held in the *Caremark* case[7] (discussed later in this chapter) that one of the board's fiduciary duties is to implement a compliance program to prevent violations of the law. The court also stated that a director's duties include "an attempt in good faith to assure that a corporate information reporting system, which the Board concludes is adequate, exist[s]."

No system for identifying risks is perfect. Likewise, there is no one-size-fits-all analysis possible. Each organization has peculiar risks, which must be identified and prioritized. A multiplicity of civil and criminal statutes, rules, and regulations (federal, state, and local) require that experienced legal counsel be used to assist in this risk analysis. At a minimum, every director should be generally aware of the more significant federal, state, local, and foreign statutes applicable to the business of the organization.

A good source for organizational risk identification is to review the problems that have previously occurred in the organization or in other similar organizations. Directors should require an industry report at each board meeting that will not only review the status of competitors, but will discuss any government investigation or any regulatory or other legal issues affecting organizations in the same industry. If another company in the industry has disclosed a government investigation, directors should inquire as to whether the practices being investigated are also being practiced by the organization. If the organization is engaged in the same practice, or the organization does something similar, it is likely that the organization will be dragged into the government investigation of the other company in the industry.

Some risks are insurable; therefore, any risk analysis must include an analysis of existing insurance coverages (see Chapter 3).

One method of analyzing risk is by using balance sheet accounts and rating the various risks which can affect these accounts. An example of this analysis is contained in Appendix B, which was provided by Accume, an internal audit outsourcer. Many other methods of analyzing risks should also be considered.

Once the major risks have been identified, methods should be developed by the board and management to attempt to control these risks. Although no risk control system is perfect, the attempt to analyze and control risks will help the organization to comply with the U.S. Department of Justice Sentencing Guidelines discussed in Chapter 4. Compliance with these guidelines helps to protect the organization from criminal indictment and fines.

BEST PRACTICE

The board must establish a succession plan for the chief executive officer.

One of the primary functions of the board of directors is to develop a succession plan for management, particularly the chief executive officer. A well-thought-out succession plan can protect the organization from the consequences of the sudden death or disability of the CEO or his or her ultimate retirement.

BEST PRACTICE

The board is responsible for obtaining an annual operating plan from management, including annual budgets, and monitoring the performance of the annual operating plan.

The board should obtain an annual operating plan from management that includes specific budgets. The board must oversee the performance of this annual operating plan and management's adherence to its proposed budgets.

BEST PRACTICE

The board has a responsibility for making certain that the organization has a long-term strategic plan and overseeing the implementation of such strategic plan by management.

It is management's responsibility to develop a long-term strategic plan, and it is the board's responsibility to make certain that management does so. The board must also regularly monitor management's execution of the strategic plan.

BEST PRACTICE

The board of directors and the chief executive officer should have a clear understanding of the types of decisions that can be made by management without board approval and those which require board approval.

Many decisions that have to be made by the organization clearly require board approval; these include mergers, major acquisitions, declaration of dividends, election of senior officers, and so on. However, in the absence of clear guidelines, many other important decisions can be made by the CEO pursuant to the CEO's power to manage the organization on a day-to-day basis. The CEO must have clear guidelines, whether monetary or otherwise, that delineate when board approval must be obtained for a particular decision.

BEST PRACTICE

When conducting internal investigations that may involve top management or may be potentially embarrassing to the organization or top management, such investigations must be conducted by an independent board committee (typically the audit committee) and completely independent counsel should be used.

If suspicious events occur that may involve top management or may be potentially embarrassing to the organization or top management, it is important for the organization to investigate them before a government agency does so. The fiduciary duties of the directors may require them to do so. In addition, there are significant advantages to conducting an internal investigation, including an ability to discover and correct problems for the organization that may be discovered later by a government agency. In order for the courts and government agencies to respect the organization's internal investigation, a special committee of the board must be formed consisting solely of completely independent directors.

BEST PRACTICE

When the organization is in the "vicinity of insolvency," directors should seek the advice of counsel to assist them in performing their potential fiduciary duties to creditors.

When private or public companies or not-for-profit organizations are in the "vicinity of insolvency," a line of court cases supports the position that they owe their fiduciary duties to creditors and not to equity holders or members (in the case of not-for-profit organizations). The concept of the "vicinity of insolvency" is not well defined and derives primarily from bankruptcy court cases. If there is any suspicion as to the financial viability of the organization, directors should seek the advice of counsel to assist them in performing their potential fiduciary duties to creditors (see Chapter 17).

BEST PRACTICE

Directors should not authorize personal loans or other personal extensions of credit to management or directors of private or not-for-profit organizations, or to management or directors of public companies not subject to Sarbanes-Oxley, except in the most compelling circumstances and only with arm's-length terms and documentation.

Sarbanes-Oxley prohibits personal loans or other personal extensions of credit to the directors or executive officers of public companies subject to that law (subject to certain exceptions). It is a bad practice for any organization (except a bank or other financial institution engaged in that business) to make personal loans or grant extensions of credit to management or directors of the organization. Such loans create conflicts of interest that can be harmful to the organization.

Not-for-profit organizations that solicit public contributions are particularly vulnerable to criticism for making any such personal loans or extensions of credit.

Obviously, this prohibition would not apply to single-owner private companies or to private companies that make proportional loans to all shareholders who also happen to be directors or officers. Likewise, this prohibition on personal loans or other extensions of credit would not apply to compensation plans that have a loan feature or to employment contracts with new executives in which the loan is part of their compensation package (except to the extent the prohibitions of Sarbanes-Oxley apply).

OTHER CORPORATE GOVERNANCE PRACTICES

BEST PRACTICE

Corporate culture is the key to corporate governance. The key to corporate culture is leadership from the top and a compensation system that rewards not only financial performance but provides positive and negative incentives to employees to report legal risks and wrongdoing up the ladder. All organizations should adopt a law compliance and ethics policy that states the policies and values of the organization and should effectively enforce such policy.

The demise of Enron and WorldCom resulted in large part from their numbers-driven cultures. The culture of the organization must be monitored by the board of directors or one of its committees (such as the nominating/corporate governance committee). Moreover, the U.S. Sentencing Commission Guidelines require the board of directors to establish an ethical, law-abiding culture as a condition for avoiding criminal indictment of the organization (see Chapter 4).

BEST PRACTICE

A whistleblower policy should be established for all organizations (except to the extent prohibited by certain foreign laws) since, according to a 2004 survey by the Association of Certified Fraud Examiners, fraud is detected 40 percent of the time by tips (see Chapter 4).

Whether the organization is public, private, or not-for-profit, it is important for the board of directors or one of its committees to make itself accessible to employees by establishing a whistleblower policy. Properly handling employee complaints helps to avoid lawsuits (including class actions) and government investigations.

Retaliation against whistleblowers may violate various federal and state laws, including Sarbanes-Oxley. The antiretaliation provisions of Sarbanes-Oxley apply to retaliation against any person providing a law enforcement officer any truthful information relating to the commission or possible commission of a federal offense, whether the retaliation is by a public, private, or not-for-profit organization, and create criminal penalties for such a violation. Sarbanes-Oxley also prohibits retaliation in fraud cases involving reporting public companies against whistleblowers by "any officer, employee, contractor, subcontractor, or agent" of such reporting public company. Thus, even private subcontractors to a reporting public company are prohibited from such retaliation.

BEST PRACTICE

All organization should have an emergency operations plan, in case of fire, flood, explosion, and the like.

Good corporate governance requires advance planning for all emergencies.

BEST PRACTICE

All organizations should adopt a press and media policy that sets forth the titles of the one or possibly two individuals who have the authority to speak for the organization. Any spokesperson for the organization must be properly trained for that role.

Every organization should have a press and media policy that describes who will be the spokesperson for the organization. Failure to have such a policy can result in mixed messages and be embarrassing to the organization. Advanced training of any spokesperson for this role is essential.

BEST PRACTICE FOR PUBLIC COMPANIES

Public companies should adopt a by-law that provides that if a majority of the shareholders actually voting withhold their votes for a particular director, such director will not be elected.

If a majority of the shareholders of a public company actually voting withhold their votes for a particular director, such director obviously does not have the support of the shareholders and should not be seated. In November 2005, Institutional Shareholders Services (ISS) stated that it would generally support shareholder proposals to public companies asking the company to implement a majority voting standard in uncontested director elections unless the public company satisfied certain tests, which could in part be satisfied by adopting the by-law just recommended.[8]

CONDUCTING INTERNAL INVESTIGATIONS

One of the basic duties of the board of directors is to conduct internal investigations as a result of whistleblower or other complaints that are received from employees of the organization. Typically these internal investigations should be assigned to the audit committee or the corporate governance committee and should be conducted by independent directors who are on those committees. In some cases a special committee of independent directors can be created to conduct an investigation.

Many boards of directors are content to delegate these investigations to other management personnel. Unless the board is certain that there is no involvement of top management and that the complaint, if true, would not be embarrassing to the organization, the board should not delegate these investigations to other management personnel.

The Enron Investigation

On August 22, 2001, Kenneth Lay, Enron's chairman, received a letter from an Enron accounting executive, Sherron Watkins, which contained these allegations:

> I am incredibly nervous that we will implode in a wave of accounting scandals. My eight years of Enron work history will be worth nothing on my resume, the business world will consider the past successes as nothing but an elaborate accounting hoax. Skilling is resigning now for "personal reasons" but I would think he wasn't having fun, looked down the road and knew this stuff was unfixable and would rather abandon ship now than resign in shame in two years.

> I realize that we have had a lot of smart people looking at this and a lot of accountants including AA & Co. have blessed the accounting treatment. None of that will protect Enron if these transactions are ever disclosed in the bright light of day. (Please review the late 90's problems of Waste Management—where AA paid $130 million plus in litigation re: questionable accounting practices.)

> Involve Jim Derrick and Rex Rogers to hire a law firm to investigate the Condor and Raptor transactions to give Enron attorney-client privilege on the work product. (Can't use V & E [Vinson & Elkins] due to conflict—they provided some true sale opinions on some of the deals.)

> Law firm to hire one of the big 6, but not Arthur Andersen or Pricewaterhouse-Coopers due to their conflicts of interest: AA & Co. (Enron); PWC (LJM).[9]

The following is the actual timeline of what happened thereafter:

1. The Watkins letter triggered an investigation by Vinson & Elkins (notwithstanding Watkins's request not to use V&E), which began in August 2001 and ended with a verbal report on September 21 and a written report on October 15, 2001.
2. The V&E report concluded that the facts revealed in its preliminary investigation did not warrant a "further widespread investigation by independent counsel or auditors," although it did note that the "bad cosmetics" of the Raptor related-party transactions, coupled with the poor performance of the assets

placed in the Raptor vehicles, created "a serious risk of adverse publicity and litigation."

3. On October 16, 2001, Enron publicly announced a $44 million after-tax charge against earnings and a reduction of its shareholders equity by $1.2 billion.

4. On December 2, 2001, Enron Corporation, then the seventh largest publicly traded corporation in the United States, declared bankruptcy.

The investigation of Enron by Vinson & Elkins LLP is a good example of a bad decision by the Enron board. The board delegated the investigation to the general counsel of Enron, even though the complaints by Sherron Watkins, the whistleblower, involved top management at Enron. Vinson & Elkins LLP, the primary outside counsel for Enron, and the Enron general counsel agreed on a very limited investigation that did not involve obtaining an independent accountants' opinion on the work of Arthur Andersen, even though accounting issues were the heart of Watkins's complaint and even though she had specifically requested that Arthur Andersen not be involved in the investigation. Indeed, Watkins also requested that Vinson & Elkins LLP not be involved in the investigation; Enron's general counsel also ignored this request. At the end of the very limited investigation, Vinson & Elkins LLP gave Enron a report that, in general, found no substance to Watkins's complaint. A separate investigation completed shortly after Enron's bankruptcy by an independent board committee, using completely independent counsel, found significant substance to Watkins's complaint.[10]

Cornell University Medical School

The need for independent board investigations, rather than management investigations, as well as the need for effective whistleblower policies is also illustrated in the case against Cornell University Medical School. This scandal is reported in *The Wall Street Journal* of August 16, 2005,[11] and we will assume, for our purposes, that the story is correct.

The Wall Street Journal reported that Cornell had agreed to pay $4.4 million to settle U.S. government charges relating to the misuse of grant money from the National Institutes of Health (NIH), without admitting wrongdoing. According to the article, Dr. Kyriakie Sarafoglou, a member of the faculty of Cornell's Weill Medical College, claimed that Cornell was defrauding American taxpayers by taking grant money for studies from the National Institutes of Health and using it to support standard care for patients at New York-Presbyterian Hospital, a Cornell affiliate on Manhattan's Upper East Side. Dr. Sarafoglou had the role of "research subject advocate," an NIH-funded position designed to ensure patient safety during research. She allegedly brought her complaints in the Spring of 2002, first to the program director (who allegedly was misusing the funds) and subsequently two internal review boards within Cornell's medical school, but claimed that she received no reply. In September 2002, Dr. Sarafoglou filed another complaint, which was followed by an internal investigation by a medical school professor. The internal investigation concluded that nobody at Cornell had engaged in scientific misconduct and that there had been no "financial impropriety."

Dr. Sarafoglou claims that she was socially ostracized as a result of her complaints and subsequently filed a so-called qui tam lawsuit, which is a lawsuit brought by an individual on behalf of the U.S. government alleging fraudulent activity involving U.S. government funds; the U.S. government has the option to join such lawsuits. As a result of her lawsuit, federal prosecutors became interested in the case and concluded that they had a strong case to bring against Cornell. Prosecutors allege that Cornell "fraudulently doubled-billed the government" in 37 cases by charging Medicaid for patient treatments while allotting NIH funds for the same treatment. Dr. Sarafoglou received a portion of the $4.4 million settlement ($877,000) for her role in bringing the qui tam action.

The moral of this story is that the whistleblower policy at Cornell was arguably defective since it is not clear that the whistleblower's complaint was ever investigated by the independent audit committee of the governing board of Cornell. Instead, the investigation was performed by another medical school professor (presumably not using independent counsel), and it is not clear that the audit committee of the governing board at Cornell was even aware of the whistleblower complaint.

STATE LAW FIDUCIARY DUTIES

Directors and officers of all organizations owe fiduciary duties to their organizations. Establishing good corporate governance practice may be considered part of these fiduciary duties.

State law imposes various fiduciary duties on all directors. The most important of these duties are due care and loyalty. In Delaware, the courts have also imposed a duty of candor, which is a subset of the duty of loyalty.

The American Law Institute Principles of Corporate Governance characterizes the statement that follows as the "black letter law" consistent with the duty of care standards articulated in most jurisdictions today:

§ 4.01 Duty of Care of Directors and Officers; the Business Judgment Rule

(a) A director or officer has a duty to the corporation to perform the director's or officer's functions in good faith, in a manner that he or she reasonably believes to be in the best interests of the corporation, and with the care that an ordinarily prudent person would reasonably be expected to exercise in a like position and under similar circumstances. This subsection (a) is subject to the provisions of subsection (c) (the business judgment rule) where applicable.

(1) The duty in subsection (a) includes the obligation to make, or cause to be made, an inquiry when, but only when, the circumstances would alert a reasonable director or officer to the need therefor. The extent of such inquiry shall be such as the director or officer reasonably believes to be necessary.

(2) In performing any of his or her functions (including oversight functions), a director or officer is entitled to rely on materials and persons in accordance with §§ 4.02 and 4.03 (reliance on directors, officers, employees, experts, other persons, and committees of the board).

(b) Except as otherwise provided by statute or by a standard of the corporation . . . and subject to the board's ultimate responsibility for oversight, in performing its functions (including oversight functions), the board may delegate, formally or informally by course of conduct, any function (including the function of identifying matters requiring the attention of the board) to committees of the board or to directors, officers, employees, experts, or other persons; a director may rely on such committees and persons in fulfilling the duty under this Section with respect to any delegated function if the reliance is in accordance with §§ 4.02 and 4.03 (reliance on directors, officers, employees, experts, other persons, and committees of the board).

(c) A director or officer who makes a business judgment in good faith fulfills the duty under this Section if the director or officer:

(3) is not interested . . . in the subject of the business judgment;

(4) is informed with respect to the subject of the business judgment to the extent the director or officer reasonably believes to be appropriate under the circumstances; and

(5) rationally believes that the business judgment is in the best interests of the corporation.

(d) A person challenging the conduct of a director or officer under this Section has the burden of proving a breach of the duty of care, including the inapplicability of the provisions as to the fulfillment of duty under subsection (b) or (c), and, in a damage action, the burden of proving that the breach was the legal cause of damage suffered by the corporation.[12]

FIDUCIARY DUTIES UNDER DELAWARE LAW

Under Delaware law, which has the most developed body of state corporate law, the fiduciary duties are not only owed to the organization, but also are generally owed to the equity holders of that organization. Under Delaware law, fiduciary duties can be divided into these categories:

- A duty of care (which can be modified by the certificate of incorporation), which includes various other duties including a duty to supervise and a duty to stay informed
- A duty of loyalty, which has several subsets, including:
  - A duty to act in good faith
  - A duty of candor
  - A duty to stay informed
  - A duty to avoid conflicts of interest
  - A possible duty to avoid entrenchment

The duty to stay informed is one of the most important duties from the corporate governance viewpoint and is discussed in more detail later. The duty to act in good faith and the duty of loyalty and each of their subsets cannot be modified under Delaware law by the certificate of incorporation.

In many states other than Delaware, fiduciary duties are owed only to the organization and not to its equity holders. In addition, approximately 40 states (excluding Delaware) permit directors to consider the interest of constituencies other than equity holders in complying with their fiduciary duties. These so-called constituency states permit the board to consider the interests of employees, community, suppliers, creditors, and so on in making their decisions, thereby giving greater discretion to directors. Pennsylvania's constituency statute specifically provides that the interests of shareholders do not have to be given greater weight than the interests of these other constituencies in the process of making board decisions.

BUSINESS JUDGMENT RULE

The so-called business judgment rule protects directors from having their decisions second-guessed by the courts. In Delaware, the business judgment rule is a presumption that directors act in good faith, on an informed basis, honestly believing that their action is in the best interest of the organization. However, there are significant limitations on the business judgment rule, particularly where the directors have violated their duty to stay informed, are not independent, have a conflict of interest, or have breached their other fiduciary duties. In Delaware, the courts have said that the business judgment rule may be overcome by showing either irrationality or inattention. In addition, a plaintiff may overcome the Delaware presumption that the directors acted in good faith by establishing that a decision was so egregious as to constitute corporate waste.

The Delaware business judgment rule generally does not apply to these transactions:

- Transactions in which a majority of the board has financial or other interests adverse to the corporation
- Transactions in which an individual director or a minority of the board have financial or other interests adverse to the corporation, *if* the interested director or directors control or dominate the board as a whole
- Transactions in which a majority of the directors receive a special or personal benefit, if material, that may be incidental to an arms' length transaction; and
- Transactions with a controlling stockholder

In these transactions, the Delaware courts will more carefully scrutinize the transaction for fairness to the corporation and its shareholders. These types of transactions require the formation of a committee of independent directors, which is discussed more fully in Chapter 8.

DUTY OF DIRECTORS TO STAY INFORMED

Directors have a duty to stay informed about their organization. They cannot rely solely on the information provided to them in so-called board packages by management. Likewise, directors cannot rely solely on the independent auditor because independent auditors perceive that their legal duties are much more circumscribed than directors believe.

Directors must advise management as to what information they require to perform their fiduciary duties and insist on receiving that information. Directors must have eyes and ears within the organization through an internal audit function.

Two prominent Delaware cases—*Smith v. Van Gorkom* and *Caremark*—illustrate the need for directors to remain fully informed, to assess management critically, and to establish adequate corporate information and reporting systems.[13] Although these cases dealt with public companies incorporated in Delaware, similar principles are generally applicable to private and not-for-profit organizations:

Smith v. Van Gorkom

Jerome Van Gorkom was chairman and CEO of the Trans Union Corporation, a public holding company. In September 1980, Van Gorkom sat down with a friend, Jay Pritzker, who specialized in corporate takeovers. He proposed a sale of Trans Union to Pritzker at $55 a share, and Pritzker accepted this offer a couple of days later. They worked out a deal over the next few days in which Trans Union's shareholders would receive $55 cash for each of their shares, and Pritzker would have the option to buy 1 million shares of Trans Union's unissued treasury stock at $38 per share, 75 cents above market price. Pritzker demanded a response from the board by September 21, 1980, just three days away.

On September 20, 1980, Van Gorkom called a senior management meeting. Almost all of the other managers thought the idea was ridiculous. The chief financial officer (CFO) objected to the $55 per share price and to the option to buy treasury shares.

Immediately after the management meeting, Van Gorkom summoned the board. He outlined the deal to them without handing over the actual agreement. He brought in a lawyer from an outside firm, who instructed the board that they might face a lawsuit if they did not take the offer; after all, it was for a shareholder meeting to decide. The CFO told the board that $55 was "at the beginning of the range" of a fair price. The board approved the merger offer after two hours, on the condition that Trans Union would be able to accept any better offer brought within the next 90 days. Van Gorkom signed the merger agreement that night at a party. Neither he nor any members of the board had actually read it.

After the deal was made public on September 22, 1980, many officers threatened to resign. Van Gorkom quieted them down by negotiating amendments that would allow Trans Union to solicit other bids through its investment banker, Salomon Brothers. The board approved these amendments on October 8, 1980. Two other offers came in, but neither ultimately led to anything. The merger was approved by Trans Union shareholders in February 1981 and completed.

Smith v. Van Gorkom involved a shareholder class action seeking rescission of the cash-out merger of the corporation into a new corporation or, alternatively, damages against the directors and others. The Delaware Supreme Court determined the duty of candor was breached by the directors' "failure to make true and correct disclosures of all information they had, or should have had, material to the transaction submitted for stockholder approval." The court also made the following observation about the duty of directors to be informed:

> Under the business judgment rule there is no protection for directors who have made "an unintelligent or unadvised judgment." . . . A director's duty to inform himself in preparation for a decision derives from the fiduciary capacity in which he serves the corporation and its stockholders . . . Since a director is vested with the responsibility for the affairs of the corporation, he must execute that duty with the recognition that he acts on behalf of others. Such obligation does not tolerate faithlessness or self-dealing. But fulfillment of the fiduciary function requires more than the mere absence of bad faith or fraud. Representation of the financial interests of others imposes on a director an affirmative duty to protect those interests and to proceed with a critical eye in assessing information of the type and under the circumstances present here. . . .

> In the specific context of a proposed merger of domestic corporations, a director has a duty under [the law], along with his fellow directors, to act in an informed and deliberate manner in determining whether to approve an agreement of merger before submitting the proposal to the stockholders. Certainly in the merger context, a director may not abdicate that duty by leaving to the shareholders alone the decision to approve or disapprove the agreement. Only an agreement of merger satisfying the requirements of [the law] may be submitted to the shareholders.

Among the findings that led the court to conclude that the directors were liable for gross negligence were:

• The board accepted the $55 price without question.

> No director sought any further information. No director asked [the CFO] why he put $55 at the bottom of his range. No director asked him for any details as to his study, the reason why it had been undertaken or its depth. No director asked to see the study; and no director asked him whether Trans Union's finance department could do a fairness study within the remaining 36-hour period available under the Pritzker offer. Had the Board, or any member, made an inquiry of him, he presumably would have responded as he testified: that his calculations were rough and preliminary; and, that the study was not designed to determine the fair value of the Company, but rather to assess the feasibility of a leveraged buy-out financed by the Company's projected cash flow, making certain assumptions as to the purchaser's borrowing needs.

• While the board claimed to have provided a 90-day "market test" to ensure the fairness of the deal, the court did not buy this argument.

> There is no evidence that the Merger Agreement was effectively amended to give the Board freedom to put Trans Union up for auction sale to the highest bidder, or that a public auction was in fact permitted to occur. The minutes of the Board meeting make no reference to any of this. Indeed, the record compels the conclusion that the directors had no rational basis for expecting that a market test was attainable, given the terms of the Agreement as executed during the evening of September 20.

- The court refused to take the directors' high level of business experience into account, adopting an earlier precedent that "found those factors denoting competence to be outweighed by evidence of gross negligence."

- As for the lawyer, who allegedly "advised [the board] that Delaware law did not require a fairness opinion or an outside valuation of the Company before the Board could act on the Pritzker proposal," the court ruled that such advice would have been correct. Nonetheless, "unless the directors had before them adequate information regarding the intrinsic value of the Company, upon which a proper exercise of business judgment could be made, mere advice of this type is meaningless; and, given this record of the defendants' failures, it constitutes no defense here." The court also said that "we cannot conclude that the mere threat of litigation, acknowledged by counsel, constitutes either legal advice or any valid basis upon which to pursue an uninformed course."

"We do not suggest that a board must read in haec verba every contract or legal document which it approves," the court said in a footnote, "but if it is to successfully absolve itself from charges of the type made here, there must be some credible contemporary evidence demonstrating that the directors knew what they were doing, and ensured that their purported action was given effect."

The court in *Van Gorkom* ultimately concluded that the directors breached their affirmative duty to inform themselves of all information reasonably available to them and relevant to their decision to approve the merger. The case was ultimately settled for $23.5 million, $10 million of which was paid from director and officer liability insurance and the remaining $13.5 million of which was paid by Jay Pritzker, on condition that the directors would pay $1,350,000 (10 percent of $13.5 million) to charity.

In addition to the liability associated with a director's failure to remain fully informed before acting on an issue before the board, the duty of care also imposes on directors an affirmative duty to monitor the ongoing operation of the corporation's business. The obligation to implement a corporate reporting system recognizes the need for relevant and timely information as an essential predicate for satisfaction of the board's supervisory role under Section 141 of the Delaware General Corporation Law. A thorough discussion of the relationship between fulfilling one's duty of care and the obligation to actively gather accurate information can be found in the seminal case of *In re Caremark International, Inc.*

Caremark

Caremark is a large, for-profit healthcare corporation engaged in the business of providing patient care and managed care services. In 1994, Caremark and some of its officers and employees were criminally indicted in multiple jurisdictions for violations of federal healthcare laws, including the Anti-Kickback Act and criminal false claims statutes. Caremark pled guilty to various offenses and agreed to pay $250 million in civil penalties, criminal fines, and restitution to private parties.

Following the corporation's entry of the guilty plea and its payment of nearly $250 million in civil penalties and criminal fines, Caremark's shareholders filed suit against the company's directors alleging that the directors breached their fiduciary duties to the corporation by allowing the criminal misconduct to occur. In evaluating this allegation, the court analyzed the directors' duties to institute compliance programs to prevent and detect violations of the law. Notably, the court expressed its view that:

> A director's obligation includes a duty to attempt in good faith to assure that a corporate information and reporting system, which the Board concludes is adequate exists, and that failure to do so under some circumstances may, in theory at least, render a director liable for losses caused by non-compliance with applicable legal standards.

The court in *Caremark* carefully examined the corporation's compliance program and found the existence and effectiveness of that program crucial to its holding that the directors did not breach their duties. Absent the directors' development of the company's elaborate compliance program, the court suggested the directors could have been held individually liable.

FEDERAL LAW

Federal statutes can also affect the duties of directors and officers and create potential civil or criminal liability for directors. Federal (and state) environmental statutes are one example. Another example is federal securities laws. If a public company is liable under the federal securities laws for material misstatements or omissions in documents filed with the Securities and Exchange Commission (SEC), directors of that public company may also be liable if:

- The director is considered to be in control of the public company.
- The director signed the document filed with the SEC.
- In either case, they failed to establish a personal due diligence defense.

The U.S. Department of Justice Sentencing Guidelines, discussed in Chapter 4, govern situations in which an organization will be indicted for violating a federal law. These guidelines dictate the corporate governance culture that the governing body of every organization must seek to develop.

NEW YORK STOCK EXCHANGE CORPORATE GOVERNANCE RULES

The corporate governance rules of the New York Stock Exchange should serve as a model for all organizations, whether public, private, or not-for-profit.[14]

The Nasdaq Stock Market corporate governance rules are not as strict as the rules of the New York Stock Exchange.[15] They should be used for private and not-for-profit organizations, as well as companies listed on the Nasdaq Bulletin Board or traded on the so-called Pink Sheets, which want to obtain some corporate governance structure but do not wish to go as far as the New York Stock Exchange rules.

ENDNOTES

1. For the Business Roundtable's best practices for 2005 go to: www.businessround-table.org/publications/index.aspx and click on the document entitled "Principles of Corporate Governance," November 3, 2005.
2. "A Closer Look at Lead or Presiding Directors" (Spencer Stuart, 2006, vol. 1, issue 4).
3. Id. at 9.
4. *In re Tele-Communications Inc. Shareholders Litigation*, Del. Ch., C.A. No. 16470 (December 21, 2005).
5. Id. at 1.
6. *Smith v. Van Gorkom*, 488 A.2d 858 (Del. 1985).
7. *Caremark International, Inc. Derivative Litigation*, 1996 WL 549894 [Del. Ch.].
8. ISS Releases, "2006 Corporate Governance Policy Updates: Section 404, Director Performance and Tally Sheet Policies Are Added, while Majority Vote, Burn Rate and Other Policies Are Tuned," Press release, November 21, 2005, www.issproxy.com/pressroom/2005archive.jsp.
9. "Sherron Watkins eMail to Enron Chairman Kenneth Lay, January 20, 2002," www.itmweb.com/f012002.htm.
10. Ackman, "Sherron Watkins Had Whistle, But Blew It," *Forbes*, February 14, 2002, www.forbes.com/2002/02/14/0214watkins.html.
11. Bernard Wysocki, Jr., "As Universities Get Billions in Grants, Some See Abuses," *Wall Street Journal*, August 16, 2005.
12. "Principles of Corporate Governance: Analysis and Recommendations," American Law Institute, April 1, 1994.
13. *Smith v. Van Gorkom*, supra at 4; *Caremark International, Inc.*, supra at 5.
14. View these rules on the New York Stock Exchange Web site: www.nyse.com/pdfs/finalcorpgovrules.pdf.
15. View these rules on the Nasdaq Web site: www.nasdaq.com/about/CorporateGovernance.pdf.

Chapter 3

Best Practices to Monitor Risk in Different Organizational Departments

This chapter summarizes best practices to monitor risk within these departments or units of an organization:

- Human resources (HR)
- Sales
- Purchasing
- Insurance
- Tax
- Legal
- Corporate development

The information technology department is discussed in Chapters 9 and 10. Obviously, not all organizations maintain each of these departments or units. Some of these functions, such as legal, may be outsourced. Nevertheless, the best practices discussed in this chapter are applicable whether the function is inside the organization or outsourced.

BEST PRACTICE

The organization should periodically employ an attorney to provide an overall review of the practices within each of the departments or units of the organization to determine if best practices are being followed.

Having a detailed legal review periodically of the departments or units of an organization helps to identify risk areas and assists the board of directors and management to focus on methods of mitigating these risks.

HUMAN RESOURCES

A summary of the major best practices within the HR department follows.

BEST PRACTICE

Maintain employee liability insurance in an amount adequate to protect the organization against claims, have such policy reviewed by an attorney specializing in this area, and require the insurer to permit the organization to use its regular counsel to defend claims.

Aggrieved employees frequently resort to lawsuits with demands for jury trials. They are represented by attorneys who are willing to take the case on a contingent fee basis (i.e., no legal fees unless the lawsuit is successful). Egregiously high jury verdicts, which can include significant punitive damages, rendered on employee claims can financially strain if not bankrupt even well-capitalized organizations. Insurance is the best answer. However, not all policies will respond to punitive damage claims, and a number of them have major defects. Therefore, it is important to have an attorney specializing in this area carefully review the policy.

The insurance policy should contain a clause permitting the organization to use its own counsel to defend claims. In the absence of such a clause, the insurer will appoint its own counsel, who may have little experience in defending labor and employment claims and who owes an allegiance to the insurer for having selected them.

BEST PRACTICE

Provide to each employee a handbook of organizational policies that has been reviewed by an attorney and is signed by the employee.

The handbook avoids misunderstandings as to the policies of the organization. A carefully constructed employee handbook can prevent claims by employees and result in favorable settlements of such claims.

BEST PRACTICE

Each employee should execute an employee agreement that, at a minimum, should spell out the employee's salary and benefits, the fact that the employee can be terminated at any time for any reason, the employee's duty of confidentiality, the employee's duty to assign ideas and inventions to the organization, and any nonsolicitation of customer provisions (or noncompete provisions) that will be applicable after termination of employment.

Many disputes with employees result from the failure to specify the terms of employment. A form letter, which has been reviewed by an attorney, can be used to spell out all of the specific terms of employment of each employee and avoid arguments by the employee that they are not employees at will.

BEST PRACTICE

Establish and maintain, on an ongoing basis, a supervisory and employee training program that would include topics such as legal compliance, ethics, antiharassment (sexual and other forms), litigation avoidance, and, where appropriate, union avoidance.

Continuous training of supervisors and other employees is extremely important to any organization interested in maintaining an ethical, law-abiding culture. Sexual harassment claims are one of the claims most frequently brought against organizations, and sensitizing supervisors and other employees to this issue is essential. It is important to establish an active education program for supervisory and other employees, which all employees are required to attend at least once a year.

BEST PRACTICE

If there is an intention to terminate an employee, written records of warnings to the employee must be maintained, an attorney should be consulted on the overall strategy, and the employee should be given time to correct the conduct that will serve as a basis for the termination.

Wrongful termination suits by employees are becoming more frequent. One of the major problems in defending these suits is the lack of a written record demonstrating that the employee was given adequate warning and a chance to correct his or her conduct. The absence of a thoroughly documented written record by HR makes it difficult to defend these claims and results in high settlements. It is important to bring an attorney into the process of termination at an early time so that a good record can be established.

BEST PRACTICE

An attorney specializing in labor and employment law should review the status of all so-called independent contractors working for the organization, to determine that these individuals are really independent contractors and not employees.

Many organizations have found that they have misclassified persons as "independent contractors" who are really employees. These organizations could then be subject to employment and income taxes, interest, and penalties upon a subsequent review by the IRS or the U.S. Department of Labor. The potential liability of the organization for the misclassification can be huge; therefore, preventive steps should be taken.

BEST PRACTICE

Top management must have periodic meetings with employees to inculcate a law-abiding corporate culture.

Under U.S. Department of Justice Guidelines (discussed in Chapter 4), the board of directors is responsible for establishing and monitoring a law-compliant culture. The HR department should be initially responsible for organizing these meetings and for providing mechanisms to assist in monitoring the corporate culture.

BEST PRACTICE

All organizations should publish an employee complaint procedure that is easily accessible for all employees. The complaint procedure must contain provisions for confidentiality and against retaliation. All whistleblowers should be treated with respect and their allegations investigated. The investigation must be conducted by an independent attorney if the allegations may involve misconduct by top management or may affect the financial statements of the organization.

It is important that all organizations maintain an employee complaint procedure that is well advertised and that permits the confidential submission of complaints. Retaliation against whistleblowers may violate federal or state laws and must be carefully guarded against. The Sarbanes-Oxley Act of 2002 made such retaliation a criminal act with respect to public companies. All employee complaints should be investigated. Independent counsel should conduct investigations involving alleged misconduct by top management or allegations that may affect financial statements in order to obtain the respect of the courts and regulatory agencies and to preserve the attorney-client privilege and the work product doctrine.

BEST PRACTICE

The HR department should immediately notify the board of directors of the identity of any children of directors or officers who become employed by the organization, their compensation, and any change in their compensation.

Securities and Exchange Commission (SEC) proxy rules require disclosure of the children of directors or officers who earn over $60,000 per year from the public company. On December 20, 2004, The Walt Disney Company settled a case brought against it by the SEC for failure to disclose the fact that the corporation employed three children of its directors, who received annual compensation ranging from $60,000 to more than $150,000.[1]

Even if the organization is not a public company or children receive less than $60,000 per year, it is a good practice for the audit, corporate governance, and compensation committees of the board of directors to be aware of the employment of close relatives by the organization. In some cases this may be viewed as an indirect increase in the compensation of the director or officer.

BEST PRACTICE

To avoid the problem of backdating stock option grants, have the board or its compensation or stock option plan committee grant authority to the chief executive officer (CEO) or the HR department head, within certain parameters, to grant stock options to new hires.

The terms of employment of senior executives are typically negotiated by the CEO or by the head of HR and documented by the HR department. The CEO or head of HR will typically promise a certain number of stock options, and the new executive will expect that the options will have exercise prices equal to the market price on the grant date (usually the first date of employment). However, most stock option plans do not grant such authority to the CEO or the head of HR, but only to the board or its compensation or stock option plan committee, which typically meets infrequently. If there is a rise in the market price of the stock after the proposed grant date, the option will have to contain the higher exercise price caused by the increase in the market price, resulting in an unhappy new executive. In view of the SEC's current campaign against backdating options, it is preferable to grant limited authority, within certain parameters, to the CEO or the head of HR to grant stock options to new hires. Public companies should seek the advice of the securities lawyers in establishing the parameters in order to satisfy the requirements of Rule 16b-3 under the Securities Exchange Act of 1934.

BEST PRACTICE

Do background checks as well as alcohol and drug testing on all new hires.

It is much easier to screen out bad potential hires than to terminate them after they have been hired. Background checks, as well as alcohol and drug testing, help to reduce the risk of hiring troublesome employees.

BEST PRACTICE

Prior to hiring any former partner, principal, shareholder, or professional employee of the auditing firm, obtain an opinion as to whether such hiring will affect the independence of the auditor.

As explained in Chapter 16, the hiring of a former partner, principal, shareholder, or professional employee of the auditing firm may, under certain circumstances, cause the auditing firm to no longer be considered "independent" under the SEC's rules. Similar rules may apply to auditors of nonpublic companies, such as private companies and not-for profit organizations, that are located in states or are members of professional organizations that have adopted the SEC standards.

BEST PRACTICE

Confirm that HR is complying with all applicable federal, state, and local laws including, but not limited to:

- Fair Labor Standards Act (minimum wage, overtime classifications, child labor, I-9's [immigration], record keeping)
- Employee Retirement Income Security Act (ERISA) (Are blackouts employed, properly managed, etc.?)
- Uniformed Services Employment and Reemployment Rights Act (applies to veterans)
- Title VII (prohibition on discrimination based on race, sex, national origin, religion)
- Age Discrimination In Employment Act
- Americans with Disabilities Act

If the organization is a U.S. government contractor, are EEO1 reports of employee sex, race, and other ethnic categories properly completed and filed? Are affirmative action plans in place/updated/maintained? Who is responsible for handling audits by the Office of Federal Contract Compliance Programs? Is the organization complying with any applicable prevailing wage regulations?

There are a myriad of federal, state, and local laws that the HR department must comply with. The board of directors can sensitize the head of HR to the need to comply with these laws by asking these kinds of questions.

SALES

The sales department represents a major corporate governance challenge, since the employees are typically paid a commission on sales rather than a straight salary.

The commission structure tends to motivate employees to be creative in maximizing their income and can lead the organization, particularly public companies, into accounting frauds. The SEC action brought against Symbol Technologies, Inc. illustrates some of the problems with the sales department.[2] A description of that action follows the summary of best practices within the sales department.

A summary of the major best practices to monitor risks within the sales department follows.

BEST PRACTICE

Have an attorney familiar with revenue recognition policies review all form sales contracts. An attorney should also review how sales contracts are formed.

Sales contracts with customers can contain very onerous terms, such as extremely long warranties and other provisions that can constitute major risks for the organization. It is important to have an attorney review all form sales contracts as well as any significant amendments. The purpose of reviewing how sales contracts are formed is to make certain that the organization's sales terms apply in a so-called "battle of the forms" that is discussed in more detail under "Purchasing."

The SEC has required a number of public companies to restate their financial statements because of improper revenue recognition. The provisions of the sales contracts used by the organization will determine when revenue can be recognized for accounting purposes, assuming there are no side letters. The provisions of these sales contracts must conform to the policies of the organization with regard to revenue recognition.

BEST PRACTICE

Customers must be advised in writing who in the organization has the authority to modify sales contracts or enter into side letters, preferably by inserting such provisions into the terms of the sales contract.

It is not unusual for a salesperson to modify contract terms or to enter into a side letter to try to effectuate a sale and thereby earn a commission. It is important that customers be specifically advised in writing as to who has the authority to modify contract terms or enter into side letters.

BEST PRACTICE

Return policies, if any, should be set forth in the sales contract and must be adhered to.

If a practice develops with a customer of permitting the customer to return goods beyond the contractual return period, that practice can arguably modify the terms of the sales contract and lead to major disputes.

BEST PRACTICE

To avoid the so-called bill and hold abuse, which results in improper revenue recognition, there should be periodic review of bills to determine if the inventory has been shipped.

A number of public companies have engaged in accounting fraud called "bill and hold" in which customers are billed but are told that they are not required to pay the bill and the inventory is never shipped.

BEST PRACTICE

To avoid the so-called channel stuffing abuse and similar manipulations, which results in improper revenue recognition, major customers should be contacted periodically to determine whether they have actually purchased the shipped inventory.

The SEC has brought several cases against public companies that engaged in channel stuffing, which involves shipping goods to customers that have not really been sold or that have extremely liberal return privileges, in order to maximize the revenue of the public company for a particular period. It is difficult to prevent this practice unless relationships are maintained with major customers by the internal auditor or another designated person who can monitor such activity.

BEST PRACTICE

Internal audit should annually review the expense reports of all sales personnel to determine if they are engaged in improper or illegal sales activities, including commercial bribery or other illegal activities (e.g., use of prostitutes).

Improper or illegal activities by the sales department can be very embarrassing to the organization and may ultimately cause the loss of customers. Some of these activities may be induced by the compensation system utilized by the organization, which typically includes sales commission arrangements. The prospect of a detailed review of expense reports by the internal auditor may deter a salesperson from engaging in any improper or illegal actions.

BEST PRACTICE

No member of the sales department should be permitted to sign an audit confirmation from a third party. Any audit confirmation must be signed by the internal auditor or chief corporate governance officer.

Sarbanes-Oxley makes it a crime to mislead the auditor of a public company. Public company auditors may send audit confirmations to the sales department of an organization to verify certain information provided to the auditor by the public company. The public company may place pressure on the sales department to sign the audit confirmation, and a signature on a false audit confirmation can result in an SEC action against the persons who executed the false confirmation.

In 2005, the SEC filed an enforcement action against seven individuals, alleging they aided and abetted a massive financial fraud by signing and returning materially false audit confirmations sent to them by the auditors of the U.S. Foodservice, Inc. subsidiary of Royal Ahold.[3] The SEC's complaints allege that U.S. Foodservice personnel contacted vendors and urged them to sign and return the false confirmation letters, which overstated the amounts owed to U.S. Foodservice, Inc. by the supplier. In some cases U.S. Foodservice, Inc. pressured the vendors; in other cases it provided side letters to the vendors assuring the vendors that they did not owe U.S. Foodservice, Inc. the amounts reflected as outstanding in the confirmation letters. In November 2005, the sales manager of Crowley Foods LLC, a supplier to U.S. Foodservice, Inc., pleaded guilty to criminal conspiracy for signing an audit confirmation that overstated what was owed by Crowley to U.S. Foodservice, Inc.[4]

PURCHASING

A summary of the major best practices within the purchasing department follows.

BEST PRACTICE

An attorney should review the terms of purchase orders.

The legal provisions of purchase orders provide protection to the organization against defective goods and services as well as help protect the organization against claims by customers who may repurchase such goods or services.

BEST PRACTICE

Use overriding agreements with suppliers.

A particular problem for the purchasing department is the so-called "battle of the forms," in which the supplier does not execute the purchase order, but instead sends its own form, which contains contradictory terms. Likewise, the purchaser does not execute the supplier's form so that there is no single document which contains all of the terms of purchase. The best way to win the battle of the forms is to negotiate an overriding agreement with the supplier where both parties agree to a uniform set of purchase terms.

BEST PRACTICE

If overriding agreements cannot be consummated with all major suppliers, an attorney should review the procedures for forming contracts to ascertain that the purchasing department's terms will prevail in a battle of the forms. In the battle of the forms, the first offer typically wins. Having the purchasing department utilize request for quotation forms that contain the organization's purchase terms will assist in winning the battle of the forms.

INSURANCE

A summary of the major best practices within the insurance department follows.

BEST PRACTICE

Only deal with insurance agents who maintain an errors and omission (E&O) insurance policy for the agency with sufficient coverage, and require the E&O carrier to give the organization notice of any changes in the E&O policy.

Insurance is typically purchased through an insurance agent. The insurance agent also provides significant advice to the organization on what policy to purchase and a summary of the terms of the policy, and recommends coverage. If a significant mistake is made by the insurance agent and the agent does not carry an adequate E&O policy, the organization will not have coverage for the losses caused by the agent's error or bad advice.

BEST PRACTICE

The amount of business interruption insurance to be carried by the organization and risk covered should be carefully reviewed by the board of directors.

Inadequate coverage on a business interruption policy can be devastating to an organization. Fire, flood, explosion, and other events can cause major problems to the continuation of a business, including loss of customers and key suppliers, loss of intellectual property, and the like. This coverage deserves careful review of the highest levels of an organization. Off-site storage is necessary to avoid destruction of records necessary to support a claim in the case of fire, flood, explosion, etc.

BEST PRACTICE

In order to attract independent directors, the organization should maintain a director and officer liability policy with adequate coverage that should not be disclaimable by the insurer at least as to innocent independent directors.

Competent independent directors may be unwilling to serve on the board of an organization that does not provide adequate insurance coverage. Some insurance companies have attempted to rescind coverage after a claim has been made on the ground that the insurance application contained false financial information about the organization. Director and officer (D&O) liability policies that prohibit disclaimer of coverage for innocent independent directors are available and should be purchased, even though the premium cost is generally higher than for policies that are disclaimable.

BEST PRACTICE

Directors should review with the insurance department what insurance coverages are available that the organization has elected not to purchase, including any endorsements that broaden coverage and that the organization elected not to purchase.

Directors must weigh the cost of insurance against the benefit of covering specific organizational risks. In order to keep the directors informed as to what cost-benefit decisions have been made, the insurance department should advise the directors as to what coverages are available that the organization elected not to acquire. Likewise, the insurance department should advise the directors as to what endorsements to existing policies are available that broaden coverage. The decision not to broaden coverage with such endorsements should also be discussed at the board level.

BEST PRACTICE

An attorney and insurance consultant should periodically review the adequacy of the organization's insurance coverage and the adequacy of the documentation needed to support a claim.

The person within the organization in charge of purchasing insurance coverage is usually under significant pressure to lower insurance costs. This cost pressure may lead to purchasing inadequate insurance coverage or utilizing insurance companies that do not have the financial strength to respond to claims. A good example of this phenomenon was the insolvency of Reliance Insurance Company, which issued a significant amount of D&O insurance policies at low prices in order to obtain market penetration, and subsequently defaulted.[5]

One should view an insurance policy as the right to sue the insurance company and not necessarily a guarantee of coverage. Since major organizational risks are insured, it is extremely important that there be a review by an attorney and an insurance consultant as to the adequacy of coverage. The attorney and insurance consultant would typically work on an hourly basis subject to a budget. Of particular importance is what endorsements are available to the organization that have not been purchased as part of the policy and the financial strength of the insurance company.

TAX

A summary of the major best practices within the tax administration department follows.

BEST PRACTICE

The tax administration department should identify all high-risk areas to the audit committee, particularly the use of tax shelters and tax practices that are likely to be challenged by the IRS.

The amount of the provision for taxes and the adequacy of tax reserves are key components in the preparation of financial statements. It is important to understand the reasonableness of the position taken in the preparation of these accounts. Major accounting firms have, in the past, sold high-risk tax shelters to organizations, particularly public companies, that were attempting to maximize their earnings. It is important to understand the risk involved in any such tax shelter.

BEST PRACTICE

State and local tax issues should be carefully reviewed by an attorney or an accountant who specializes in this area.

Many organizations find that they have significantly underpaid their sales tax liability and other local taxes, resulting in significant interest and penalties being assessed against the organization. A careful review of all state and local tax issues should be made periodically by an attorney or an accountant to be certain that sales taxes and other local taxes are being properly paid.

LEGAL

A summary of the major best practices within the legal department or, if there is no legal department, best practices with outside counsel follows.

BEST PRACTICE

Major legal risks of the organization should be prioritized and methods of preventing or mitigating such risks developed proactively.

Legal risks are some of the major risks facing any organization. The board of directors or its audit or compliance committee must obtain an understanding of the major legal risks, including their priority against one another.

It is not sufficient to wait until the risk results in a major lawsuit or other legal catastrophe for the organization. The board of directors and management must authorize the legal department to proactively develop methods to prevent or mitigate such risks.

BEST PRACTICE

The board of directors or its audit or compliance committee must be informed immediately of any major new legal risks or significant lawsuits.

Mechanisms must be established to keep the board of directors or its audit or compliance committee informed of new legal risks or significant lawsuits. Such information will assist them in making business judgments concerning issues facing the organization and will help them fulfill their duty of monitoring management.

BEST PRACTICE

The legal department must review, on a periodic basis, the standard terms and conditions of purchases and sales and how contracts are formed by the purchasing and sales department.

Laws and court decisions relating to purchasing and selling activities are constantly changing and may require changes in the standard terms and conditions of purchase and sales.

BEST PRACTICE

The legal department must be kept informed of all new marketing efforts, so that it can determine the legal risks and methods of mitigating those risks.

It is not unusual for an organization to undertake a marketing effort without fully understanding the legal risks involved. Open and frequent communication with the legal department will permit the organization to identify and ameliorate such risks.

BEST PRACTICE

The legal department should develop a record retention policy customized to the business of the organization, which should include a requirement to consult with the legal department prior to any document destruction.

All organizations should have a document retention policy, with specific times at which documents should be destroyed. However, to avoid any possible charge of obstruction of justice, no document should be destroyed without a prior legal review to determine if there are any outstanding or threatening investigations that would require production of documents intended for destruction.

Under Sarbanes-Oxley, any person who alters, destroys, mutilates, conceals, covers up, falsifies, or makes a false entry in any record, document, or tangible object with the intent to impede, obstruct, or influence the investigation or proper administration of any matter within the jurisdiction of any department or agency of the United States or any Chapter 11 bankruptcy case will be fined, imprisoned for up to 20 years, or both. This provision applies to all organizations, whether public, private, or not for profit.

BEST PRACTICE

Intellectual property assets of the organization (trade secrets, patents, trademarks, service marks, copyrights, logos, licenses, etc.) should be identified, classified, and protected.

Intellectual property assets are financial assets of the organization, help to protect it from competitors, and in many cases represent the most valuable assets of the organization. Many companies identify, classify, and protect their plant, property, and equipment but completely neglect their intellectual property. Public companies also may have an obligation to value such intellectual property.

CORPORATE DEVELOPMENT

A summary of the major best practices to monitor risks within the corporate development department follows.

BEST PRACTICE

All letters of intent used in connection with corporate acquisitions, whether intended to be legally binding or not, should be reviewed by an attorney.

Even letters of intent that purport not to be legally binding can nevertheless create legally binding obligations. There have been numerous court cases in which letters of intent were found to be legally binding, notwithstanding language in the letter to the contrary.

BEST PRACTICE

Background checks must be performed on all principals and important executives of significant target acquisitions, preferably using private detective agencies.

There have been several instances where significant acquisitions have been made only to find after the closing that some of the principals or important executives of the target have criminal backgrounds or have lied on their resumes. This can be both embarrassing and risky for the acquiring organization.

What Can Symbol Technologies, Inc., Teach Us?

Lessons

- Audit committees must be sensitive to channel stuffing and interview the head of the sales department as part of their due diligence.
- Any proposed sale of company stock or risk-reducing transaction (e.g., a collar) by key executives is a warning event that requires the audit committee to authorize more intensive auditing.
- Audit committees must be sensitive to "cookie jar" reserves.
- Audit committees must fully understand the culture of their organization and must change the culture of organizations that are exclusively numbers driven.

Symbol Technologies, Inc., was the eighth largest public company on Long Island, employing in 2004 approximately 5,600 employees worldwide. It was one of the world's leading manufacturers and distributors of wireless and mobile computing and bar code

---

(continued)

reading devices and other networking systems. Its stock was traded on the New York Stock Exchange.

On June 3, 2004, the U.S. Attorney for the Eastern District of New York announced that Symbol and seven of its top-level executives (including the firm's former general counsel as well as Tomo Razmilovic, former president and chief executive officer) had been criminally indicted, and that Symbol had agreed to pay a fine of $139 million in stock and cash for purposes of compensating shareholders for losses arising out of the company's criminal conduct. Five other Symbol executives, including Robert Asti (a vice president of sales finance) previously had pleaded guilty to conspiracy charges arising out of an accounting fraud.[6]

On June 3, 2004, SEC complaints were filed alleging that from at least 1998 until early 2003, Symbol and the other defendants engaged in numerous fraudulent accounting practices and other misconduct that had a cumulative net impact of over $230 million on Symbol's reported revenue and over $530 million on its pretax earnings and had manipulated stock option exercise dates to minimize the tax impact for executives, with the help of Symbol's general counsel.[7] The complaint alleged the following, among other things:

> To lock in profits on his Symbol stock, Razmilovic entered into so-called European "zero cost collar" transactions with a brokerage firm, an option strategy designed to protect against a decline in the stock price. Razmilovic "collared" thousands of Symbol shares that he owned by selling a call option and buying a put option, thereby establishing a minimum and maximum price range for the stock. Razmilovic received substantial sums in proceeds from multiple collar transactions he arranged while engaged in the fraud. In each case, Razmilovic falsely certified to the brokerage firm that he did not possess material non-public information about Symbol. Upon his departure from the company, he also sold thousands of shares of Symbol stock that he acquired by exercising stock options priced below the inflated market price.

Other defendants used their control over operations to create fraudulent cookie jar reserves, by concealing surpluses in operations in an inventory reserve account known as Account 9106. When quarterly expenses and operations were lower, the defendants inflated accrued expenses and credited the surplus amount to this account. Other defendants directed a subordinate in December 2001 to make an entry that improperly shifted $3 million from a deferred revenue account to a recognized revenue account. In March 2002, the defendant then directed the subordinate to book an improper entry to inflate revenue by nearly $3 million.

Channel Stuffing

Robert Asti was vice president of sales finance for The Americas Sales and Services (TASS) at Symbol, which included Symbol's sales operations in North and South America.

Among other fraudulent accounting practices, Asti and others allegedly "stuffed" Symbol's distribution channel at the end of each quarter to help meet revenue and earnings targets imposed by Symbol's president at that time. According to the SEC complaint, Asti, with others, engineered phony sales in which resellers placed large "purchase" orders but were given the right not to pay for the products, either orally or in "side letters." Asti also arranged for Symbol to make payments to certain resellers to induce them to place orders and accept shipments in excess of their financial means. Asti also allegedly employed other fraudulent devices to accelerate revenue on sales to end users when the product the end user wanted was unavailable or could not be shipped before the end of the quarter for other reasons. Asti and his "sales finance" staff allegedly improperly controlled critical aspects of Symbol's revenue recognition process, such as the booking of orders and the issuance of invoices and credits.

According to the SEC complaint, the scheme worked this way:

> During the late 1990s, Symbol reported rapid growth in its business, including a $150 million contract in late 1998 with the United States Postal Service. The revenue recorded on that contract contributed to an increase in Symbol's annual revenue of nearly thirty percent over the prior year. There was significant pressure to maintain a comparable reported rate of growth in subsequent years.
>
> Symbol's president at the time established ambitious revenue and earnings targets that either drove or mirrored Wall Street expectations, and he aggressively enforced those targets. As a result, Symbol was a "numbers driven" company whose executives and key employees were obsessed with meeting financial projections. Asti reported to the head of TASS, whose main job was to make sure that TASS met the president's targets. During the relevant period, there was often a mad scramble at the end of financial reporting periods to "hit the number."
>
> Symbol's lack of adequate internal controls exacerbated the situation. Each area of the company performed its own finance function that fed directly into the financial reporting done at the corporate level. The so-called "sales finance" function had a significant impact on the revenue recognition process at the end of financial reporting periods. For example, members of Symbol's sales and service operation had the authority to decide, in the first instance, whether and when purchase orders and service contracts were booked for revenue recognition purposes. In addition, the sales finance group had virtually unfettered access to Symbol's general ledger through its automated accounting system, known as SAP. As a result, the sales finance function also exercised significant control over the issuance of credits for product returns and the aging of accounts receivable. Asti ran the finance department at TASS during the relevant period . . . .
>
> Asti's supervisor and other members of senior management looked to Asti and his staff to ensure that any large quarter-end transactions needed to meet the president's targets were structured and documented so that the orders could be processed, and the revenue recognized, that quarter. As a result, Asti often became involved in negotiating the details of transactions. At the same time, he made, or directed his staff to make, the necessary entries to SAP to book the order, generate an invoice and authorize shipment. At the end of each reporting period, Symbol's corporate finance department downloaded the data entered into SAP and consolidated the data to generate the company's financial statements . . .
>
> To help meet senior management's targets, the head of TASS counted on a group of resellers to submit to Symbol, at his or his staff's request, large "purchase" orders for product that Symbol had available and could ship before the end of the quarter. Asti and others arranged these transactions to make it appear that Symbol was selling the product to these resellers, while they simultaneously eliminated the resellers' obligation to pay for it.
>
> These resellers typically did not need and often could not even afford to pay for the product they ordered, but Asti and others negated any risk to the resellers by granting

(continued)

them contingent payment terms and unconditional return rights. The resellers did not have to pay Symbol unless and until they resold the product and received payment from an end user. The resellers also had the right to return any unsold product to Symbol at no cost. These special terms did not appear anywhere in the purchase orders or resulting invoices, which typically recited Symbol's standard "net 45 day" payment terms.

To reduce the risk of detection, Asti and others preferred to keep these side agreements oral, but sometimes the resellers requested and received written confirmation. For example, Asti handled multimillion dollar orders placed by a certain reseller ("Reseller A") in June and September 2000. Although Asti and another Symbol executive both told Reseller A that it could return any unsold product at no cost, Reseller A asked for documentation of the true terms to ensure that Reseller A incurred no risk in placing the orders. Asti sent emails to Reseller A at the end of both quarters agreeing that Reseller A had "stock rotation rights" with "no restocking fee" for these orders. Asti and Reseller A both understood that the phrase "stock rotation rights" meant unconditional return rights, a fact that the latter confirmed in a September 2000 email to Asti: "[A]s we discussed, 'stock rotation' as used in your e-mail of the terms means complete stock return privilege." This side agreement superseded the stock rotation terms that Symbol normally granted to channel partners in its standard contracts, which did not permit unlimited returns and provided for a restocking fee in many circumstances.

In many cases, resellers also received substantial price discounts in addition to the standard reseller discount, thereby guaranteeing a huge risk-free profit on any sales they might make to an end user. In most cases, Symbol also agreed to share leads and attempt to arrange for end users to purchase the product held by the resellers. In effect, Symbol offered the resellers a large commission on any future sale to an end user in exchange for storing the product on the resellers' premises. In some cases, Asti also gave resellers immediate "rebates" in the form of credits or cash as compensation simply for placing the order. Some resellers used a portion of the payments to cover the costs of storing and insuring Symbol's product.

For example, one reseller ("Reseller C") placed a $5 million order in September 2000 after receiving an email from Asti that specified the identity and quantity of the product it was supposed to order, and that stated as follows: "I agree that should you have to return this product, we will issue full amount [plus] 1%." At the end of the next quarter, Asti confirmed in a letter that Reseller C could use the "$50,000 rebate for our Q3 quarter end-deal" as a credit. Reseller C did not even have to return the product to receive the rebate, because Symbol never shipped the product. Symbol employees called such transactions "ship-in-place" deals, since the product never left Symbol's warehouse.

Asti and others also employed a channel stuffing device using what were known as "candy" deals. In these three-way transactions, Symbol paid off resellers to "purchase" large volumes of Symbol product from another distributor at the end of a quarter so that Symbol could induce that distributor to place orders to meet this illusory demand. This fraudulent scheme had the following essential components.

Asti and others first arranged for a reseller to order a specified volume of Symbol product from a distributor. In exchange, Asti and others agreed that Symbol would cover the cost of the reseller's purchase from the distributor, which included a substantial markup, and pay the reseller an additional amount—the "candy"—equal to

1% of the purchase price. Once the reseller placed its purchase order with the distributor, Asti or another Symbol executive solicited an order from the distributor to fill the reseller's order or restock the distributor's supply. The price that Symbol charged the distributor was lower than the cost of repurchasing the product from the reseller, which included both the distributor's mark-up and the "candy" payment.

During FY 2000, Asti arranged "candy" transactions in which Symbol's improper payments to the resellers totaled approximately $15 million. Symbol's recognition of revenue on the corresponding purchase orders placed by the distributors was also fraudulent and misleading. Symbol did not actually make any money—and, in fact, lost money—on these sham three-way transactions. Moreover, Symbol did not disclose that it generated this revenue by buying back its own products at a higher price and paying a bribe.

Other Fraudulent Actions

According to the SEC Complaint, Asti and others also used fraudulent devices to accelerate revenue on sales to end users when the product the end user wanted was unavailable or could not be shipped before the end of the quarter for other reasons. For example, in June 2000, Asti and others arranged a $3.8 million phony sale to Reseller D because an upgraded version of the product that a supermarket chain planned to purchase was not due to be ready until July 2000. Asti and others arranged for Reseller D to order an equivalent amount of the existing product in June 2000 with the explicit understanding that Reseller D's order would be cancelled and replaced by a real order from the supermarket chain the following quarter for the upgraded product.

On other occasions when the ordered product was unavailable, Symbol personnel deliberately shipped the wrong product to the customer and manipulated the accounting system to capture the revenue that quarter. To enable the invoice to be generated—and revenue to be recognized—Asti's staff did one of two things. They either altered the order information on SAP to reflect product that was available or they incorrectly "cycled" excess inventory into the system as the ordered product. When the desired product later became available, Symbol did what was known there as a "zero dollar" return, leaving the original transaction intact.

Asti and others were also involved in Symbol's fraudulent practice of recognizing revenue on orders that were processed in one quarter but not shipped until the following quarter. From January 2000 through March 2001, Asti had his staff accrue revenue on orders when they attained "post goods issued" (PGI) status on the SAP system, which indicated that the order was packed by the factory and ready for shipping. Because the shipments did not occur until the next quarter, the practice of accruing revenue based on an order's PGI status prematurely added millions of dollars of revenue to Symbol's reported financial results.

Symbol often had to perform what were called product "staging" services for a customer before the product was ready for use. Symbol performed these services, such as the loading of software and adding customer-specific configurations, at its own staging facilities. Although Symbol typically invoiced the customer upon shipment to the staging facility, some customers declined to accept the risks of ownership or to agree to pay Symbol until they received the product. With large orders requiring significant staging work, the staging process often continued into the next quarter. To circumvent revenue recognition rules and make it appear as though the sales process was complete in the quarter in which Symbol delivered the product to staging, Asti

(continued)

and others artificially treated transfer of title to the goods as if it were a matter separate from the risk of loss.

For example, in September 2000, Symbol agreed in a side letter that "title to the products" ordered by a retailer "transfers upon shipment of the products to Symbol's staging area, provided that Symbol maintains the risk of loss until the products are received at [the retailer's] designated locations." Based on this side agreement, Asti authorized his staff to book the retailer's multimillion dollar order that quarter. Asti and others used a similar agreement to improperly book a multimillion dollar order placed by a private delivery service in November 1999, where the risk of loss remained with Symbol until the finished product was installed in the customer's vehicles.

Asti and others managed the issuance of credits, which reduced net income, to ensure that they did not interfere with the earnings target. For example, in April 2000, a member of Asti's staff issued a memorandum instructing TASS executives that, absent prior approval by the sales finance department, "[t]here will be no processing of credit requests or return authorizations on the last two days and the first two days of a month, and the last two weeks and the first two weeks of a new quarter." Sales finance preferred to defer processing returns and credits during the first two weeks of a quarter for a second reason—to avoid raising red flags for auditors who might be skeptical about the timing of such entries.

Asti and others also used the credit process to conceal the age of certain reseller receivables generated by channel stuffing. For example, in the last two quarters of FY 2000, Asti directed his staff to issue credits to certain resellers whose accounts were overdue and then issue new invoices to them in the same amount. This "credit and rebill" artifice "refreshed" the age of specific receivables and reduced Symbol's overall "days sales outstanding" number, eliminating two additional red flags.

Cover-up and Stock Sales

The SEC complaint alleged both cover-up activities by Asti and stock sales:

To reduce the risk of detection, Asti also directed others to delete invoices totaling approximately $34 million from SAP. These invoices were issued in December 2000 and were deleted in the next quarter. Many of the canceled invoices related to "channel stuffing" and other improper transactions.

Asti sold Symbol stock while engaged in the scheme to manipulate Symbol's reported financial results. On five occasions from October 26, 1999 to March 2, 2001, Asti sold thousands of shares of Symbol stock that he had acquired by exercising employee stock options priced below the inflated market price.

Lessons from Symbol Technologies, Inc.

The Symbol audit committee presumably relied on the independent auditor to detect cookie jar reserves and channel stuffing. That reliance was obviously misplaced. A strong and independent internal audit staff, with responsibility for financial accounting as well as operational issues, may have alerted the audit committee to what was happening inside the company.

Sales of a significant amount of stock or other risk-reducing transactions by top executives should be viewed as a warning event by the audit committee, which should trigger more intensive auditing. It is not clear that the Symbol audit committee was aware of the "zero cost dollar" entered into by Razmilovic, and it is not always possible to discover this transaction unless there is a strong and independent internal audit function.

In view of the widespread criminal activity at Symbol, it is clear that the firm's independent directors lacked any knowledge of the culture of the organization.

Organizations whose culture is exclusively driven by numbers are at high risk for accounting manipulations, such as cookie jar reserves and channel stuffing. The board of directors must take action to change the culture of such an organization.

ENDNOTES

1. Securities Exchange Act of 1934, Rel. No. 50882, December 20, 2004, www.sec.gov/litigation/admin/34-50882.htm.
2. U.S. Securities and Exchange Commission, Litigation Rel. No. 18734, June 3, 2004, www.sec.gov/litigation/litreleases/lr18734.htm.
3. "SEC Charges Seven Individuals with Aiding and Abetting Financial Fraud at Royal Ahold's U.S. Foodservice Subsidiary for Signing and Returning False Audit Confirmations," U.S. Securities and Exchange Commission, News Release, November 2, 2005, www.sec.gov/news/press/2005-157.htm.
4. U. S. Securities and Exchange Commission, Litigation Rel. No. 19454, November 2, 2005, www.sec.gov/litigation/litreleases/lr19454.htm.
5. "Reliance Insurance Company in Liquidation," Louisiana Department of Insurance, October 4, 2001, www.ldi.state.la.us/whats_new/reliance_ins_co_liquidation.htm.
6. Press Release, United States Attorney's Office, Robert Nardoza, June 3, 2004, www.usdoj.gov/usao/nye/pr/2004jun3.htm.
7. U.S. Securities and Exchange Commission, Litigation Release No. 18734, June 3, 2004, www.sec.gov/litigation/litreleases/lr18734.htm.

Chapter 4

Monitoring and Changing the Corporate Culture

Perhaps the most important corporate governance tool is creating a corporate culture within an organization (whether public, private, or not-for-profit) that is both law-abiding and sensitive to legal risks. Such a culture must be created within an organization without discouraging entrepreneurship or risk taking, which are essential to organizational growth and profitability.

BEST PRACTICE

Create an ethical, law abiding culture within the organization without discouraging entrepreneurial risk taking. A key element of such a culture is the tone at the top of the organization.

This delicate balance between encouraging entrepreneurial risk taking and discouraging the assumption of material legal risks is one of the most difficult challenges for both the board of directors and management. It is clear that Enron encouraged entrepreneurial risk taking but failed to sensitize the employees to avoiding unreasonable legal risks and the need to communicate such risks to the highest level in the organization. A similar culture caused the implosion of Arthur Andersen LLP, according to Barbara Ley Toffler, author of *Final Accounting.*[1]

The culture of an organization is generally reflective of its compensation system. There must be positive incentives for employees to report possible legal risk or wrongdoing. If the only rewards are for financial performance, the organization may wind up with an Enron-type culture. Employees must believe that the risk to their careers of reporting legal risks or wrongdoing up the ladder is worth it. Saving an organization from lawsuits, legal fees, fines, and bad publicity must be equally rewarding as increasing revenues or profits.

To create an ethical, law-abiding corporate culture, negative incentives must also be supplied. Action must be taken to discipline or fire employees who are not sensitive to legal risks or wrongdoing or who fail to disclose such risks to the highest level of the organization. It is important that any disciplinary action against an employee be communicated (without necessarily naming the employee) throughout the organization so as to demonstrate the commitment of the organization to a law abiding culture.

BEST PRACTICE

Employees must be sensitized to the need to communicate significant legal risks to management and to the audit committee or nominating/corporate governance committee of the board of directors.

For example, if an employee of a pharmaceutical company is aware of adverse reactions to a drug sold by that organization, he or she must be able to easily communicate that concern not only to that employee's immediate supervisor but also to the audit committee or nominating corporate governance committee as well as a higher level of management, such as the general counsel. The communication of this information to higher levels beyond the employee's immediate supervisor helps to ensure that the highest levels of authority within the organization are aware of the problem and can develop appropriate business strategies.

Merely communicating a significant legal risk to one's immediate supervisor is not sufficient, since in many cases the supervisor may have financial or other motivation to avoid further disclosure of this information. Therefore, mechanisms must be developed to encourage an open corporate culture that rewards and does not punish employees who communicate adverse information beyond their immediate supervisors.

One of the problems with this type of open corporate culture is that some employees will abuse their ability to communicate to the highest level of management. The employee may have a misunderstanding of the significance of the legal risk. In some cases, employees who have poor performance ratings or are worried about being laid off will communicate legal risks in order to later claim that any action taken against them was really in retaliation for the disclosure of the legal risk, thereby protecting themselves from any disciplinary action or layoff. These situations must be handled on a case-by-case basis and are a necessary disadvantage of having an ethical, law-abiding culture.

The advantage of having an open corporate culture is that the board of directors and management are less likely to have unpleasant surprises because of the realization of legal risks of which lower-level employees may have knowledge. The realization of legal risks can result in significant costs to the organization, a drop in stock price, criminal and civil actions, and embarrassing governmental investigations. If directors and management are given early warning about these legal risks, they have time to take appropriate action to prevent or ameliorate the risk and avoid bad publicity for the organization.

The creation of an ethical, law-abiding culture within an organization is not only good business; it is also mandated by the U.S. Sentencing Guidelines, discussed later, in order to avoid the criminal indictment of the organization.

SENSITIZING EMPLOYEES IN THEIR DEALINGS
WITH PUBLIC COMPANIES

It is hoped that the board of directors of the banks and investment bankers that helped finance Enron's off-balance sheet entities have learned an important and expensive lesson. Creating an ethical, law-abiding corporate culture requires not only an emphasis on internal activities by employees but also a sensitivity to their external actions. The assistance provided to Enron's fraud by these financial institutions have cost them dearly, including these reported settlements, with more to come:

- Canadian Imperial Bank of Commerce (CIBC): $2.4 billion[2]
- Citigroup and J.P. Morgan Securities and Exchange Commission (SEC) fines: $305 million[3]
- J.P. Morgan Chase: $2.2 billion[4]
- Citigroup: $2 billion[5]
- Lehman Bros.: $225 million[6]
- Toronto Dominion Bank: $70 million[7]
- Bank of America: $69 million[8]
- Five investment banks by Alabama Pension Funds: $49 million[9]

To the extent that the Enron settlement payments by these financial institutions cause their own stock to drop, they will likely face shareholder lawsuits. The drop in CIBC's stock price, following the announcement of its eye-popping $2.4 billion settlement, is expected to result in CIBC shareholder suits against their board of directors.

BEST PRACTICE

Employees of any organization (whether public, private, or not for profit) must be sensitized to the problem of dealing with public companies that are customers, suppliers, or have other relationships with the organization. This is a lesson that was painfully learned by the Enron financial institutions.

The SEC has in recent years brought action against organizations that aid or abet a public company in falsifying its financial statements or gave false statements to the auditor of the public company.[10] One example is the case against Ronald Davies, an executive vice president of Ikon Office Solutions, who provided a false audit confirmation to the auditor of Hybrid Networks. Davies participated in Ikon's purchase of products from Hybrid and obtained a letter from Hybrid's sales representative that gave Ikon an absolute right to return any products purchased from Hybrid. When Hybrid's auditor sought confirmation that Ikon had received no right of return, Davies allegedly provided a misleading audit response.[11] Another example is the case against Amazon.com, a vendor to

Ashford.com. Amazon.com employees allegedly caused a securities law violation by settling a contract dispute that was documented, at Ashford's request, using two separate documents, one of which Ashford failed to disclose to its auditors. The SEC, in its opinion, found that Amazon employees *should have known* that the purpose of splitting the settlement into two letters was to help Ashford in improperly deferring expenses.[12]

Care must be taken by all organizations to educate their employees concerning the dangers in responding to audit confirmations from public companies and the dangers in structuring transactions to assist public companies in falsifying their financial statements.

ENRON'S CORPORATE CULTURE

Portions of an interview of Sherron Watkins published in the April 2003 issue of *Internal Auditor* are revealing of Enron's corporate culture:

"Ms. Watkins, how did Enron's corporate culture contribute to the corruption of its governance infrastructure?"

On paper, Enron had everything you would imagine from a Fortune 50 company. It had the right code of conduct and ethics program. CALpers, one of the largest public pension funds, was an investor and performed its own due diligence on Enron before investing; CALpers gave Enron passing grades on its corporate governance.

Outwardly, our corporate values were respect, integrity, communication, and excellence. The problem was the other component of our culture, which was known as a "loose-tight" management structure. "Loose" meant that with regard to commercial revenue-generating endeavors, Enron did not superimpose a strict hierarchy. The goal was for great ideas to float up and be heard, rather than be stifled by an unimaginative boss. This was a big reason we all loved working at Enron—we could each be something of an entrepreneur. The "tight" aspect of this management style referred to tight risk management and spending controls to make sure the company was not wasting time or money on half-baked ideas.

Over time, however, another management model, informally called "rank and yank" and instituted by Enron's Performance Review Committee (PRC), had a way of marginalizing what were supposed to be tight controls. The PRC applied a forced bell curve that comprised about 5 percent of employees at the top and 40 percent spread out in the next two groups—these three groups were the primary bonus categories. Then there was about 30 percent in the middle and two groups toward the end, with at least 8 percent of the employees getting "yanked" (meaning fired) for poor performance. *As for those individuals in charge of control, they soon learned that if they did not help commercial dealmakers achieve financial goals by pushing deals through the system, the PRC would complain about them. The culture should have dictated that the control professionals with the most complaints be rewarded for doing their job and throwing up red flags on suspicious deals.* But that didn't happen at Enron and in time, the tight controls fell away. [Emphasis added]

For their part, the dealmakers had to chase new business ferociously or be persecuted by the PRC. Another company less focused in this way might have stopped and explored deals that were confusing and difficult to understand, just to make sure they held water.

"Describe the overall decision-making process at Enron."

The decision-making procedures were correct, but the controls were marginalized. In my opinion, the biggest problem was that Enron outsourced its internal audit function. On top of that, it outsourced the internal audit function to the company's external auditors, Arthur Andersen. The fact was junior auditors at Andersen were not going to challenge deals that senior Andersen auditors and senior Enron executives had approved.

Companies must have a strong internal audit function, one that reports directly to the audit committee. In the last year before Enron's bankruptcy, the company hired vice presidents for each business unit to coordinate with the Andersen internal auditors to review controls and procedures. These vice presidents went to Richard Causey, Enron's then executive vice president and chief accounting officer, and asked him what kept him awake at night. Causey said, "Nothing." [Emphasis added]

"Did you ever go to the internal auditors with your questions and concerns about the 'creative accounting' you uncovered?"

Who knew who they were? *There was no place for me to voice my concerns, either to the internal audit function or the audit committee.* Remember, I was not in the accounting department. But even if I were, I think I would have known it would have been fruitless, because I would have had access to junior auditors who were simply not in the position to raise the flags that would have hurt their senior auditors and account executives. [Emphasis added]

"What corporate governance advice would you pass along to internal audit departments?"

The three main problems at Enron were that the company had an accommodating and passive board, an unhealthy drive to meet earnings targets and—probably the most damaging quality—a penchant for hiring only the best and the brightest and rewarding them lavishly if they proved they could innovate, innovate, innovate. Unfortunately, the dark side of innovation is fraud.

With this in mind, I would tell internal auditors *that undue earnings pressure—that is, the drive to absolutely not miss earnings targets—is a dangerous sign.* To detect this, I suggest employee surveys, which can help an internal audit function reveal discrepancies among top management, middle management, and lower staff with regard to expectations and earnings pressure. [Emphasis added]

Once upper management starts applying undue pressure and exerting inappropriate influence, people begin to stop questioning authority because they think it is futile to do so. Also, people tend to assuage themselves of guilt when they are controlled by authority—they start hiding behind the mask of the corporation. This is what I think happened at Enron. The tone at the top really is crucial, and if the people at the top are disregarding corporate ethics, so will everyone else. At Enron, there was a vacuum in leadership. [Emphasis added]

Also, internal auditors have to examine compensation arrangements to make sure employees are not committing fraud to be financially rewarded. For example, managing directors at Enron received huge cash rewards when the company outperformed its peer group in Standard & Poor's 500 three years running. In this performance program, a managing director could receive up to $900,000. *Of course, the director is going to suppress objections, questions, or concerns if it puts a bonus of that size in jeopardy.*[13] [Emphasis added]

A number of Enron employees invested in LJM Partnerships and made a significant return. According to the Report of Investigation by the Special Investigative Committee of the Enron Board of Directors dated February 1, 2002 (Powers Report), Michael Copper, who worked for the chief financial officer, Andrew Fastow, received more than $10 million from Enron for a $125,000 investment in some of the off-balance sheet entities. Other employees, including an accountant and an in-house lawyer, also made investments in off-balance sheet entities with extraordinary returns.

Lessons from Enron's Culture

The board of directors must learn the culture of their organization. Any of these elements in the culture should raise a red flag:

- Meeting financial goals is the only thing that creates rewards for employees.
- Internal audit function reports only to management and not to the audit committee of the board of directors.
- The internal audit function is performed by the external auditors rather than by organization employees or an independent outsourcer.

The culture of an organization will be reflected in its compensation system. The board must fully understand the compensation system used by management to reward lower level employees.

U.S. SENTENCING GUIDELINES

Audit committee members must, either alone or together with any nominating/corporate governance committee of the board of directors, inquire from management about their efforts to comply with the revised U.S. Sentencing Commission Guidelines. These U.S. Sentencing Guidelines, effective in November 2004, require that, in order to obtain a reduction in the culpability of the organization for a criminal violation of the securities or anti-trust laws (or other federal criminal laws), the organization must "exercise due diligence to prevent and detect criminal conduct; *and otherwise promote an organizational culture that encourages ethical conduct and a commitment to compliance with the law.*"[14] To satisfy this standard, the organization, at a minimum, must do the following:

(1) The organization shall establish standards and procedures to prevent and detect criminal conduct.

(2) (A) The organization's governing authority shall be knowledgeable about the content and operation of the compliance and ethics program and shall exercise reasonable oversight with respect to the implementation and effectiveness of the compliance and ethics program.

(B) High-level personnel of the organization shall ensure that the organization has an effective compliance and ethics program, as described in this guideline. Specific individual(s) within high-level personnel shall be assigned overall responsibility for the compliance and ethics program.

(C) Specific individual(s) within the organization shall be delegated day-to-day operational responsibility for the compliance and ethics program. Individual(s) with operational responsibility shall report periodically to high-level personnel and, as appropriate, to the governing authority, or an appropriate subgroup of the governing authority, on the effectiveness of the compliance and ethics program. To carry out such operational responsibility, such individual(s) shall be given adequate resources, appropriate authority, and direct access to the governing authority or an appropriate subgroup of the governing authority.

(3) The organization shall use reasonable efforts not to include within the substantial authority personnel of the organization any individual whom the organization knew, or should have known through the exercise of due diligence, has engaged in illegal activities or other conduct inconsistent with an effective compliance and ethics program.

(4) (A) The organization shall take reasonable steps to communicate periodically and in a practical manner its standards and procedures, and other aspects of the compliance and ethics program, to the individuals referred to in subdivision (B) by conducting effective training programs and otherwise disseminating information appropriate to such individuals' respective roles and responsibilities.

(B) The individuals referred to in subdivision (A) are the members of the governing authority, high-level personnel, substantial authority personnel, the organization's employees, and, as appropriate, the organization's agents.

(5) The organization shall take reasonable steps—
(A) to ensure that the organization's compliance and ethics program is followed, including monitoring and auditing to detect criminal conduct;
(B) to evaluate periodically the effectiveness of the organization's compliance and ethics program; and
(C) to have and publicize a system, which may include mechanisms that allow for anonymity or confidentiality, whereby the organization's employees and agents may report or seek guidance regarding potential or actual criminal conduct without fear of retaliation.

(6) The organization's compliance and ethics program shall be promoted and enforced consistently throughout the organization through (A) appropriate incentives to perform in accordance with the compliance and ethics program; and (B) appropriate disciplinary measures for engaging in criminal conduct and failing to take reasonable steps to prevent or detect criminal conduct.

(7) After criminal conduct has been detected, the organization shall take reasonable steps to respond appropriately to the criminal conduct and to prevent further similar criminal conduct, including making any necessary modifications to the organization's compliance and ethics program.

The U.S. Sentencing Guidelines apply to all organizations, whether private, public, or not-for-profit.

Audit and corporate governance committees should also be aware of the U.S. Department of Justice's position entitled "Principles of Federal Prosecution of Business Organizations" (January 20, 2003, also called the Thompson Memorandum). That memorandum provides this guide to federal prosecutors in determining whether to criminally indict an organization:

> Prosecutors should therefore attempt to determine whether a corporation's compliance program is merely a "paper program" or whether it was designed and implemented in an effective manner. In addition, prosecutors should determine whether the corporation has provided for a staff sufficient to audit, document, analyze, and utilize the results of the corporation's compliance efforts. In addition, prosecutors should determine whether the corporation's employees are adequately informed about the compliance program and are convinced of the corporation's commitment to it. This will enable the prosecutor to make an informed decision as to whether the corporation has adopted and implemented a truly effective compliance program that, when consistent with other federal law enforcement policies, may result in a decision to charge only the corporation's employees and agents.[15]

INEFFECTIVE COMPLIANCE PROGRAMS

On September 29, 2003, a suit was brought by the United States against Merck-Medco Managed Care, one of the largest pharmacy benefit managers in the United States, alleging that the company had engaged in a broad range of fraudulent practices, including submitting false claims to the United States for payment of pharmacy benefit management services. Among the conduct cited by the United States as a basis for False Claims Act liability was the company's failure to develop and enforce an appropriate compliance reporting system. The complaint recited, among other things, that the employees were not made aware of the compliance program, there were no specific high-level personnel with direct responsibility for overseeing compliance and with direct access to the chief executive and the board of directors, there were no regular reports to the board concerning internal investigations, there was no effective anonymous hotline, there was no effective protection for whistleblowers, and so on. The moral of this story is that an ineffective compliance program may itself constitute a violation of the False Claims Act.[16]

CHANGING THE CORPORATE CULTURE

This article from *Communication World* explains how the new leadership of Adelphia attempted to change the corporate culture after the scandals involving the Rigas family:

ETHICAL MISCONDUCT AT ADELPHIA REQUIRES NEW LEADERSHIP AND REBUILDING

by Ray Dravesky

> In May 2002, Adelphia's founder and CEO resigned amid accusations that he and his sons had borrowed and used billions of company dollars for personal items. In June 2002, Adelphia declared bankruptcy. Nine months later, two experienced cable industry veterans came on board to lead the company. They started a turnaround effort to rebuild the company's reputation internally.

The new leaders wanted to ensure that the actions that had almost destroyed the company would never happen again. They worked closely with Adelphia's board of directors to adopt a new code of business conduct and ethics. In April 2003, the board adopted the code and mandated that the company share it with all Adelphia employees.

INTENDED AUDIENCES

Adelphia employees made up the main audience for the new code of business conduct and ethics. Especially important to reach were executives, supervisors, board members, HR staff and new hires. The team also aimed its messages at the legal community and the media.

GOALS/OBJECTIVES

To build greater awareness of ethics issues at all levels of the organization, it was important to reinforce Adelphia's new values and new business mission, which included developing a reputation as a company with outstanding corporate governance. As role models, the company's managers and supervisors needed to make changes in support of the desired corporate culture change. It was also paramount to minimize Adelphia's risk of exposure in the event of an investigation or lawsuit by demonstrating that the company had proactively communicated ethics policies to all employees. Finally, the new management team wanted to further distance itself and the board from former executives and board members.

The team identified four main objectives related to these goals:

* getting 100 percent of executives and managers and as many frontline employees as possible to acknowledge the new code of business conduct and ethics by 31 Dec. 2003
* generating active use of a new hot line for employees
* having no employee lawsuits filed around ethical issues
* making outside experts, including the press, notice that Adelphia was serious about improving its reputation.

SOLUTION OVERVIEW

The solution contained many elements, including a communication strategy to plan and guide communication and to assure the board that corporate was working to restore employees' confidence in Adelphia. The team conducted a pulse survey of approximately 200 internal communication professionals, asking about their recent experiences with ethics communication. The results influenced the communication approach.

The team held town hall meetings to involve managers and inform them of the planned rollout of the conduct code and their roles in communication. Adelphia's management team answered questions and provided managers with points to use in talking both informally and formally with others.

Adelphia's electronic executive newsletter announced three major business initiatives, including ethics. By including ethics with the other initiatives, the team emphasized that ethics were intertwined with Adelphia's business strategy and 2003 operating initiatives, and not a standalone event.

The team created a folder that included the official code of conduct, along with a highlights sheet and a wallet card. In addition, the team arranged for an online acknowledgement form that employees would complete to show that they had received the folder, read it and were committed to following the new code . . .

IMPLEMENTATION AND CHALLENGES

Concerned about its cash flow, Adelphia had extremely small budgets for special projects. Therefore, it was important to design a kit that would attract attention, signify the substance and importance of the information, yet appear calming and modest.

Throughout all communication, the team emphasized that the policy change applied to everyone. The goal was to ensure that employees understood that the new code of business conduct and ethics was not just for executives (even though the recent lapse of ethics was with former executives). The team also had to ensure that employees realized that the new way of doing business was not a special one-time activity to please the bankruptcy court and impress the media.

The online system used to collect employee acknowledgement forms streamlined and sped up the process, while reinforcing the organization's focus on adopting more technological solutions. However, the system was accessible only through Adelphia's intranet, InSite. About 50 percent of employees did not have easy access to InSite, and at that time, the intranet was not totally reliable. To overcome these challenges, the team encouraged employees to go to supervisors, managers or HR representatives if they had trouble getting the form online.

To support HR staff in rolling out and explaining the policy, the team made the communication as self-contained as possible so that HR staff members in the field could meet face to face with employees and deliver messages with their own local flavor, without having to spend time creating custom messages and materials.

MEASUREMENT/EVALUATION

To measure the success of the code of conduct rollout, the team tracked performance against their objectives. As of 31 Dec. 2003

- About 95 percent of leaders had completed the acknowledgement form, and electronic signatures from 54 percent of the frontline employees had been collected.
- The hot line received about 300 calls from September through December 2003. Almost all of these calls were about HR matters and problems with tools and other on-the-job resources. Very few were related to potential violations of the code of conduct.
- No Lawsuits Had Been Filed.

The company also received favorable press coverage from several news outlets about the new code of conduct and ethics. In addition, employees offered positive unsolicited feedback.

As a result, the board and the company leadership viewed the policy change as a successful endeavor with an extremely high return on investment. Good ethical practices have become part of the new culture at Adelphia.

The communication team at Adelphia developed a comprehensive communication plan to educate and involve employees with the company's new code of conduct and ethics.

Among their efforts:

- setting up a hot line for employees to call to report possible ethics problems or ask questions
- designing a poster that highlighted the anonymous hot line number, reinforced the company's new business values and showed how the new values supported ethics
- producing a train-the-trainer kit. which included an employee presentation that HR managers could give at staff meetings to strengthen the messages contained in the folder, and to provide an opportunity for employees to ask questions
- preparing FAQs for HR managers and line managers to familiarize them with the issues, and to share with their employees if they so desired.[17]

ENDNOTES

1. Barbara Ley Toffler, *Final Accounting: Ambition, Greed, and the Fall of Arthur Andersen* (New York: Broadway Books, 2003).
2. "Canadian Bank to Settle Enron Case," *Washington Times*, August 3, 2005.
3. Matthew Goldstein, "Citigroup, J.P. Morgan Fined $305 Million for Enron Role," The Street.com, July 28, 2003, www.thestreet.com/pf/markets/matthewgoldstein/10103933.html.
4. Criswell, "US: J. P. Morgan Chase to Pay Investors $2.2 Billion," *New York Times*, June 15, 2005.
5. Isadore, "Citigroup to Pay $2B in Enron Case," CNNMoney.com, June 16, 2005, http://money.cnn.com/2005/06/10/news/fortune500/citigroup_enron/?section=money_latest.
6. Matthew Goldstein, "Lehman Forks Out $225 Million to Enron Shareholders," The Street.com, October 29, 2004, www.thestreet.com/stocks/brokerages/10191585.html.
7. "Two More Banks Settle Enron Claims," Washingtonpost.com, August 17, 2005, www.washingtonpost.com/wp-dyn/content/article/2005/08/16/AR2005081601701.html.
8. "Bank of America Settles Enron Suit for $69M," *Houston Business Journal*, July 2, 2004.
9. Rawls, "RSA Settles Enron Lawsuit," *The Decatur Daily News*, (June 15, 2005) www.decaturdaily.com/decaturdaily/news/050615/rsa.shtml.
10. Securities Exchange Act of 1934 Release No. 42987 / June 29, 2000 www.sec.gov/litigation/admin/34-42987.htm.
11. In re *Ronald G. Davies*, Release No. 34-42987 (June 28, 2000).
12. In re Ashford.com, Release No. 3446052 (June 10, 2002).
13. Watkins "If Capitalists Were Angels," *Internal Auditor*, (April 2003). www.allbusiness.com/periodicals/article/521380-1.html. This article was reprinted, with permission from April 2003 issue of *Internal Auditor*, published by The Institute of Internal Auditors, Inc. www.theiia.org.
14. "2004 Federal Sentencing Guideline Manual," United States Sentencing Commission (November 1, 2004) www.ussc.gov/2004guid/TABCON04.htm. Emphasis added.
15. www.usdoj.gov/dag/cftf/corporate_guidelines.htm.
16. "Can Ineffective Compliance Programs Violate the FCA?," Compliance Week, Financial Media Holdings Group, Inc. (January 2006), page 1.
17. "Ethical Misconduct at Adelphia Requires New Leadership and Rebuilding," *Communication World* (Nov-Dec 2004). www.allbusiness.com/periodicals/article/380165-1.html. Reprinted with permission.

Chapter 5

The Internal Audit Function

After creation of an ethical, law-abiding culture, the second most important corporate governance action is to create an internal audit function. The auditor should act as the eyes and ears of the board of directors, particularly the audit committee, the compensation committee, and the nominating/corporate governance committee (if any) of the board of directors.

The audit committee of the board of directors is an essential part of the internal control structure of an organization. The basic problem with audit committees is that, no matter how competent their members, they can only operate on the information they receive. In addition, they cannot devote full time and effort to the organization and typically meet anywhere from a minimum of 4 to 10 times a year. It is clear from the discussion of the corporate scandals that audit committees cannot rely exclusively on either the outside auditors or management to perform that role. Audit committees must have their own independent sources of information to properly perform their monitoring role.

BEST PRACTICE

Establishing an effective internal audit function, reporting to the audit committee, is probably the most important thing that can be done by an audit committee. The most important source of independent information for the audit committee is the internal auditor. Some companies outsource their internal audit function and some companies maintain a full employed staff of internal auditors.

It is clear from the WorldCom fiasco that the audit committee must control the operations of the internal audit department to the extent that those functions deal with the audit of financial reporting. The WorldCom audit committee allowed management to control the internal audit department and created an incentive structure that required the internal audit group to emphasize operational audits which saved money for WorldCom or otherwise produced "value." This resulted in an internal audit group that did not have the staffing or funding to provide adequate information to the audit committee on financial reporting issues.

COMPENSATION COMMITTEE AND NOMINATING CORPORATE GOVERNANCE COMMITTEE

The compensation committee of the board of directors also needs the eyes and ears of the internal auditor to supply and verify the information it receives on executive compensation. The Tyco scandal might have been avoided had the Tyco compensation committee required the internal auditor to verify the information of executive compensation contained in the Tyco proxy statement.[1] The nominating/corporate governance committee (if any) of the board of directors also needs its own flow of information from the internal auditor. If the nominating/corporate governance committee is monitoring the corporate culture, this information is invaluable to determining whether the organization maintains an ethical, law-abiding culture.

INTERNAL AUDIT COSTS

An internal audit function is currently not required by law, rule, or regulation, except for companies listed on the New York Stock Exchange. Many companies do not wish to establish an internal audit function because of the cost of doing so. Although it is true that establishing a strong internal function can be expensive, scandals are even more expensive.

Many companies establish or beef up their internal audit function after an accounting scandal that has cost them millions of dollars in legal fees, huge amounts of executive time, fines, and damage to the corporate reputation. An effective internal audit function should help to prevent these disastrous costs.

Perhaps management should look at internal audit as a substitute for scandal insurance. If scandal insurance were available (which it is not), many companies would purchase it if the premium costs were reasonable. Internal audit costs should be viewed as a form of insurance.

Operational internal auditing can itself save the company money in uncovering duplication, waste, and wrongdoing at lower levels of the company. Structuring the internal audit function to include financial reporting (to avoid the WorldCom problem) could also be viewed as an additional cost of having an informed board of directors who are legally required to monitor top management of the company to prevent wrongdoing.

CREATING AN INDEPENDENT AUDIT FUNCTION

The concept of having the internal auditor report both to management and to the audit committee is flawed unless the audit committee plays a proactive role in controlling the internal audit function. Management needs the internal audit function to provide operational audits and to provide management with important information. The audit committee needs to obtain independent information from the internal audit function to enable the audit committee to perform its role of monitoring management, particularly with regard to financial reporting.

Thus, based on the lessons of the corporate scandals, the audit committee should adhere to the best practices that follow.

BEST PRACTICE

Play a major role in the selection, retention, and evaluation of the internal auditor or the internal audit group (whether in-house or outsourced).

BEST PRACTICE

Determine the compensation of the head of internal auditing in consultation with management.

BEST PRACTICE

Meet separately with the head of internal audit, without management present, to determine the adequacy of the staffing and funding of the internal audit function.

BEST PRACTICE

Play an active role in reviewing and approving the annual internal audit budget and services.

BEST PRACTICE

Question the head of internal auditing, without management present, on significant risk areas within the business.

BEST PRACTICE

Compensate the internal auditor without regard to cost savings or efficiencies uncovered in the internal audit process, based solely on the quality of the services rendered by the internal auditor.

BEST PRACTICE

Require the internal auditor to provide more intensive services with regard to financial reporting if certain warning events occur (e.g., the company barely made its earning projection, which produced a large bonus from management, as discussed more fully in Chapter 15).

BEST PRACTICE

Be certain that the internal auditor and the independent outside auditor are fully exchanging information and are otherwise coordinating with each other.

BEST PRACTICE

The chairman of the audit committee and the head of internal audit should exchange cellular numbers.

OPERATIONAL VERSUS FINANCIAL INTERNAL AUDITING

The audit committee and the board of directors need financial and other internal auditing work performed by the internal audit department in order to have an independent source of information. However, management typically also requires internal audit departments to do operational auditing and to report to management on these operational audits, which are very important to the day-to-day operation of the business.

These requirements may necessitate that the internal audit department be bifurcated between those performing operational internal audits and those performing financial statement audits, and a separate budget established for each function. If there is a bifurcation of the internal audit department, there must be a single head of the department who can provide the results of the operational audits, as well as the financial statement audits, to the audit committee and the board of directors.

BEST PRACTICE

The audit committee and the head of the internal audit department must prevent any interference by management, as occurred in WorldCom, according to the Second Interim Report of Dick Thornburgh, dated June 9, 2003 (Thornburgh Report), in the financial statement audits.[2]

WORLDCOM'S INTERNAL AUDIT DEPARTMENT

The Second Thornburgh Report found that the WorldCom Internal Audit Department was not really independent and was focused by management on operational issues, rather than financial reporting. The report stated:

> It is now clear that the Internal Audit Department, despite some dual reporting responsibility to the Company's Audit Committee, was never truly an independent department but rather reported and was answerable to senior Management including the CFO [chief financial officer], or Mr. [Charles] Cannada [Senior Vice President of Corporate Development], and the CEO [chief executive officer]. Members of the Internal Audit Department did not believe that Mr. Ebbers initially accepted the necessity of an Internal Audit Department at his Company and claim that he had to be convinced of its value. The viability of the Internal Audit Department was thus largely dependent on the whim of senior Management, and especially the CFO and CEO, with little more than deference being given to the Audit Committee. For years, the leadership of the Internal Audit Department sought to gain acceptance as team players by focusing the work of the Department on audits and projects that would be seen as adding "value" to the Company, rather than fulfilling any role as the Company's "internal control police."
>
> Internal Audit focused primarily on finding ways to assist the Company in maximizing revenue, reducing costs and improving efficiencies. As a result, most of the audits conducted by Internal Audit were strictly operational audits with these objectives in mind. Over the years, Internal Audit did conduct some operational audits with financial components. However, we could not discern any methodology used to determine those operational audits that would also include a financial component.
>
> While Internal Audit reviewed the relevant financial amounts generated in the detail subsidiary journals, it did not, for the most part, trace transactions to the general ledger . . .
>
> In this way, Internal Audit focused its audits primarily on areas expected to yield cost savings and additional revenues . . .
>
> Internal Audit's narrow focus may have contributed, in part, to the Company's failure to detect some of the accounting improprieties reported by WorldCom at an earlier stage. Even though a line cost audit appears to have been annually scheduled by the Internal Audit Department, it was always the first to be rescheduled due to other priorities. When it performed the line cost audits, Internal Audit focused on the operational level without apparently any review or verification of the Company's general ledger and the journal entries that supported those line costs . . .
>
> As a result, internal controls with an impact on the Company's accounting policies were not systematically evaluated and monitored by Internal Audit and certainly were not communicated to the external auditors for their review.

Chief Financial Officer Control of Internal Audit Department

The WorldCom CFO, rather than the audit committee, controlled the internal audit department. According to the Second Thornburgh Report:

> The CFO oversaw all personnel actions for the Department, approving promotions and changes in officer titles, as well as salary increases, bonuses, and stock options,

and provided guidance to the development of the scope of the Department's audits and audit plans, the conduct of its audits, and the issuance of its conclusions and recommendations. The Audit Committee approved the charter for the Internal Audit Department in November 1999 and annually approved audit plans but, in contrast to the CFO or to Mr. Cannada, had little to no input regarding the modification of those plans during the audit year. Internal Audit presented to the Audit Committee its final conclusions and recommendations developed in cooperation with Management, in the form of summaries and oral presentations and, occasionally, final reports. The Audit Committee had no input in either the development of the scope of each audit or the findings and recommendations issued at its conclusion. Nor did the Audit Committee play any role in determining the day-to-day activities of the Internal Audit department. At times, Mr. Ebbers or Mr. Sullivan would assign "special projects" to the Internal Audit Department. Some of these projects were not audit-related and the Audit Committee does not appear to have been consulted about such assignments. In a glaring and disturbing example, in the fall of 2000, Mr. Ebbers assigned to the Internal Audit Department responsibility for generating the ERP, which was a compilation of schedules and trend analyses for tracking orders, activations, disconnections and cancellations received by the Company from its customers each month, and estimating the Company's revenues associated with those orders. This reporting package was purely operational in nature and had no audit purpose or use, but enabled senior Management, and Mr. Ebbers in particular, to track on a monthly basis increases or decreases in orders placed with the Company by its customers and potential swings in revenue associated with those orders.

The production of the ERP was time-intensive, consuming most of the time of Internal Audit's staff for at least the first six months of its inception. This effort drained scarce departmental resources and delayed scheduled audits. Internal Audit staff have indicated that, at times, they would work on the ERP during the day and stay late into the evening to perform the audit functions they were unable to perform during the day. The use of Internal Audit for the ERP was reportedly defended by Ms. Cooper to a complaining staff member as an important effort that added "value" to the Company, was in keeping with her department's consulting function within the Company, and could demonstrate to the Company's leadership the indispensability of the Internal Audit Department. . . . the Audit Committee does not appear to have ever been consulted about this assignment or informed of its impact on the Department's scarce resources until the decision was made to transfer responsibilities for preparation of the ERP to a different department nearly two years later. Significantly, Internal Audit did not meet its audit plan objectives, in part, because of the time and resources devoted to the ERP. . . .

Staffing and Funding of Internal Audit Department

The Second Thornburgh Report noted that the WorldCom Internal Audit Department was understaffed and underfunded and had to justify its operations by whether they added "value" to WorldCom. The report stated:

> According to the 2002 Global Auditing Information Network peer study ("Gain Study") conducted by The Institute of Internal Auditors ("IIA"), WorldCom's Internal Audit Department, at a staff of 27 by 2002, was half the size of the internal audit departments of peer telecommunications companies. In May 2002, after Mr. Ebbers' departure from the Company, Ms. Cooper presented the results of the Gain Study to

the Audit Committee, advising them that her Department was understaffed and underpaid. . . .

An Internal Audit function operating with such limited resources appears particularly inappropriate from an internal controls perspective given the international breadth and scope of the Company's operations and the challenges posed by the Company's status as a conglomeration of recently merged or acquired companies. . . .

In sum, an audit area's level of risk was determined by assessing whether the audit would add value to the Company and enhance revenue. If it did not meet these criteria, the audit would be considered to have a low level of risk and would not be performed. . . .

The annual internal audit planning process was wholly deficient for a number of reasons. Typically, an annual audit planning process should start with the review of a company's audit universe, which is a risk-rated, comprehensive list of all auditable areas within a company. Risks should be assessed based on the perceived strengths and weaknesses of the internal controls, the security over systems, and the reliability of the personnel responsible for such controls and systems. At WorldCom, risk analysis was instead performed with the goal of selecting audits that could add "value" to the Company by emphasizing revenue enhancements and cost reductions. Moreover, the lack of any consultation with Arthur Andersen resulted in gaps in audit coverage. Given the absence of a comprehensive risk-based internal audit plan, there was no apparent relationship between the audits scheduled annually and the risk and the effectiveness of internal controls associated with these audit areas.

Failure of Audit Committee to Review Internal Audit Plan

The WorldCom committee did not truly participate in reviewing the adequacy of the firm's annual internal audit plan. According to the report:

> Of concern is the lack of any effective participation by the Audit Committee in reviewing the adequacy of the annual internal audit plan, with the Audit Committee appearing to have approved the final plan as a formality. Based upon requests of Management, other audits, not part of the Audit Committee-approved plan, were added while some audits originally scheduled were not completed. At most, the Audit Committee was advised of such changes after the fact. Under such circumstances, senior Management could influence the focus of the Internal Audit Department away from sensitive areas without the oversight that the Audit Committee would normally be expected to provide.

> An Audit Plan Universe, or the equivalent, should have been presented to the Audit Committee annually for its review and approval. WorldCom apparently had no such procedure. Indeed, we have not identified any effective participation by the Audit Committee in setting the internal audit plan. Under such circumstances, the ability of senior management to influence the focus of the Internal Audit Department away from sensitive areas may be left without the control check which the Audit Committee is expected to provide.

> Our investigation to date has shown only perfunctory attention by the Audit Committee to the audits performed by the Internal Audit Department. Moreover, the Audit Committee minutes and other records did not include reference to the status of significant and unresolved internal control weaknesses cited in prior audits. We are

still seeking to identify whether such weaknesses were resolved. If the Audit Committee did not maintain such records, it denied itself a ready means to determine whether the identified weaknesses were subsequently addressed. There is no evidence that the Audit Committee requested from the Internal Audit Department updates on the status of internal control weaknesses. The records of the Audit Committee also appear devoid of timetables for corrective action and resolution.

Dealings with Arthur Andersen

The report noted the failure of the internal audit department to coordinate with the independent auditor, stating:

> We found little evidence of substantive interaction between Arthur Andersen and the Internal Audit Department. This would violate a core requirement of GAAS [generally accepted accounting standards] if Arthur Andersen placed any reliance on the internal audit function for monitoring and testing the status of the Company's internal controls . . . We are still investigating to determine whether Arthur Andersen relied on any reports or activities by the Internal Audit Department. However, they did have access to internal audit reports distributed at meetings of the Audit Committee. Despite these reports, Arthur Andersen represented to the Audit Committee and the Board of Directors that there were no material weaknesses regarding the Company's system of internal controls.

Budgetary Resources

According to the Thornburgh Report, the WorldCom audit committee failed to follow through on discussions with internal auditing about the adequacy of staff. As previously noted, WorldCom's internal audit department was half the size of internal audit departments in peer telecommunication companies, according to the 2002 Global Auditing Information Network study conducted by the Institute of Internal Auditors.

BEST PRACTICE

It is the responsibility of the audit committee to ask the head of internal audit as to the adequacy of his or her personnel and budget to perform the task assigned to the internal audit department and to make appropriate changes where necessary.

Interaction with External Auditors

According to the Thornburgh Report, there was little interaction between the company's external auditors and the company's internal auditors after 1997, other than quarterly audit committee meetings where both gave presentations. This would suggest that there should be regular communication between the internal and external auditors outside of the formality of the audit committee meeting. The audit committee should be responsible to make sure that this happens.

Annual Internal Audit Planning

BEST PRACTICE

Create an annual plan for the internal audit process, taking into account significant risk areas of the organization.

According to the Thornburgh Report, the risk assessment used during the World-Com internal audit planning process did not involve quantitative factors to measure risk with respect to internal control weaknesses or prior audit findings. The level of risk was determined by assessing whether the audit would add value—that is, enhance revenue or detect significant cost savings—or not. If an audit area's level of risk did not meet these criteria, the audit would be considered low risk and would not be performed.

The audit committee and the head of internal audit must carefully annually plan the internal audit process to take into account the areas of significant risk to the business.

Internal Audit Function: Employees versus Independent Contractors

Many public companies do not wish to have a large internal audit staff of full-time employees and instead use independent contractors. There are many fine outsourcers of internal audit services.

One of the key pieces of information that an audit committee needs is some sense of the culture of the organization. It is extremely difficult to obtain that information solely by using outsourcers. Therefore, it is a good practice to have at least one full-time employee as head of internal audit, who can supply such information to the audit committee, even if the balance of the internal audit services are performed by an outsourcer.

Uncooking the WorldCom Books

Appendix C contains the exciting story of Cynthia Cooper, WorldCom's vice president of internal audit, and her team, who discovered the accounting World-Com fraud, and provides some insight as to the benefits of having an alert and motivated internal auditing staff.

ENDNOTES

1. "SEC Sues Former Tyco CEO Kozlowski, Two Others for Fraud," U.S. Securities and Exchange Commission, September 12, 2002, www.sec.gov/news/press/2002-135.htm.
2. "Second Interim Report of Dick Thornburgh, Bankruptcy Court Examiner" (Bankr. SDNY June 9, 2003), *In re WORLDCOM, INC., et al*, Chapter 11 Case No. 02-15533 (AJG), Jointly Administered.

Chapter 6

Compensation Committees of Public, Private, and Not-for-Profit Organizations

---

BEST PRACTICE

The compensation committee's responsibilities should include overseeing the organization's overall compensation structure, policies, and programs (including board compensation); establishing or recommending to the board performance goals and objectives for the chief executive officer (CEO) and other members of senior management; and establishing or recommending to the independent directors compensation for the CEO and senior management.

The compensation committee is equally as important as the audit committee in the corporate governance structure. Since the culture of an organization is reflective of its compensation policies, the policies adopted by the compensation committee can be instrumental in establishing an ethical, law-abiding culture.

The compensation committee (or possibly the corporate governance committee) must study the entire compensation system within the organization to determine whether the incentives and disincentives are consistent with an ethical, law-abiding culture. Unfortunately, many compensation committees limit their activities to the compensation just of the top executives. This is a mistake unless some other committee (e.g., corporate governance committee) has been assigned the duty of monitoring the entire compensation structure of the organization.

BEST PRACTICE

The compensation committee should have the authority to retain compensation consultants, counsel, and other advisors to provide the committee with independent advice.

The compensation committee cannot rely on experts provided by management and should have its own independent access to outside experts, including compensation consultants, counsel, and other advisors. To avoid conflicts of interest, it is particularly important for the compensation committee to use independent experts to assist the committee in establishing reasonable compensation for the members of the board of directors.

CREATING INCENTIVES FOR GOOD CORPORATE GOVERNANCE

If the only incentives given to top management by the compensation committee are numbers driven, the board of directors should not be surprised if the corporate culture of the organization is also numbers driven. An excessively numbers-driven culture will produce an Enron or a WorldCom.

The board must recognize that top management of public companies is under greater pressure than ever before from securities analysts to hit the numbers in order to keep the share price up. The board must balance this pressure by creating incentives for ethical behavior and good corporate governance as well as incentives that are driven by financial results.

BEST PRACTICE

Incentives must be provided by the compensation committee for top management of all organizations (whether public, private, or not-for-profit) to create good corporate governance. These incentives should include significant economic rewards for achieving these goals:

- Creating an ethical, law-abiding corporate culture
- Assisting the board in establishing an effective internal control function that monitors management on financial statement issues

---

Most boards of directors would be loath to reward top management whose economic performance is poor just because they have also accomplished corporate governance goals. Therefore, there has to be a balance in the compensation system between rewards created for financial performance and rewards for satisfying corporate governance objectives. At a minimum, even if the compensation committee does not reward reaching corporate governance goals, top management should be penalized for the failure to achieve such objectives.

How does the compensation committee measure the achievement of corporate governance goals for the purpose of determining management rewards or penalties? Such measurements may require the use of outside consultants on corporate culture, input from the internal auditor, and direct conversations between board or compensation committee members and lower-level employees. The attitude of the sales and marketing group within the organization is of particular importance, since such employees may have some of the greatest incentives for unethical behavior.

It is crucial to good corporate governance that the board balance management incentives to satisfy financial goals with the incentives to accomplish corporate governance objectives. However, the financial incentive to management for good governance will never equal the financial incentives to management for creating shareholder value—nor should they. Therefore, other mechanisms for overseeing management must be utilized (e.g., internal audit).

EXECUTIVE COMPENSATION ISSUES[1]

Compensation committees have been the focus of an intense media and public criticism for providing what is viewed as excessive compensation to top executives. Some of the corporate scandals have also resulted from compensation committees establishing financial compensation objectives that are met by cooking the books. (See Huntingdon Bancshares, Inc. in Chapter 13.) The compensation committee of Tyco's board of directors failed to verify that the compensation paid to its two top executives was not greater than what the committee had approved.[2]

Compensation of executives of tax-exempt organizations has also become a major issue for the media, Congress, and state attorney generals. Moreover, the IRS has focused its attention on executive compensation practices of tax-exempt organizations and has developed an aggressive audit and compliance program in which 2,000 charities and foundations will be asked about their compensation practices. See Chapter 18 for more details.

BEST PRACTICE

The compensation committee should have a tally sheet of all executive compensation components, which should be created by the human resources (HR) department and verified by the internal auditor.

Executive compensation packages are complex. The compensation committee must understand all aspects of an executive's compensation package. Likewise, the compensation committee should understand the maximum payment due to the executive under different scenarios, such as change of control, retirement, termination with or without cause, and so on. An analysis must be obtained by the compensation committee of the maximum payout due under each of these different situations. This analysis is typically performed by the HR department, often with the assistance of counsel and either the internal or external auditor.

The tally sheets should include all elements of compensation, including the annual increase in the value of pension plans as well as annual gains from deferred benefit plans.[3]

Any analysis should be verified by the internal auditor and presented to the compensation committee annually. The analysis should include not only the cash payments to the executive under various potential scenarios, but also the accounting effect so that shareholders are not shocked by a very material charge to income.

COMMON MISTAKES OF COMPENSATION COMMITTEES

Some of the common mistakes made by compensation committees follow.

- *The failure to understand all of the components of the compensation of the key officers.* As noted, a comprehensive tally sheet should be created by the HR department for the compensation committee and verified by the internal auditor, so all of these components are in one place. Include in such tally sheet such obscure items as annual interest on deferred compensation and annual dividends on restricted stock grants.
- *Overreliance on surveys by compensation consultants.* In this regard, compensation committees should read the speech by Fred Cook posted on the Website of CompensationStandards.com.[4]
- *Failure to consider internal pay equity.* How does the compensation of the CEO compare to other executives and lower-level employees of the organization during the past five or ten years? However, internal pay equity considerations should not inhibit a compensation committee from payment of competitive compensation to talented executives.
- *Failure to understand the true value of perquisites* (such as personal use of a company airplane as described in the Tyson Foods case described later in the chapter).

No single executive compensation formula works for all companies. Some boards have been aligning executive pay with short-term performance by keeping salaries competitive, paying bonuses that can amount to half the annual compensation, and tying bonuses directly to performance against budgets. To keep executives from focusing only on short-term results, some boards of public companies are also awarding stock options or restricted stock grants based on how the company's stock is doing compared to its competitors. However, from a corporate governance perspective, public companies should not tie too large a share of the CEO's compensation to the company's stock price for fear of creating incentives that are contrary to good corporate governance.

It is currently in fashion for public companies to grant restricted stock rather than stock options to executives. This can be a mistake unless the restrictions on the restricted stock are based on satisfying financial goals. Although stock options have received bad press as a result of the corporate scandals, they have the advantage of rewarding executives only if the public market valuation of the public company increases. Restricted stock awards where the restrictions lapse solely over time (regardless of financial performance) reward executives even if the shareholders suffer a decrease in their market price. In addition, restricted stock awards may permit the executive to receive dividends on the restricted stock, which are not available to the holder of an unexercised stock option.

In any event, the compensation committee must retain discretion since no compensation formula works perfectly. For example, a company could have a great year because one of its competitors goes out of business and a terrible year that may set the stage for future growth.

BEST PRACTICE

Require executives who receive stock options or stock grants to hold the stock until retirement and cease granting stock options or rewards once the executive receives a sufficient level of equity.

Some companies are implementing hold-until-retirement provisions in their stock options and stock grants and placing an overall limit on the equity rewards to executives. The advantage of the hold-until-retirement provisions is that they align the interest of the executive with the interests of the long-term shareholders. Any such provisions should contain an exception for personal emergencies of the executive, as determined by the board of directors. The advantage of placing a cap on the total amount of equity rewards is to limit the total amount of equity received by the executive to an amount sufficient to motivate him or her properly, but not in excess of that amount.

LAKE WOBEGON EFFECT[5]

Compensation committees should avoid what has been characterized as the Lake Wobegon effect (after the mythical Minnesota village dreamed up by radio personality Garrison Keillor, where "all the children are above average"). Not all executives are above average and not all executives deserve to be above the 50th percentile in compensation.

BEST PRACTICE FOR PUBLIC COMPANIES

Require shareholder approval of executive severance agreements that would constitute an excess golden parachute payment under Section 280G of the Internal Revenue Code.

Companies that have adopted this policy or a variant include the Coca-Cola Company, Bank of America Corp., Raytheon Co., Hewlett-Packard, Electronic Data Systems, American Electric Power, Union Pacific, and AutoNation.[6] Under the Internal Revenue Code, no deduction is allowed to a public company with respect to an "excess parachute payment," which is typically a payment to a disqualified individual (generally officers or other highly compensated individuals) contingent on a change in the ownership or effective control of the corporation, or in the ownership of a substantial portion of the assets of the corporation, that equals or exceeds three times the "base amount" of such individual.

This policy has the incidental benefit of deterring requests for "excess parachute payments" from executives or so-called gross-up clauses to cover the golden parachute taxes. The disadvantage of this policy is that the cost of the shareholders' meeting sometimes can exceed the golden parachute payment and can interfere with the hiring of key executives. However, on the whole, seeking shareholder approval is generally going to be the best policy in today's atmosphere.

PRACTICAL STEPS FOR COMPENSATION COMMITTEES

Good corporate governance requires that the board of directors establish an independent compensation committee that would in turn create a substantial record of good faith and due diligence in making its decisions. The compensation committee should consider obtaining separate independent counsel to help create such a record.

Decisions of the compensation committee will be fully respected by the courts only if the members are truly independent. This may suggest that the compensation committee members should have no interrelationships with management, even relationships that are permitted by the rules of the New York Stock Exchange or the Nasdaq Stock Market.

It is important that the compensation committee think and act independently with regard to compensation issues. Compensation committees should adhere to the words of Chief Justice Veasey, of the Delaware Supreme Court, who stated that "directors who are supposed to be independent should have the guts to be a pain in the neck and act independently."[7]

To create a record of good faith and due diligence, the compensation committee should follow these best practices.

BEST PRACTICE

Choose an independent compensation consultant who has not previously worked for management or has any relationship with management.

BEST PRACTICE

Members of the compensation committee must receive materials well in advance of any meeting at which compensation is to be discussed, and the package should include a full draft of the proposed agreement, a summary of the key provisions, an analysis of the aggregate cost of the agreement to the company, and any other documents that shed light on the reasonableness of its terms.

BEST PRACTICE

Before approving any employment agreement or any severance or similar agreement, the compensation committee should insist that it receives the advice of an attorney in writing on at least these issues:

- What would be the maximum cost to the organization if the executive were terminated without cause?

(continued)

- Can the executive terminate the agreement following a change of control if there has been no change in his or her title, authority, duties, or compensation?
- What would be the maximum cost to the organization if the executive elected to terminate following a change of control?
- Would the maximum cost to the organization materially increase or decrease depending on the time of the event?

It is typical for the board of directors to receive a legal summary of the provisions of an executive employment contract or similar agreement before approving such an agreement. The legal summary sometimes is so complicated that it obscures the most important issues to the board, namely, what is this going to cost the organization.

Requiring a simple statement of the maximum cost to the organization sometimes shocks the directors into realizing the importance of their decision whether to approve the contract or not. This is particularly true if there is a so-called gross-up clause in the agreement for any golden parachute taxes. Such a simple statement would have helped the Disney directors in the litigation to be described. The maximum cost to the organization should include not only the cash cost but also the accounting effect on the income statement.

Likewise, the directors should be advised as to whether the executive can quit the organization for a good cause if there is a change of control, even if the executive's title, authority, duties, or compensation are not affected by the change of control. Executives should not normally be given the right to terminate their employment for good cause solely because there has been a change of control, if their position and compensation were not affected by the change of control.

BEST PRACTICE

Place maximums on the amounts of severance and retirement benefits available to an executive and on any tax gross-up payments.

Severance benefits should not be unlimited, as illustrated in the Disney case to be discussed. A maximum dollar amount should be placed on severance benefits in any executive employment agreement. Likewise, a maximum dollar amount should be placed on retirement benefits, including supplemental executive retirement plans (SERPs), and any tax gross-up provisions in the executive employment agreement. In the absence of such maximums, the complex formulas in some executive employment agreements can lead to absurdly high payments to the executive.

BEST PRACTICE

Make certain that the minutes of the compensation committee meeting reflect a full consideration of each of the elements of the current compensation structure (not just base salary and bonus but all of the pension benefits, including SERPs, fringe benefits, and other perquisites) of the executive and the total value of the existing compensation package, and allow adequate time at different compensation committee meetings to discuss each of these elements.

BEST PRACTICE

The minutes should reflect a record of arm's-length negotiations with the executive and his or her attorney, with each proposal and counteroffer fully documented.

BEST PRACTICE

If the final form of the agreement differs materially from the version submitted to the compensation committee, a separate meeting should be held to consider the material changes.

BEST PRACTICE

The report of the compensation consultant must compare the compensation package with industry standards.

BEST PRACTICE

Use the internal auditors to verify that the compensation actually paid to the top executives is not greater than what was approved by the compensation committee (i.e., avoid a Tyco situation).

BEST PRACTICE

Obtain information on the compensation of lower-level employees to determine if the compensation arrangements reward not only financial performance but also being good corporate citizens.

It is typical for compensation committees to deal only with the compensation of top executives. If that is the case, then another committee of the board of directors (such as the nominating/corporate governance committee) should monitor the compensation of other employees. Lower-level employees must be rewarded for risking their careers to report legal risk or evidence of wrongdoing.

BEST PRACTICE FOR PUBLIC COMPANIES

Use the internal auditor to verify that any proxy statement filed with the Securities and Exchange Commission (SEC) fully reflects all of the compensation elements and that they are properly valued.

The compensation committee should rely on the internal auditor to verify all compensation information provided to it by management. As cited in the last section of this chapter, Dr. LeMaistre, chairman of Enron's compensation committee, had tremendous difficulty in obtaining information on Mr. Fastow, Enron's chief financial officer (CFO). An independent internal auditor, hired and compensated by the audit committee and reporting directly to the audit committee, should be the eyes and ears of the compensation committee as well as the audit committee.

BEST PRACTICE FOR PRIVATE COMPANIES

In the case of private companies granting stock options to employees, the compensation committee should obtain an independent appraisal to determine the fair market value of the option stock in order to establish the option exercise price.

The proposed regulations under Section 409A of the Internal Revenue Code of 1986 treat options with exercise prices below fair market value as deferred compensation that may be subject, among other things, to a 20 percent additional tax to the employee unless certain tax requirements are satisfied. Using an independent appraiser assists in avoiding this result. Appraisals should also be considered for so-called public companies that have no trading volume or only sporadic or infrequent trades in their stock.

COMPENSATION COMMITTEE LITIGATION

A discussion of significant litigation involving the compensation committee follows. Thereafter, SEC disclosure rules and major stock market listing rules concerning the compensation committee are described.

Disney Litigation

The Disney case involved the decision of the Disney compensation committee and of the full board to approve a compensation agreement with Disney's former president, Michael Ovitz, *without having ever seen a draft of the agreement*, only an incomplete summary, following a compensation committee meeting that lasted only an hour.[8] The complaint alleged: there were no analyses to show the potential compensation over the term of the agreement; there were no analyses of the potential cost of the severance package under various termination scenarios, including no-fault termination; no outside consultant advised the board; comparable peer compensation was not considered; and there was no review of the final employment or stock option agreements, which differed from the summaries previously provided.[9]

The Delaware Chancery Court in 2003 initially denied Disney's motion to dismiss the complaint against the directors, holding that "[w]here a director consciously ignores his or her duties to the corporation, thereby causing economic injury to its shareholders, the director's actions are either 'not in good faith' or 'involve international misconduct.'" In August 2005, after a full trial, (including 37 days of testimony) the Delaware Chancery Court dismissed the complaint against the directors and others because the plaintiffs failed to prove the factual allegations in the complaint, holding that ordinary negligence by the directors is not sufficient to prove lack of good faith. The court found that although the board's conduct fell significantly short of the "aspirational ideal of best practices," the directors did not breach their fiduciary duties.[10]

Although the Disney directors were successful after a full trial, the Disney case probably would have been dismissed at an earlier stage (or perhaps not brought at all) had the Disney compensation committee used best practices in approving Michael Ovitz's compensation agreement. Use of best corporate practices would have avoided the distraction and disruption of Disney's operations and of the lives of its director defendants resulting from lengthy depositions and the full trial.

Some commentators have noted that the actions of the Disney board took place in the twentieth century and that the application of twenty-first-century notions of best practices for compensation committees might have changed the result. Therefore, compensation committees should update and improve their practices to current standards to safeguard themselves from personal liability.

New York Stock Exchange Alleged Scandal

Dick Grasso, chairman and chief executive officer of the New York Stock Exchange (NYSE), was ousted from his position in September 2003 as a result of a public outcry over his compensation package. The NYSE is a not-for-profit organization, formed under New York law. Prior to his ouster, it was determined that Grasso's $187.5 million pay package was excessive. A suit was subsequently filed by New York state's attorney general, Eliot Spitzer, to recover some of the money.

According to *The Wall Street Journal* of July 20, 2005, 9 of the 12 directors who served on the compensation committee during a crucial period in 2001 and

2002 did not realize that the big pay raises awarded to Grasso would cause his retirement benefits to soar when his total compensation rose to $26.8 million in
2000 and $30.6 million in 2001. Many of the members of the compensation com-
mittee were reportedly surprised by how large the pension package had become.
The growth in Grasso's pension plan, known as a SERP (supplemental executive
retirement plan), was not envisioned when the SERP was established because
the plan was modeled after one for U.S. government employees earning far less
money.

The moral of this story is that the compensation committee of the New York
Stock Exchange apparently failed to fully understand Grasso's entire pay package
when they gave him large increases in his compensation and should have placed
a cap on his SERP.[11]

SEC Action against Tyson Foods

The SEC is particularly concerned about the failure to properly disclose and value
all compensation elements in the proxy statement sent to the company shareholders. For example, the SEC has taken the position in litigation against Tyson Foods,
Inc., and Don Tyson (who is a director and a member of the executive committee
of the board) that there was a failure of internal controls because of inadequate disclosure of Don Tyson's perquisites in the company's proxy statement. According
to the SEC complaint, Tyson Foods' internal accounting controls were deficient
because they failed to cause the disclosure of approximately $424,000 in per-
quisites and because $1,500,000 in personal benefits and perquisites had not been
raised with or authorized by the compensation committee of the board of directors. The SEC alleged that the company's proxy statement mischaracterized certain perquisites as "performance-based" bonuses whereas in fact they were not
performance-based. According to the SEC, certain of Tyson's personal expenses
and his use of homes owned by Tyson Foods should have been specifically reported in the footnotes to the compensation disclosures in the proxy statement but
were not. Also, the SEC alleged that Tyson's use of a company airplane was improperly valued because it did not take into consideration the incremental cost of
his private use of the airplane and instead used the Standard Industry Fare Level
(SIFL) method of calculated value. When the sole purpose of the flight is for the
individual's personal use, the incremental cost will significantly exceed the SIFL
valuation.[12]

SEC DISCLOSURE RULES FOR PUBLIC COMPANY
COMPENSATION COMMITTEES

Public companies that report to the SEC must disclose to their shareholders certain
information about the compensation committee, including the following:

- Compensation policies applicable to executive officers, including the specific
  relationship of corporate performance to executive compensation, are required
  with respect to compensation reported for the last completed fiscal year.

- Discussion is required of the compensation committee's basis for the CEO's compensation reported for the last completed fiscal year, including the factors and criteria upon which the CEO's compensation was based. The committee must include a specific discussion of the relationship of the registrant's performance to the CEO's compensation for the last completed fiscal year, describing each measure of the registrant's performance, whether qualitative or quantitative, on which the CEO's compensation was based.

- The required disclosure must be made under the name of each member of the compensation committee.

- If the board of directors modified or rejected in a material way any action or recommendation by such committee with respect to such decision in the last completed fiscal year, the disclosure must so indicate and explain the reasons for the board's actions, and be made over the names of all members of the board.

Much more extensive compensation information is required under SEC proposed rules, which have not yet been adopted as of May 2006.

STOCK MARKET LISTING REQUIREMENTS FOR COMPENSATION COMMITTEES

The New York Stock Exchange requires, as part of its listing requirements, that the listed company have a compensation committee composed entirely of independent directors. The NYSE also requires that the compensation committee have a written charter that addresses the committee's purpose and responsibilities—which, at minimum, must be to have direct responsibility to:

- Review and approve corporate goals and objectives relevant to CEO compensation, evaluate the CEO's performance in light of those goals and objectives, and, either as a committee or together with the other independent directors (as directed by the board), determine and approve the CEO's compensation level based on this evaluation

- Make recommendations to the board with respect to non-CEO executive officer compensation, and incentive-compensation and equity-based plans that are subject to board approval

- Produce a compensation committee report on executive officer compensation as required by the SEC to be included in the listed company's annual proxy statement or annual report on Form 10-K filed with the SEC

- Produce an annual performance evaluation of the compensation committee

The Nasdaq Stock Market listing rules do not specifically require a compensation committee and permit a majority of the independent directors to establish the compensation of the CEO and other executive officers without the formation of a compensation committee. If the Nasdaq Stock Market company has a compensation committee, it must be composed solely of independent directors, subject to a limited exception. The CEO may not be present during voting or deliberations.

ENRON—WORST PRACTICES

The Enron compensation committee was chaired by Dr. Charles A. LeMaistre, former president of the M.D. Anderson Cancer Center, a large, well-respected, and complex medical facility in Texas. The U.S. Senate Committee Report (Senate Committee Report) was scathing in its review of the work of the Enron compensation committee, particularly with respect to its oversight over the compensation of Enron's CFO, Andrew Fastow, in connection with the so-called LJM off-balance sheet partnerships.[13] Excerpts from the Senate Committee Report follow.

> The Board's role in overseeing Mr. Fastow's LJM compensation was even more lax. For the first year, the Board apparently relied on Mr. Skilling to review Mr. Fastow's LJM-related income and asked no questions. In October 2000, after LJM1 had been operating for more than one year and the Finance Committee was told that LJM1 and LJIM2 were engaging in multiple, high dollar transactions with Enron, the Finance Committee asked the Compensation Committee to conduct a one-time review of Mr. Fastow' s compensation.

> Dr. LeMaistre, then Chairman of the Compensation Committee, was present at the Finance Committee meeting, and attempted to obtain the requested information on Mr. Fastow's LJM compensation. He indicated during his interview and at the hearing that, after the Finance Committee meeting, he asked Enron's senior compensation officer, Mary Joyce, to provide him with information on the outside income of all of Enron's "16(b) officers," a reference to top company officials identified according to an SEC regulation. He said during his Subcommittee interview that he did not specifically name Mr. Fastow to Ms. Joyce because he did not want to start any office gossip. Ms. Joyce did not provide him with the information he requested. He said that he asked her a second time to obtain the information, but she again did not do so. He admitted that he never actually named Mr. Fastow to her or insisted that she obtain information about his LJM compensation. Instead, Dr. LeMaistre let the matter drop.

> At the hearing, Subcommittee Chairman Levin and Dr. LeMaistre had the following exchange.

> Dr. LeMaistre: I asked Mary Joyce about it.

> Sen. Levin: And what did she tell you?

> Dr. LeMaistre: She said she did not have the information.

> Sen. Levin: Did you say, well, I want it?

> Dr. LeMaistre: She knew that I wanted it.

> Sen. Levin: Did you get it?

> Dr. LeMaistre: I did not.

> Sen. Levin: This is the heart of the problem. You have got a Board that says, I want it. You have got a request for it. It does not come and you do nothing. That is an approach which is unacceptable for a Board.

> One year later, despite the Finance Committee's directive, Dr. LeMaistre had not obtained any information about Mr. Fastow's LJM compensation. Nor had any other Board member taken any steps to obtain this information. In October 2001, a *Wall Street Journal* article was published detailing Enron's transactions with LJM and

alleging that Mr. Fastow had received compensation from LJM business transactions in excess of $7 million . . . .

Dr. LeMaistre's handwritten notes on the document indicate that Mr. Fastow admitted receiving LJM compensation totalling $45 million, $23 million from LJM1 and $22 million from LJIM2. A handwritten note in the margin of the document states "incredible," which Dr. LeMaistre said was his reaction to the compensation total, which was much greater than he had been expecting. Dr. LeMaistre also noted that Mr. Fastow declined to provide information related to his LJM investment return and promised to provide that information the next day. Mr. Duncan said during his interview that when Mr. Fastow failed to telephone with the information at the time promised, Mr. Duncan called him and was told by Mr. Fastow that he had not had the chance to obtain the requested information and would provide it later. Mr. Fastow apparently never provided that information to the Board.

Dr. LeMaistre and Mr. Duncan reported the October 23 conversation to the other Board members in a telephone Board meeting the next day. The other Directors expressed surprise at the large amount of compensation, and the decision was made to place Mr. Fastow on leave immediately. Mr. Fastow was placed on leave on October 24, 2001.

During his interview, Dr. LeMaistre noted that he asked Mr. Fastow whether any Enron employee other than Mr. Fastow and Mr. Kopper had "any economic interest in or derive[d] any benefit from" the LJM partnerships. He said that Mr. Fastow had replied "no," which the Board later discovered to be untrue. He and other Board members said that it was during the Powers investigation that they first learned of the Southhampton partnership, which Mr. Fastow had established with five other Enron employees to invest in LJM1 and enabled these additional Enron employees to benefit financially at Enron's expense.[14]

If we are to believe the allegations of the Senate Report, LeMaistre allowed himself to be stonewalled and stalled by Fastow. Directors must be prepared to exercise their power as directors or resign from the board. LeMaistre should have brought the failure to receive the Fastow compensation information immediately to the attention of the entire board of directors.

ENDNOTES

1. See, generally, Lucian A. Bebchuk and Jesse Fried, *Pay without Performance: The Unfulfilled Promise of Executive Compensation* (Cambridge, MA: Harvard University Press, 2004).
2. United States Securities and Exchange Commission, Litigation Release No. 17722, September 12, 2002, www.sec.gov/litigation/litreleases/lr17722.htm.
3. Lucian A. Bebchuk, "How Much Does the Boss Make?" *Wall Street Journal,* January 18, 2006, and the study by Lucian A. Bebchuk and Robert J. Jackson entitled "Executive Pensions," http://papers.ssrn.com/sol3/papers.cfm?abstract_id=694766. The SEC has proposed disclosure of the increase in pension value but excluded defined contribution plans for reasons that are not clear. Securities Exchange Act Release No. 34-53185, January 27, 2006.
4. www.compensationstandards.com/home.asp.
5. "Lake Wobegone Effect," http://en.wikipedia.org/wiki/Lake_Wobegon_effect.

6. Gretchen Morgenson, "Severance Pay Doesn't Go Better with Coke," *New York Time*, December 25, 2005.

7. E. Norman Veasey, "What's Wrong with Executive Compensation," *Harvard Business Review* (January 2003): 68, 76.

8. *In re Walt Disney Company* Derivative Litigation, No. 15452 (Del. Ch. August 9, 2005) at 27.

9. The Walt Disney Derivative Litigation, 825 A.2d 275 (Del. Ch. 2003).

10. See Note 8 at 1.

11. Landon Thomas Jr. and Jenny Anderson, "Report Details Huge Pay Deal Grasso Set Up," *New York Times*, February 2, 2005; Krysten Crawford, "Spitzer Seeks $100 Million from Grasso," *CNNMoney*, May 24, 2004, http://money.cnn.com/2004/05/24/markets/spitzer_grasso. See also William Donaldson, "Statement by the Chairperson: Letter to NYSE Regarding NYSE Executive Compensation," U.S. Securities and Exchange Commission, Washington, D.C., September 2, 2003.

12. U.S. Securities and Exchange Commission, Litigation Release No. 19208, April 28, 2005, www.sec.gov/litigation/litreleases/lr19208.htm.

13. "The Role of the Board of Directors in Enron's Collapse," Permanent Subcommittee on Investigations of the Committee on Governmental Affairs, United States Senate, July 8, 2002.

14. Id. p. 34 et seq.

Chapter 7

Other Committees

Many organizations have other committees on the board of directors in addition to the audit committee and the compensation committee. Typically, there is a compliance or risk management committee, in certain cases a trust committee, and in other cases a nominating/corporate governance committee. Not every organization requires each of these committees. The board of directors should establish these committees where necessary for purposes of good corporate governance, or where it is necessary to have extra scrutiny of particular areas of the organization.

BEST PRACTICE

Board committees should have functions and authority that match the activities and major risks of the organization.

Committee functions and authority must be tailored to the organization's business activities and risks profile. For example, if a not-for-profit organization administers trust funds, a board committee should oversee this function. However, there is no need for a trust committee if the organization has no trust funds.

For example, the board of directors of a bank that offers consumer loans should have a committee of the board that oversees compliance with the numerous federal and state consumer statutes and regulations, including: Truth in Lending Act and Regulations M (leasing) and Z (credit) of Federal Reserve Board; Real Estate Settlement Procedures Act; Equal Credit Opportunity Act; Home Mortgage Disclosure Act; Community Reinvestment Act; Fair Credit Reporting Act; Fair Debt Collection Practices Act; Electronic Funds Transfer Act; Title V to Gramm-Leach-Bliley Act (the privacy provisions) and Regulation P; Bank Secrecy Act; state unfair trade practice law.

The New York Stock Exchange (NYSE) and other public securities markets require listed public companies to have a nominating/corporate governance committee as discussed later or to allocate the responsibilities of that committee to other board committees composed entirely of independent directors. Private, not-for-profit, and nonlisted companies are not required to have a nominating/corporate governance committee.

BEST PRACTICE

If a separate corporate governance committee is created, it is important that
the chair of the audit committee be a member of the corporate governance
committee in order to coordinate the activities of the two committees.

The duties of the nominating/corporate governance committee can be performed by the independent directors of the board of directors or by other committees composed of independent directors, such as the audit committee or
compensation committee. In some respects, creating a separate corporate governance committee can create confusion and overlap with the audit committee functions. If a separate nominating/corporate governance committee is formed, the
chair of the audit committee should be a member of that committee in order to
avoid any overlap of functions between the two committees.

BEST PRACTICE

Any nominating/corporate governance committee should generally consist
of independent directors and should recommend director nominees to the full
board; oversee the structure, operation, and membership of board committees; and play a leadership role in corporate governance.

NYSE companies are required to have a nominating/corporate governance
committee composed entirely of independent directors. No similar requirement is
imposed on other public companies or in private or not-for-profit organizations,
even though this is a best practice.

Some organizations have a separate nominating committee, which is typically
combined with the corporate governance committee. The nominating/corporate
governance committee has the function of searching for new independent directors
and, in certain cases, evaluating the effectiveness of the directors currently on
the board. Directors who miss too many meetings or fall asleep at meetings must
be removed from the board if the board is to function properly. The nominating/
corporate governance committee plays a leadership role in shaping the corporate
governance of the organization and may also oversee the compensation of board
members if the compensation committee does not do so.

The nominating/corporate governance committee can also serve as the vehicle
for monitoring the corporate culture, as required by the U.S. Department of Justice Sentencing Guidelines.[1] This committee can monitor legal risks within the organization and suggest methods to minimize such risks. Moreover, the nominating/
corporate governance committee can also suggest an appropriate committee structure to the full board and the membership and chair of each committee. If a nom-
inating/corporate governance committee is formed, the internal auditor should
have reporting responsibilities to that committee as well as the audit, compensation, and other board committees.

> ## BEST PRACTICE
>
> The nominating/corporate governance committee should establish criteria for board and committee membership and recommend those criteria to the board. It also should assist the board in identifying potential director candidates.

The nominating/corporate governance committee of the directors of the organization should make at least an annual review to determine whether additional expertise is required, who should be eliminated from the board, and what method should be used to attract new independent directors to the board. The nominating/corporate governance committee should take the lead in interviewing new potential candidates for the board of directors. This committee should also anticipate the departure of directors (e.g., as a result of mandatory retirement age requirements or term limits, etc.) so that the board can fill any vacancies quickly.

The nominating/corporate governance committee will typically also annually review the organization's employee code of conduct, suggest changes in the code of conduct, and determine whether to grant waivers from that code of conduct.

> ## BEST PRACTICE FOR PUBLIC COMPANIES
>
> The nominating/corporate governance committee should monitor the independence of the board and compliance with applicable listing standards and oversee the effective functioning of the board and its committees.

The nominating/corporate governance committee should oversee the evaluation of the board and its committees and periodically make recommendations to the board to improve its functioning. The Business Roundtable, in its "Principles of Corporate Governance 2005," has excellent recommendations for the specific functions of the nominating/corporate governance committee of public companies.[2] These practices should generally be followed by nominating/corporate governance committees of private and not-for-profit organizations.

COMMITTEE STRUCTURE, MEMBERSHIP, AND REPORTING

> ## BEST PRACTICE
>
> Each board committee should have a written charter that is approved by the board, which contains any special qualifications for committee membership and which is reviewed annually.

Creating a written charter for a committee forces the committee members to focus on the duties of the committee, its powers, and its membership criteria, all of which are helpful in educating the committee members. The NYSE listing rules require a written charter for the audit, compensation, and nominating/corporate governance committees, as described later. The charter should be reviewed annually and changes recommended to the full board when necessary.

BEST PRACTICE

Decisions about committee membership, including the chair of each committee, should be made by the full board. If there is a corporate governance committee, the board should receive a recommendation from the corporate governance committee on the membership of each committee, including the chair.

Each year the board should establish the specific committees of the board that will oversee areas of the organization in more depth than is possible at a full board meeting. The board should consider whether periodic rotation of committee membership and chairs is appropriate in order to provide fresh perspectives and to enhance overall director familiarity with the organization. If the organization is a public company, Securities and Exchange Commission (SEC) and listing rules must be complied with in the selection and rotation of committee members. As previously discussed, one of the functions of any corporate governance committee is to make recommendations to the full board regarding the committee structure and the membership and chair of each committee.

BEST PRACTICE

Committees should advise the full board of their activities on a regular basis.

It is important that the full board be kept fully apprised of the work of its committees through verbal or written reports. In view of potential litigation risks, if written reports or minutes of committee meetings are provided to the full board, such written documents should first be reviewed by counsel for the organization prior to their submission to the full board.

STOCK MARKET LISTING RULES

New York Stock Exchange listed companies are required by its rules to have a nominating/corporate governance committee composed entirely of independent directors or to delegate the responsibilities of that committee to other committees composed entirely of independent directors. If there is a separate nominating/corporate governance committee, this committee must have a written charter that addresses:

- The committee's purpose and responsibilities—which, at minimum, must be to: identify individuals qualified to become board members, consistent with criteria approved by the board, and to select, or to recommend that the board select, the director nominees for the next annual meeting of shareholders; develop and recommend to the board a set of corporate governance guidelines applicable to the corporation; and oversee the evaluation of the board and management
- An annual performance evaluation of the committee

New York Stock Exchange listing rules contain this commentary concerning the importance of the nominating/corporate governance committee:

> _Commentary:_ A nominating/corporate governance committee is central to the effective functioning of the board. New director and board committee nominations are among a board's most important functions. Placing this responsibility in the hands of an independent nominating/corporate governance committee can enhance the independence and quality of nominees. The committee is also responsible for taking a leadership role in shaping the corporate governance of a corporation.
>
> If a listed company is legally required by contract or otherwise to provide third parties with the ability to nominate directors (for example, preferred stock rights to elect directors upon a dividend default, shareholder agreements, and management agreements), the selection and nomination of such directors need not be subject to the nominating committee process.
>
> The nominating/corporate governance committee charter should also address the following items: committee member qualifications; committee member appointment and removal; committee structure and operations (including authority to delegate to subcommittees); and committee reporting to the board. In addition, the charter should give the nominating/corporate governance committee sole authority to retain and terminate any search firm to be used to identify director candidates, including sole authority to approve the search firm's fees and other retention terms.
>
> Boards may allocate the responsibilities of the nominating/corporate governance committee to committees of their own denomination, provided that the committees are composed entirely of independent directors. Any such committee must have a published committee charter.[3]

The Nasdaq Stock Market rules do not require listed companies to have a nominating/corporate governance committee. However, director nominees must be selected or recommended for the board's selection, either by a majority of the independent directors, or a nominations committee comprised solely of independent directors (subject to limited exceptions).

ENDNOTES

1. "2005 Federal Sentencing Guideline Manual," United States Sentencing Commission, November 1, 2005, www.ussc.gov/2005guid/TABCON05.htm.
2. For the Business Roundtable's best practices for 2005, go to: www.businessroundtable.org/publications/index.aspx and click on the document entitled "Principles of Corporate Governance" (November 3, 2005).
3. New York Stock Exchange, Final NYSE Corporate Governance Rules, 303A, p. 8. See Appendix D.

Chapter 8

Independent Directors and Their Committees

This chapter discusses two subjects that are applicable to all organizations:

1. When should the independent directors form a special committee?
2. Who qualifies as an independent director?

The primary reason to form an independent director committee (also called a special committee) is to obtain the respect of the courts for the final decision and recommendations that are made by the committee in the event of a lawsuit. Nonindependent directors are typically excluded from the committee because of a conflict of interest. For example, in a management buyout, the directors who are also part of the management buyout would have a clear conflict of interest and would be excluded from being considered independent.

In conflict of interest situations, in the event of a lawsuit, the Delaware courts typically do not apply the business judgment rule and examine the decisions and recommendations of the independent director committee in excruciating detail (as is done in Delaware pursuant to what is called the entire fairness doctrine). The actions of each individual member of the special committee may be examined by the court in what may be characterized as a legal "proctological" examination. However, even where the courts use 20/20 hindsight under the entire fairness doctrine to review the decisions and recommendations of the independent director committee, the proper creation and operation of such a committee can shift the burden of proof to the plaintiff complaining about such decisions or recommendations and assist in protecting directors from personal liability. Standing independent commission committees of the board, such as the audit or compensation committee, will also have their actions carefully scrutinized by the court in the event of a lawsuit. In the Disney case (discussed in Chapter 6), the actions of each member of the Disney compensation committee were analyzed by the court.

BEST PRACTICE

Special committees typically are formed for these reasons, among others:

- To conduct an investigation that may involve top management or other directors

(continued)

- To consider a demand on a corporation by a shareholder to bring action against other directors and officers
- To consider whether to terminate an action brought by shareholders in the name of the corporation (a so-called derivative action)
- To consider a transaction in which a majority of the board has financial or other interests adverse to the corporation
- To consider a transaction in which an individual director or a minority of the board have financial or other interests adverse to the corporation, if the interested director or directors control or dominate the board as a whole
- To consider a transaction in which a majority of the directors receive a special or personal benefit, if material, that may be incidental to an arm's-length transaction
- To consider a transaction with a controlling stockholder (e.g., a going private transaction)

If the organization is involved in any of these transactions or similar conflict of interest transactions, it is extremely important for the proposed committee to obtain for the proposed committee independent counsel experienced in representing special committees. Independent counsel should preferably be counsel who has not previously performed services for the organization and who is selected by the independent director committee. In sensitive situations (e.g., a management buyout), the independent counsel should have no prior relationship to the organization and should be selected without the recommendation of management.

Some of the mistakes that have been made by special committees of Delaware public companies, all of which would be considered negative factors by the Delaware courts in determining whether to respect the decisions and recommendations of the committee, are listed next.

- The committee employed an investment banker recommended by management.
- The chief executive officer leading a management buyout hand-picked the chairman of the special committee and other members.
- The special committee did not have the authority to engage independent advisors at the company's expense.
- The special committee did not have sufficient authority to engage in real arm's-length bargaining but could only pass on the fairness of the transaction.
- The special committee did not in fact engage in arm's-length bargaining with a controlling shareholder.
- The special committee's investment banker was paid only if a transaction occurred with a controlling shareholder.
- The special committee failed to spend a reasonable amount of time meeting and deliberating on the issue in light of its importance to the organization.

- The special committee failed to ever meet in person (versus telephone conference calls).

- All of the directors on the committee were not viewed as completely independent (see the following discussion).

The failure to properly form and operate an independent board committee can result in major personal liability to directors. For example, in 2004, certain directors and the controlling shareholder of Emerging Communications, Inc. were held liable for over $75 million in connection with a going private transaction with a controlling shareholder.[1]

TENDER OFFERS BY CONTROLLING SHAREHOLDERS

The business judgment rule (which generally respects the decisions of the board of directors) rather than the entire fairness doctrine (which examines the action of the committee with 20/20 hindsight) is applied by the Delaware courts in certain limited types of conflict of interest transactions, such as a going private transaction by a controlling shareholder if the so-called Siliconix-style structure (as modified by the *Pure Resources* case[2]) is utilized. This peculiar Delaware rule permits the business judgment rule, rather than the entire fairness doctrine, to be applied to a going private tender offer by a controlling shareholder if:

- The offer is subject to a nonwaivable condition that a majority of the disinterested stockholders tender their shares.

- The controlling stockholder commits to complete a "short form" merger at the same price if more than 90 percent of the outstanding shares are tendered in the offer.

- The controlling stockholder does not make "retributive threats" to the special committee or the minority stockholders.

- The independent directors are given complete discretion and sufficient time "to react to the tender offer, by (at the very least) hiring their own advisors," providing a recommendation to the noncontrolling shareholders, and disclosing adequate information to allow the noncontrolling shareholders an opportunity for informed decision making.

WHO IS AN INDEPENDENT DIRECTOR?

There are different standards as to who is an independent director, depending on the context, and these standards significantly differ. For example, an individual can be an independent director for purposes of New York Stock Exchange corporate governance standards but not be considered an independent director because of social ties if the individual is a member of a special management buyout committee of the board of directors. Likewise, a director can be considered an independent for purposes of the compensation committee of the board of directors of a Nasdaq Stock Market company, but not be considered independent for the audit committee because the individual is an executive of a venture capital fund that is an affiliate of the company.

BEST PRACTICE

A special committee should have an experienced attorney carefully determine the "independence" of each of its members.

Independence issues can arise in any of these contexts, each of which has a different test of independence:

- New York Stock Exchange corporate governance standards (see Appendix D). (In general, the same independence definitions apply to the requirement that the company must have a majority of independent directors, an independent compensation committee, and an independent audit committee, except that the audit committee has additional independence requirements.)

- Nasdaq National Market corporate governance standards (see Appendix D). (In general, the same independence definitions apply to the requirement that the company must have a majority of independent directors, an independent compensation committee, and an independent audit committee, except that the audit committee has additional independence requirements.)

- The determination as to whether a demand on the board of directors made by a shareholder to bring an action on behalf of the corporation (a so-called derivative action) against an insider is excused or not. (For example, if a shareholder wishes to sue directors for breach of fiduciary duty to the organization, the shareholder must first make a demand on the board of directors to sue; the demand is excused, under Delaware law, if the shareholder establishes a reasonable doubt that the directors are disinterested and independent, or that the challenged transaction otherwise was not the product of a valid exercise of business judgment.)

- The determination of whether the directors constituting a special litigation committee in derivative suits are independent or not. (For example, if the board of directors lacks independence and therefore the demand is excused, it is typical for the board to create a special committee of uninvolved directors, typically newly appointed ones, who thereafter assert control over the litigation against the other directors or other insiders, provided the special committee is independent.)

- The determination of whether the directors constituting a special committee for a management buyout or a parent subsidiary merger are independent or not. (For example, Delaware encourages the use of independent committees to represent the interests of nonmanagement shareholders in a management buyout and to represent the interests of noncontrolling shareholders in a parent-subsidiary merger.)

- The determination of whether the directors constituting a special committee for an internal investigation are independent or not.

ORACLE LITIGATION (THE STANFORD PROFESSORS CASE)[3]

The strictest test to date for independence has arisen from the Oracle Corporation Derivative Action decided in 2003 by Vice Chancellor Strine of the Delaware Chancery Court. Vice Chancellor Strine declined the recommendation of Oracle's special litigation committee that litigation alleging insider trading by certain directors should be dismissed because the court held that nonmonetary social connections between the special committee and the directors whose conduct was at issue raised a reasonable doubt as to the special committee's ability to impartially consider whether the action should be dismissed. Since this case presents the farthest reaches of the independence doctrine, we will look at the facts in detail.

In this action, shareholders of Oracle Corporation challenged the sale of Oracle stock by certain Oracle directors (the "Trading Defendants") who, according to plaintiffs, were in possession of material, nonpublic information showing that Oracle would not meet its earnings expectations for the third quarter of Oracle's fiscal year 2001. On that basis, plaintiffs asserted breach of fiduciary duty claims against the Trading Defendants. After the filing of the complaint, Oracle appointed a special litigation committee (SLC) consisting of two purportedly independent directors, Hector Garcia-Molina and Joseph Grundfest, to investigate the Trading Defendants' activities.

The SLC undertook an extensive investigation of the allegations. The committee engaged independent financial and legal advisors, reviewed a vast amount of paper and electronic records, had its counsel interview 70 witnesses, and met with its counsel for a total of 80 hours to discuss the allegations. The SLC then prepared a 1,110-page report concluding that the Trading Defendants had not breached their fiduciary duty because "even a hypothetical Oracle executive who possessed all information regarding the company's performance in . . . 3Q FY 2001 would not have possessed material, non-public information that the company would fail to meet the earnings and revenue guidance it provided the market in December."[4] Moreover, the Trading Defendants sold only between 2 and 17 percent of their extensive holdings of Oracle shares. Having found no breach of duty by the Trading Defendants, the SLC accordingly moved to terminate the litigation.

In order to terminate the litigation, the SLC was required to demonstrate that its members: (1) were independent; (2) acted in good faith; and (3) had a reasonable basis for their recommendation. The SLC attempted to demonstrate its independence by noting that neither member received compensation from Oracle other than as directors, neither was on the board at the time of the alleged improper trading, both members were willing to return any compensation received as a result of their work on the SLC if such compensation should be deemed to affect their independence, and there was an absence of any material ties between the members of the SLC, the Trading Defendants, and Oracle. The court, however, found that the SLC had not met its burden of demonstrating the absence of a material factual question about its independence because of a series of ties and relationships among Stanford University, Oracle, and the Trading Defendants.

Both Garcia-Molina and Grundfest were professors at Stanford University. The SLC's report disclosed that one of the defendants also was a professor at Stanford and that one defendant had made donations to the university. After discovery, however, other "shocking" connections between the Trading Defendants and Stanford were revealed, such as the fact that at least two of the Trading Defendants had been generous contributors to Stanford. Thus, according to the court, "[s]ummarized fairly, two Stanford professors were recruited to the Oracle board in summer 2001 and soon asked to investigate a fellow professor and two benefactors of the University."[5] The court noted that, as a result of being tenured professors, "neither of the SLC members is compromised by a fear that support for the procession of this suit would endanger his ability to make a nice living."[6] Nonetheless, applying a "subjective" actual person standard, the court explained that with their ties to Stanford, the members of the SLC were simply not situated to act with the required degree of impartiality. Indeed, "these connections generate a reasonable doubt about the SLC's impartiality because they suggest that material considerations other than the best interests of Oracle could have influenced the SLC's inquiry and judgments."

The SLC argued that none of these ties to Stanford indicates that the committee was dominated or controlled by the Trading Defendants. Moreover, there were no economically material ties between the SLC and the Trading Defendants. The court, however, rejected the idea that "domination and control"[7] is the appropriate test for independence. Vice Chancellor Strine did acknowledge that "much of our law focuses the bias inquiry on whether there are economically material ties between the interested party and the director whose impartiality is questioned, treating the possible effect on one's personal wealth as the key to the independence inquiry." Despite such precedents, the Court further explained that:

> Delaware law should not be based on a reductionist view of human nature that simplifies human motivations on the lines of the least sophisticated notions of the law and economics movement. *Homo sapiens* is not merely *homo economicus*. We may be thankful that an array of other motivations exist that influence human behavior; not all are any better than greed or avarice, think of envy, to name just one. But also think of motives like love, friendship, and collegiality, think of those among us who direct their behavior as best they can on a guiding creed or set of moral values.

> As such, "a director may be compromised if he is beholden to an interested person. Beholden in this sense does not mean just owing in the financial sense, it can also flow out of "personal or other relationships" to the interested party.[8]

In discussing how these ties to Stanford might affect the SLC's independence, the court noted that it "necessarily measure[s] the SLC's independence contextually. As such, "the Delaware approach undoubtedly results in some level of indeterminacy, but with the compensating benefit that independence determinations are tailored to the precise situation at issue."[9]

This case sends a clear signal that the court will closely scrutinize relationships between special committee members and the directors whose conduct they may be called on to review, at least in the SLC context. As such, if at all possible, it is wise when appointing special committees to select directors who possess virtually no ties to other board members and thus are of unquestionable independence.

BEST PRACTICE

Director independence standards should include evaluating the relationship of directors of the company with not-for-profit organizations that receive contributions or other support from the company.

PERSONAL FRIENDSHIP (THE MARTHA STEWART CASE)

Does personal friendship make a director nonindependent? The Delaware Supreme Court in 2004, in a demand excused case, held that the personal friendship alone is not sufficient to destroy independence unless there is evidence that the friendship produced a bias in the director.[10]

The case involving whether a demand by a shareholder of Martha Stewart Living Omnimedia, Inc. (MSO) for its board of directors to bring a claim against Martha Stewart and other board members was excused or not. The MSO board of directors consisted of six members: Martha Stewart, Sharon L. Patrick, Arthur C. Martinez, Darla D. Moore, Naomi O. Seligman, and Jeffrey W. Ubben. The plaintiff, Beam, alleged that Martha Stewart breached her fiduciary duties of loyalty and care by illegally selling ImClone stock in December of 2001 and by mishandling the media attention that followed, thereby jeopardizing the financial future of MSO, and that the demand should be excused because of personal friendship ties between other MSO board members and Martha Stewart and Sharon L. Patrick.

The Delaware Supreme Court held that the demand was not excused by mere allegations of personal friendship in the absence of allegations of bias. The court stated:

> A variety of motivations, including friendship, may influence the demand futility inquiry. But, to render a director unable to consider demand, a relationship must be of a bias-producing nature. Allegations of mere personal friendship or a mere outside business relationship, standing alone, are insufficient to raise a reasonable doubt about a director's independence. In this connection, we adopt as our own the Chancellor's analysis in this case:

> [S]ome professional or personal friendships, which may border on or even exceed familial loyalty and closeness, may raise a reasonable doubt whether a director can appropriately consider demand. This is particularly true when the allegations raise serious questions of either civil or criminal liability of such a close friend. Not all friendships, or even most of them, rise to this level and the Court cannot make a *reasonable* inference that a particular friendship does so without specific factual allegations to support such a conclusion.

> The facts alleged by Beam regarding the relationships between Stewart and these other members of MSO's board of directors largely boil down to a "structural bias" argument, which presupposes that the professional and social relationships that naturally develop among members of a board impede independent decisionmaking.[11]

The Court addressed the structural bias argument in this way:

Critics will charge that [by requiring the independence of only a majority of the board] we are ignoring the structural bias common to corporate boards throughout America, as well as the other unseen socialization processes cutting against independent discussion and decisionmaking in the boardroom. The difficulty with structural bias in a demand futile case is simply one of establishing it in the complaint for purposes of [Delaware court rules]. We are satisfied that discretionary review by the Court of Chancery of complaints alleging specific facts pointing to bias on a particular board will be sufficient for determining demand futility.

In the present case, the plaintiff attempted to plead affinity beyond mere friendship between Stewart and the other directors, but her attempt is not sufficient to demonstrate demand futility. Even if the alleged friendships may have preceded the directors' membership on MSO's board and did not necessarily arise out of that membership, these relationships are of the same nature as those giving rise to the structural bias argument.

Allegations that Stewart and the other directors moved in the same social circles, attended the same weddings, developed business relationships before joining the board, and described each other as "friends," even when coupled with Stewart's 94% voting power, are insufficient, without more, to rebut the presumption of independence. They do not provide a sufficient basis from which reasonably to infer that Martinez, Moore and Seligman may have been beholden to Stewart. Whether they arise before board membership or later as a result of collegial relationships among the board of directors, such affinities—standing alone—will not render presuit demand futile. . . . Mere allegations that they move in the same business and social circles, or a characterization that they are close friends, is not enough to negate independence for demand excusal purposes.

That is not to say that personal friendship is always irrelevant to the independence calculus. But, for presuit demand purposes, friendship must be accompanied by substantially more in the nature of serious allegations that would lead to a reasonable doubt as to a director's independence. That a much stronger relationship is necessary to overcome the presumption of independence at the demand futility stage becomes especially compelling when one considers the risks that directors would take by protecting their social acquaintances in the face of allegations that those friends engaged in misconduct. To create a reasonable doubt about an outside director's independence, a plaintiff must plead facts that would support the inference that because of the nature of a relationship or additional circumstances other than the interested director's stock ownership or voting power, the noninterested director would be more willing to risk his or her reputation than risk the relationship with the interested director.[12]

There were more specific nonindependence allegations made by the plaintiff, against two directors, namely Seligman and Moore, which the Delaware Supreme Court also rejected as follows:

"Beam alleges that Seligman called John Wiley & Sons (Wiley) at Stewart's request in order to prevent an unfavorable publication reference to Stewart. The Chancellor concluded, properly in our view, that this allegation does not provide particularized facts from which one may reasonably infer improper influence.

The bare fact that Seligman contacted Wiley, on whose board Seligman also served, to dissuade Wiley from publishing unfavorable references to Stewart, even if done at Stewart's request, is insufficient to create a reasonable doubt that Seligman is capable of considering presuit demand free of Stewart's influence. Although the court should draw all reasonable inferences in Beam's favor, neither improper influence by Stewart over Seligman nor that Seligman was beholden to Stewart is a reasonable inference from these allegations.

Indeed, the reasonable inference is that Seligman's purported intervention on Stewart's behalf was of benefit to MSO and its reputation, which is allegedly tied to Stewart's reputation, as the Chancellor noted. A motivation by Seligman to benefit the company every bit as much as Stewart herself is the only reasonable inference supported by the complaint, when all of its allegations are read in context.[13]

The Court of Chancery concluded that the plaintiff's allegations with respect to Moore's social relationship with Stewart presented "quite a close call" and suggested ways that the "balance could have been tipped."

Although we agree that there are ways that the balance could be tipped so that mere allegations of social relationships would become allegations casting reasonable doubt on independence, we do not agree that the facts as alleged present a "close call" with respect to Moore's independence. These allegations center on: (a) Moore's attendance at a wedding reception for the daughter of Stewart's lawyer where Stewart and Waksal were also present; (b) a Fortune magazine article focusing on the close personal relationships among Moore, Stewart and Beers; and (c) the fact that Moore replaced Beers on the MSO board. In our view, these bare social relationships clearly do not create a reasonable doubt of independence.[14]

The Delaware Supreme Court distinguished the *Oracle* case on the ground that this case involved whether demand was excused or not (i.e., whether a plaintiff shareholder must demand that the board act before starting a lawsuit in the name of the corporation against certain directors or officers or others), whereas *Oracle* involved whether a special litigation committee had the power to dismiss a shareholder lawsuit previously brought in the name of the corporation against certain directors or officers or others. The court held that the demand for independence is greater in the context of a special litigation committee than in a demand excusal context, since the special litigation committee has the power to dismiss corporate litigation and, therefore, has the burden of establishing its own independence, unlike the demand excusal context, where the board is presumed to be independent. The Delaware Supreme Court said that the special litigation committee must be "like Caesar's wife"—"above reproach."[15] The implication of the court's statement was that this litigation could have been decided differently had it been in the context of whether a special litigation committee could dismiss shareholder litigation.

NEW YORK STOCK EXCHANGE INDEPENDENCE RULES

The definition of an independent director for purposes of determining whether a majority of the board of directors of a NYSE company are independent and for purposes of the independence requirement for the compensation committee and the audit committee (except for the additional audit committee requirements set forth in Chapter 11) can be found on the NYSE Web site (see Appendix D).

NASDAQ STOCK MARKET INDEPENDENCE RULES

The definition of an independent director for purposes of determining whether a majority of the board of directors of a Nasdaq Stock Market company are independent and for purposes of the independence requirement for the compensation committee and the audit committee (except for the additional audit committee requirements set forth in Chapter 11) follows.

(14) "Family Member" means a person's spouse, parents, children and siblings, whether by blood, marriage or adoption, or anyone residing in such person's home.

(15) "Independent director" means a person other than an officer or employee of the company or its subsidiaries or any other individual having a relationship which, in the opinion of the company's board of directors, would interfere with the exercise of independent judgment in carrying out the responsibilities of a director. The following persons shall not be considered independent:

(A) a director who is, or at any time during the past three years was, employed by the company or by any parent or subsidiary of the company;

(B) a director who accepted or who has a Family Member who accepted any payments from the company or any parent or subsidiary of the company in excess of $60,000 during any period of twelve consecutive months within the three years preceding the determination of independence, other than the following:

(i) compensation for board or board committee service;

(ii) payments arising solely from investments in the company's securities;

(iii) compensation paid to a Family Member who is a non-executive employee of the company or a parent or subsidiary of the company;

(iv) benefits under a tax-qualified retirement plan, or non-discretionary compensation;

(v) loans from a financial institution provided that the loans (1) were made in the ordinary course of business, (2) were made on substantially the same terms, including interest rates and collateral, as those prevailing at the time for comparable transactions with the general public, (3) did not involve more than a normal degree of risk or other unfavorable factors, and (4) were not otherwise subject to the specific disclosure requirements of SEC Regulation S-K, Item 404;

(vi) payments from a financial institution in connection with the deposit of funds or the financial institution acting in an agency capacity, provided such payments were (1) made in the ordinary course of business; (2) made on substantially the same terms as those prevailing at the time for comparable transactions with the general public; and (3) not otherwise subject to the disclosure requirements of SEC Regulation S-K, Item 404; or

(vii) loans permitted under Section 13(k) of the Act.

Provided, however, that in addition to the requirements contained in this paragraph (B), audit committee members are also subject to additional, more stringent requirements under Rule 4350(d).

(C) a director who is a Family Member of an individual who is, or at any time during the past three years was, employed by the company or by any parent or subsidiary of the company as an executive officer;

(D) a director who is, or has a Family Member who is, a partner in, or a controlling shareholder or an executive officer of, any organization to which the company made, or from which the company received, payments for property or services in the current or any of the past three fiscal years that exceed 5% of the recipient's consolidated gross revenues for that year, or $200,000, whichever is more, other than the following:

(i) payments arising solely from investments in the company's securities; or

(ii) payments under non-discretionary charitable contribution matching

(E) a director of the listed company who is, or has a Family Member who is, employed as an executive officer of another entity where at any time during the past three years any of the executive officers of the listed company serve on the compensation committee of such other entity; or

(F) a director who is, or has a Family Member who is, a current partner of the company's outside auditor, or was a partner or employee of the company's outside auditor who worked on the company's audit at any time during any of the past three years.

(G) in the case of an investment company, in lieu of paragraphs (A)–(F), a director who is an "interested person" of the company as defined in Section 2(a)(19) of the Investment Company Act of 1940, other than in his or her capacity as a member of the board of directors or any board committee.[16]

PUBLIC COMPANY AUDIT COMMITTEES

There are special independence and other requirements for the audit committee of a company whose securities are listed in the New York Stock Exchange, American Stock Exchange, or other national securities exchange, or the Nasdaq Stock Market. These special requirements are discussed in detail in Chapter 11.

ENDNOTES

1. *In re Emerging Communications, Inc.*, Shareholders Litigation, 2004 WL 1305745 (Del. Ch., May 3, 2004, Revised June 4, 2004).
2. *In re Pure Resources, Inc.*, Shareholders Litigation, 808 A.2d 421 (Del. Ch., Oct. 7, 2002).
3. *In re Oracle* Derivative Litigation, 824 A.2d 917 (Del. Ch. 2003).
4. Id. at 926.
5. Id. at 947.
6. Id. at 930.
7. Id. at 937.
8. Id. at 938.
9. Id. at 941.
10. *In re Beam ex rel. Martha Stewart Living Omnimedia, Inc. v. Stewart*, 845A.2d 1040 (Del. 2004).

11. Id. at 1050.
12. Id. at 1051–1052.
13. Id. at 1052–1053.
14. Id. at 1054.
15. Id. at 1055.
16. The Nasdaq Stock Market, Inc., Corporate Governance Rules 4200, 4200A, 4350, 4350A, 4351, and 4360 and Associated Interpretive Material, www.nasdaq.com/about/ CorporateGovernance.pdf.

Part II

Information Technology Corporate Governance

Chapter 9

IT Content: Best Corporate Governance Practices

Information technology (IT) is one of the major risk areas facing every organization (whether public, private, or not-for-profit). According to a University of California Berkeley study, 92 percent of new information is stored on magnetic media, primarily hard disks.[1] The most significant IT risk for all organizations results from the misuse of e-mails by management and employees of the organization and document retention and destruction policies.

Plaintiff attorneys have found e-mails to be the most fruitful source of damaging information against organizations. U.S. courts are imposing increasingly harsh punishments on organizations that fail to comply with subpoenas and other private lawsuits and government discovery requests to produce e-mail documents. For example, in 2004, a federal district court judge ordered Philip Morris and others to pay $2.75 million in discovery sanctions for deleting e-mails relevant to a pending litigation, barred 11 corporate employees from testifying at trial, and sanctioned each of those employees $250,000.[2]

Moreover, public companies are required by Securities and Exchange Commission (SEC) and Public Company Accounting Oversight Board (PCAOB) regulations, adopted under Section 404 of Sarbanes-Oxley, to provide effective internal controls over financial reporting, including IT general controls. Finally, Section 409 of Sarbanes-Oxley and related SEC rules have required the reporting on Form 8-K of material contracts and other items within four business days. The four-business-day rule places enormous pressure on the effectiveness of the IT structure of the public company.

Proposed changes to the Federal Rules of Civil Procedure were recently recommended that permit discovery of "electronically stored information" and are likely to go into effect on December 1, 2006. However, these proposed rules merely codify the practices that have been in effect for many years and do not really change the basic legal landscape.

EDUCATION IS KEY

Although most organizations have adopted extensive written e-mail and voice-mail policies, many of these policies are ignored. A written policy on e-mails and voice-mail is only the start of the process of minimizing risk and establishing good internal controls.

The board of directors and management must sensitize employees to the serious risk of casual e-mails. Employees should be educated that they should say nothing in an e-mail or voice-mail that they would not want repeated in a newspaper. If sensitive matters are to be discussed, such matters should be discussed verbally. A failure to so educate employees can be viewed as a weakness in internal controls.

BEST PRACTICE

Discourage the use of e-mails or voice-mail for sensitive information and, in any event, utilize enterprise content management software that permits the permanent destruction of e-mails and voice-mail at the appropriate time.

E-mails and voice mail are the single most fruitful source of damaging information against an organization. They are regularly subpoenaed in any litigation against the organization. Employees must be educated not to use sensitive information in e-mails or voice mail. Since such education is rarely completely effective, all content must be managed through enterprise content management software that permits the permanent destruction of e-mails and voicemail. This subject is discussed later in this chapter in more detail.

BEST PRACTICE

Establish a company policy that prohibits certain kinds of e-mail or computer use and warns that employees' e-mail, computer use, and employee Internet blogs may be monitored.

It is important to warn employees in a formal company policy about certain kinds of e-mails (e.g., sexually explicit) and personal computer use and Internet blogs. It is also appropriate for employers to monitor employees' e-mail and computer use on certain occasions and to constantly review employee Internet blogs for sensitive information. To avoid employee claims of improper monitoring or invasion of privacy, establish a clear policy that states that such monitoring may occur.

MORGAN STANLEY FIASCO[3]

In May 2005, a Florida jury held that investment banker Morgan Stanley had to pay the full $604.3 million claim made against it by billionaire financier Ronald Perelman, plus $850 million in punitive damages. The jury verdict for Perelman was not because the jury had been convinced by Perelman's claim that Morgan Stanley had defrauded him of the money in 1998 when it brokered his sale of the Coleman camping equipment company to the since-collapsed Sunbeam domestic appliance maker. Rather, the jury verdict was the result of an instruction by the presiding judge solely to decide whether Perelman had relied on Morgan Stanley. This instruction was given by the presiding judge because Morgan Stanley failed repeatedly to locate and hand over e-mails deemed vital to Perelman's case.

In May 2004, an employee of Morgan Stanley stumbled on 1,423 backup tapes in a storage cupboard in a Brooklyn office building. But before these were searched for relevant data, Morgan Stanley certified to the court that it had complied with the judge's instructions in full. Although the tapes were from the period of the dispute, Morgan Stanley allegedly did not reveal their existence to the Perelman attorneys for six months. In February 2005, with only weeks to go before the trial, another 129 tapes turned up in a mid-Manhattan office and a further set of uncataloged tapes were found at Morgan Stanley's headquarters on Broadway.

Morgan Stanley stated to *The Wall Street Journal* that its "discovery problems" were the result of honest mistakes, such as computer problems encountered during backup and recovery and the misplacing of tapes.

This is not the first time this has happened to Morgan Stanley. When New York Attorney General Eliot Spitzer investigated the research departments of Wall Street firms approximately five years previously, Morgan Stanley was fined a little under $10 million for not having a proper e-mail retention policy in place.

LAURA ZUBULAKE V. UBS WARBURG LLC[4]

In July 2004, a judge in the U.S. District Court for the Southern District of New York found that Swiss bank UBS Warburg LLC had willfully destroyed potential e-mail evidence in a sex discrimination case brought by equity saleswoman Laura Zubulake. The judge ordered UBS to pay Zubulake's costs, and a jury later awarded her $29.2 million. The core issues in the lawsuit were whether the defendant discriminated based upon gender and whether it then retaliated against the plaintiff for reporting her discrimination claim to the Equal Employment Opportunity Commission (EEOC). A discovery dispute emerged when the defendant claimed that it had produced "all relevant e-mails" and argued against the substantial cost of restoring, and then producing, network "backup tapes" that, the defendant contended, contained only duplicative data. Plaintiff argued that the backup tapes contained e-mails that had been deleted and cited long-standing Supreme Court precedent requiring that the producing party bear the cost of production.

The U.S. District Court began by requiring the defense to produce a sampling of backup tapes. Plaintiff chose tapes from the time period between her EEOC report and her termination two months later. These backup tapes revealed 600 e-mails that had not been included in earlier productions, leading the court to "the unavoidable conclusion that there are a significant number of responsive e-mails that now exist only on backup tapes." The court also concluded that in some instances the restored e-mails proved that key witnesses deleted relevant e-mails in the hope that such deleted e-mails would not be produced in discovery.

Satisfied by the contents of the tapes that more production was warranted and employing a complex, case-specific "seven point" test, the court then ordered the defendant to bear 75 percent of the more than $165,000 restoration costs and all costs related to attorney review, an additional $107,000. The court imposed several sanctions that led to the large jury verdict, including permitting the jury to infer that the lost e-mails would have been unfavorable to the company and ordering additional depositions at the company's cost. Ultimately, a $29.2 million verdict was rendered for the plaintiff, which, according to the plaintiff's counsel, is the largest single plaintiff sex discrimination verdict in U.S. history.

LITIGATION OR INVESTIGATION HOLDS

The board of directors must be certain that the organization is capable of responding to lawsuits and investigations in order to avoid a Morgan Stanley–type problem, namely the destruction of documents in anticipation of litigation or investigation (also known as spoliation). This requires the implementation of a so-called litigation or investigation hold policy.

The most conservative view today is that whenever an organization is aware of potential litigation or investigation, it must preserve any relevant information, including paper files, databases, Microsoft Office documents, and e-mails.

BEST PRACTICE

Management must put in place a policy that covers:

- How employees will report the risk of potential litigation or investigation
- The methodology for determining what needs to be preserved
- How the information will be preserved

Notice of a potential litigation or investigation does not only occur when inside counsel or an officer receives information of a litigation or investigation, but also occurs when other employees within the organization receive such advice. In the Zubulake case, the organization was held to be on notice when one of Zubulake's bosses and coworkers were aware that she might sue UBS Warburg, even though the general counsel had no specific notice. Thus, inside counsel must properly educate the organization on how to identify potential litigation or potential investigations and have an internal business process so that counsel can react appropriately.

After notice of a potential litigation or investigation, the next step is for counsel to conduct an internal investigation and determine at a minimum who are the involved individuals. Counsel will need to make a decision as to how wide a swath of content (both electronic and physical) must be preserved. This can range from documents and e-mails of those involved in the dispute to only the specific content that appears relevant to the dispute. Many times this is a decision of practicality. Today in many organizations it is extremely difficult to identify the relevant content without incurring large expense.

BEST PRACTICE FOR HOLDS

- Counsel or their designee should interview each of the individuals who were involved in a dispute or investigation to determine locations on the network, hard drives, file cabinets, and local mail files to locate the content.

- All electronic documents and e-mail in the organization should be indexed. Then keyword searches can look for documents and e-mail that are relevant. In order to determine the relevant keywords, someone will need to interview those individuals who were involved in the dispute or investigation.

- All existing backup tapes that are relevant to the time period of the dispute or investigation should be gathered.

The first best practice listed is the standard approach. The second best practice provides an additional layer of security that all relevant content has been identified. Many times individuals will have forgotten where they have placed relevant content. The third best practice, namely gathering the backup tapes, gives the organization the security that no data are inappropriately deleted. This may require taking backup tapes out of rotation.

SEARCHING FOR CONTENT

BEST PRACTICE

In order to permit the organization to search all of its content in response to a lawsuit or investigation, the organization should invest in enterprise search software or e-mail archiving software.

Enterprise search software enables the organization to search all of the documents, e-mails, and other content sources that are currently on the network. Using enterprise search software requires that the organization's network be crawled constantly for information to index.

E-mail archiving products have been designed to perform these two functions:

- Enable the organization to reduce the size of its e-mail system in order to improve performance and permit faster disaster recovery through the removal of e-mail attachments and replacement of them with a pointer.

- Allow the organization to capture each e-mail that has been sent and received from any user or received from the outside world.

The second feature is typically called journaling and is required for financial service organizations that trade securities and that must keep all e-mails from three to six years (under SEC Rules 17a-3 and 17a-4, NASD Rule 3110, and New York Stock Exchange Rule 440). For organizations that do not desire to actively manage their content or are not required to journal by law, e-mail archiving software products provide an easy way to search all of the organization's e-mail easily.

PRESERVING CONTENT

Once the decision has been made on what needs to be preserved, several strategies can be employed to actually preserve the content:

- Leave in place and educate employees not to delete this content.
- Leave in place and use technology to prevent deletion of the content.
- Create a copy of the documents and e-mails (known as a preservation repository).

Leaving the content in place and educating employees not to delete it is the easiest and lowest-cost method to preserve content, but it is also the riskiest. The organization is completely dependent on its employees acting correctly to guarantee the preservation of the content.

The strategy to leave content in place but use technology to prevent its deletion requires that the organization has implanted technology that will accomplish this goal. This usually requires the organization to have e-mail, document, and records management technology that will be effective for this task. In addition, this technology will require that the organization build out a file plan or other organizational method to track content across the organization. User adoption is required with this type of technology; without it, the investment in the technology will have minimal value. Once implemented, this strategy offers an easy method to enact a litigation hold with little incremental cost.

BEST PRACTICE

To preserve electronic content in connection with litigation or investigation holds, create a preservation repository.

The last strategy listed, to copy all of the documents and e-mails into a preservation repository provides the greatest certainly that content will be preserved. This process removes any risk that employees will accidentally delete any relevant document or e-mail during the time of the litigation or investigative hold. Additionally, this approach does not require the implementation of an e-mail, document, or record management system. However, this approach is incrementally more expensive than the first two methods. The organization will have additional labor in copying data and the cost of the software and hardware to store preserved content. Since it provides the least risk to the organization, using a preservation repository is a best practice.

> ### BEST PRACTICE
>
> To copy electronic files, use tools that do not create new dates or modify the existing dates.

Regardless of which technique is used, any content must be copied to the task in a forensically sound manner. This practically means that, in copying the data, all of the original dates on the file must be preserved; you do not want to modify dates related to a file. There are tools on the market that facilitate this objective.

NEED TO MANAGE CONTENT

Having the ability to completely respond to discovery requests, however, is not sufficient. For example, Merrill Lynch had good backup systems in response to the investigation by New York Attorney General Eliot Spitzer and was able to produce all relevant e-mails that he requested. Unfortunately for Merrill Lynch, it had to pay over $100 million in fines because some e-mails contained compromising material.[5]

E-mails tend not to be treated with the same formality as other correspondence. E-mail is essentially used as a replacement for telephone calls, informal conversations, and meetings. E-mail and other technology tools have enabled organizations to support geographically disparate teams. While this has enabled organizations to grow on a global basis and provided for revenue growth, it has come with a cost.

When a litigation or an investigation occurs, many times a contemporaneously written document is considered to be more persuasive than oral testimony alone. In order to prove their case, each side is looking for a document that shows that the individual did or did not do the deed. Most of the time, the case is won with a very limited set of documents.

Prior to e-mails, employees would think seriously before writing a memorandum or letter. This resulted in a limited amount of communication being created. Additionally, paper is self-limiting; one can only fit so much of it on a desk. At a certain point, most people must either file it away or throw out documents that have limited value. This results in much less potential problematic documents being created and preserved.

With the advent of e-mails, the amount of content has grown tremendously. According to a study co-sponsored by the Radicati Group, in 2005 the average business user received approximately 94 e-mails a day and is likely to receive substantially more by 2008.[6] Unlike paper, electronic content is not self-limiting. The storage capacity of hard drives and other devices continues to also grow exponentially, and the cost of storage is declining. In most instances, employees are not throwing out any relevant content and are preserving everything.

The challenge for organizations is that they need electronic content from programs such as e-mails, Microsoft Office, enterprise resource planning (ERP), and customer relationship management (CRM) systems in order to run their organizations, but the by-product of these tools are more fodder for the lawyers. The result is that e-mails and other Microsoft Office documents are one of the major risks facing all organizations in the event of a lawsuit or investigation.

An easy way to think about it is that anything you keep is a record, including every stupid e-mail to your mother or rant to your boss. Anything you leave on your computer or network is something that is subject to discovery during some type of litigation or investigation. Thus, the best practice is that all content must be managed. This includes both paper, digital media (e.g., tapes, CDs, DVDs, etc.) and their electronic content.

The ability to effectively manage content will enable the organization to:

- Reduce the costs surrounding the implementation of a litigation or investigation hold, including, in case the litigation or investigation proceeds forward, the cost of copying documents and of locating information.
- Permit the organization the ability to actually make a decision as to what content should be retained and what should be destroyed (i.e., retention policies), on an organization-wide basis.

Organizations that apply retention policies without an effective content management strategy will have serious problems. Only some of the information will be destroyed, and some may remain available for discovery. Many times employees may have relevant e-mails in their inbox or local e-mail stores that will not be destroyed. The organization may destroy the documents that defend its actions while leaving other content that may harm the organization intact in an employee's inbox or local e-mail store. Retention policies should be applied only when the organization actually can delete all content relevant to a particular topic both in paper and electronic form. In order to succeed in managing all of the content, an investment in technologies, policy making, business process modeling, and possible reengineering must be made.

WHICH CONTENT, IF ANY, TO MANAGE?

BEST PRACTICE

Proactively manage all of the content throughout the organization. This is the only method to have effective retention policies.

Three basic strategies can be used in the decision to manage content:

1. Do not manage anything.
2. Manage content of high-risk actors within your organization.
3. Manage all content.

Determining which strategy to use involves an assessment of the risks and rewards. For example, if the company is in the financial service industry, it is subject to investigations and litigations all of the time, whereas the software industry has a lower risk of investigations and litigations.

Do-Nothing Strategy

An organization should choose the do-nothing strategy only if it believes that it is subject to very little risk of litigation or investigation. The result of this strategy is that if some event does occur, the organization will be required to spend significant amounts of time and money on finding the relevant content to this litigation or investigation. Organizations that adopt this strategy should not have retention policies for their content except for discrete document collections, such as tax returns. Despite the policy name, "Do Nothing," the organization should at a minimum invest in educating the employees on how their e-mail and other documents will be treated in any investigation or other litigious scenario.

Manage the Content of the High-Risk Actors

For organizations that are subject to some litigation and investigation, a logical strategy would be to identify the individuals who may be subject to litigation or investigation. In a technology company, most predictable litigation surrounds the defense or prosecution of patents and other intellectual property rights. Under this scenario, it would be logical to manage the content of the individuals (e.g., engineers and product managers) who are involved in creating inventions. This will ease the burden of finding the relevant content in order to defend these types of claims. The challenge with this kind of strategy is that the organization will really not be able to apply any kind of retention policy effectively except for very discrete content, such as tax returns. In case of a litigation or investigation, it will be necessary to seek relevant content throughout the organization. Thus, the cost will be reduced, but not significantly.

Manage All the Content

This strategy is the best practice. It requires an enterprise-wide effort to manage all of the content that exists throughout the organization in a systematic fashion. This enables the organization to respond more effectively to litigation or investigation requests. It also enables the organization to have retention policies that can be applied throughout the organizations and actually delete electronic documents effectively.

TECHNOLOGY CHOICES TO MANAGE CONTENT

In order to manage all of the content in the organization, an investment must be made in enterprise content management (ECM) software. The types of software that are categorized under the ECM label provide these functions:

- Document management
- Records management

- Web content management
- E-mail management
- Imaging
- Digital asset management

The purpose of this software is to place structure, organization, security, and retention policies around the documents. This is accomplished through integration with tools that create documents, such as e-mail software, Microsoft Office, and creative applications such as Adobe Acrobat, all of which together enable the organization to implement litigation and investigation holds and finally apply retention (and destruction) policies.

What Does It Mean to Manage All of the Content?

If the organization makes the decision to manage all of its content, a holistic strategy must be developed that stretches across all electronic and physical content throughout the organization, including backup systems. By deciding to manage all content, the organization needs assurance that when a document or e-mail is deleted, it is truly and permanently deleted.

What typically happens today is that when a user deletes a document on a network share, it is really not truly deleted. The file is still recoverable through the recycle bin, and a copy of that file exists on numerous backup tapes. We will focus our discussion principally on electronic information, which is the hardest content to manage.

In order to manage all of the content successfully, the organization will have to accomplish these tasks:

- All e-mail that has business value will be removed from the e-mail system and stored in an enterprise content management (ECM) repository, which is subject to deletion periodically pursuant to your retention policies.
- All e-mail that remains in the e-mail system (i.e., that is not stored in an enterprise content management repository) will be deleted within 30 to 180 days of its receipt.
- Users will not be able to store e-mails on their local hard drive except through software that works with the ECM system.
- All Microsoft Office documents will be stored or linked to the ECM system from initial creation through completion.
- Backup tapes are for disaster recovery and are not a tool for long-term storage of data and should be constantly rotated on a 30- to 90-day basis. Complete backups of all systems for month-end or year-end should not be maintained.
- Before each update of the organization's internally and externally managed Web site or Web sites, a snapshot should be taken or the Web site(s) duplicated so that the organization has the capability to understand how the information on the Web site(s) has changed over time.

When the organization is required to produce documents as a result of a subpoena or other request for document production, it will want the ability to easily identify all of the relevant content. The organization still may be required to search the e-mail system, but only if the request for documents falls within the last 30 to 180 days. If the organization can meet the 30- to 180-day goal, it should have some assurance that it is correctly applying retention policies on an enterprise-wide basis.

IMPLEMENTING A CONTENT MANAGEMENT STRATEGY

BEST PRACTICE

Implement a strategy to manage all content by determining what content to keep, how to organize it, and how long to retain it.

The issues that must be addressed in order to implement a strategy to manage content throughout the organization follow.

What Content to Keep

1. Determine what documents must be kept as a record to operate the business and what is required to be kept by law. An attorney must be consulted by the organization to determine the content required to be retained by law. For non-regulated or lightly regulated industries, a large percentage of the organization's content is not required to be retained by law. Therefore, it is within the discretion of the organization as to whether it should be retained or destroyed. Clearly, all e-mail spam can be deleted any time. Most people have an innate instinct as to what is worth keeping and what should be thrown out.
2. Review all content within the control of the organization and include any computer backup system.
3. Each department or business unit must determine what content is important to its business operations.

How to Organize the Content

The IT department should work with each department or business unit to determine how they need to effectively organize the information. Within each job function, there is usually an understanding on how information should be organized to make the group more effective. This work also provides an opportunity to standardize and implement better organizational processes.

The IT department should develop a file plan or taxonomy that connects each department's (or business unit's) organizational plan together and integrates such plans to create a unified organization plan. Everything must be tied together. Integration of content becomes important when the organization applies retention policies.

This strategy must stretch across both electronic and physical content of the entire organization.

How Long to Keep the Content

How long to keep content is a complex issue and varies with the nature of the organization and the nature of the content or records. Ultimately, an attorney must be consulted on the length of time that content must be retained. A retention policy should specify the life of each category of content. The policy will demonstrate what happens to the content throughout its lifetime. An example of a retention policy for a paper file is: (1) send the paper file off-site after the project ends and (2) destroy the file after three years.

Many documents are not worth keeping, and there is nothing wrong with deleting these documents.

Generally, there are two basic types of working metaphors for content: (1) project based (also known as a deal, engagement, or matter) and (2) continuous work. A good example of project-based work would be the construction of a building. The project has a beginning when someone decides that a building should be built and end when the building is finished. However, the maintenance of the building represents continuous work. With project-based work, the same file will exist and grow throughout the life of the project. When the project ends, the organization would then start the retention policy that applies to the file. For continuous work, at a regular interval the organization will cut-off or close the file related to a continuous work, create new files, and then apply a retention policy to the closed files. With the building maintenance example, the organization may have these files: 2004 Building Maintenance Request, 2005 Building Maintenance Requests, and so on. On the 2004 Building Maintenance Request File, the retention policy on that file should be in effect on January 1, 2005, when nothing further can be placed in the file.

When there is a threat of potential litigation or investigation, all document destruction activities with respect to any documents that may be relevant to the litigation or investigation must cease.

Selecting Technology Tools

In selecting technology, the organization must focus on technology that makes users more effective in performing their jobs while providing compliance. Tools that provide for compliance but do not make users more effective should be avoided. Tools that help an employee do his or her job more effectively usually are adopted while those tools that are an afterthought to the employee's daily day will be ignored or avoided. Therefore, the ideal ECM tool is one that integrates seamlessly into the employee's everyday activities as her or she organizes e-mail and creates and saves documents.

Practical Steps to Manage Content

The implementation of a strategy to manage all of the content within the organization can seem daunting. The creation of organization-wide retention policies and taxonomy is a large project and this can result in the project not moving forward. The real challenge is delivering technology solutions that enable the organization to capture *all* of the electronic content throughout the organization. Once the organization has captured the content successfully, the application of a retention policy is the easier part of the task.

In order to make the project palatable instead of daunting, the organization should focus on implementing tools to capture content on a departmental or business unit basis and should start with the highest-risk actors within the organization. Within the high-risk actors, first focus on those who already have a good process and organization of their paper files, before implementing widespread adoption of the e-mail policy. High-risk actors who do not maintain good files and organization should be saved until the end of the process.

With the good paper filers, the effort should be focused solely on translating their effective paper process into an electronic equivalent so that they can manage their electronic content effectively. This strategy is likely to provide the organization an immediate win. The organization can then expand progressively to other groups, including the bad filers. At the same time, the organization can work with counsel on determining the enterprise's retention policies and enterprise taxonomy.

ENDNOTES

1. Peter Lyman and Hal R. Varian (Senior Researchers), "How Much Information? 2003," Regents of the University of California, October 27, 2003, www.sims.berkeley.edu/research/projects/how-much-info-2003.
2. *United States v. Philip Morris, USA, Inc.*, No. CIV.A.99-2496, 2004 WL 1627252 (D.D.C. July 21, 2004).
3. "How Morgan Stanley Botched a Big Case by Fumbling Emails" *Wall Street Journal*, May 16, 2005; see also "The Morgan Stanley Email Fiasco" Securities Litigation Watch, http://slw.issproxy.com/securities_litigation_blo/2005/05/the_morgan_stan.html.
4. *Zubulake v. UBS Warburg*, 2004 WL 1620866 (S.D.N.Y. July 20, 2004); see also *Zubulake v. UBS Warburg*, 220 F.R.D. 212 (S.D.N.Y. 2003); see also *Zubulake v. UBS Warburg*, 216 F.R.D. 280 (S.D.N.Y. 2003); see also *Zubulake v. UBS Warburg*, No. 02 Civ. 1243, 2003 WL 21087136 (S.D.N.Y. May 13, 2003) (Please note: This does not relate to electronic disclosure); see also *Zubulake v. UBS Warburg*, 217 F.R.D. 309 (S.D.N.Y. 2003).
5. Khan, "Merrill Settles Charges," CNN/Money, May 21, 2002, http://money.cnn.com/2002/05/21/news/companies/merrill/.
6. "End-User Study on Email Hygene," cosponsored by The Radicati Group, Inc. and Mirapoint, Inc., April 2005, www.mirapoint.com/pdfs/whitepapers/End-User-Study-on-Email-Hygiene.pdf; see also Frauenheim, "Spam Joins Pounds on New Year's 'to Shed' List," ZDNet News, January 4, 2005, http://news.zdnet.com/2100-3513_22-5512382.html.

Chapter 10

IT Security Best Corporate Governance Practices

This chapter discusses the best practices for protecting and securing the organization's information content and technology from both internal and external threats. The discussion starts with the nature of the threats, then turns to the best practices to be adopted by smaller organizations and the best practices to be adopted by larger organizations.[1]

Electronic information is one of the most important assets of any organization. Electronic information may include sensitive data, including price lists, customer information, as well as intellectual property and other trade secrets of the organization. The loss of this sensitive information can affect the organization's competitiveness and cash flow and damage its reputation.

Information security is a business issue, not just a technology question. Organizations must ensure the confidentiality, integrity, and availability of their data. They must also ensure that information shared with other organizations is likewise protected.

BEST PRACTICE

All organizations should perform a risk analysis. Based on such analysis, high-risk organizations must take greater security precautions.

Any security risk analysis must be tailored to the nature of the business. For example, if the organization collects and stores sensitive data, such as social security numbers, credit card numbers, other personally identifiable consumer information, or is otherwise data intensive, a security breach will have more serious consequences to the organization than to organizations that are not data intensive.

In performing the risk analysis, the questions that follow should be asked. Affirmative answers indicate a high risk level from computer hackers or other polluters of information.

- Does the organization use electronic data that is protected by statute (e.g., does the organization retain health information protected by the Health Insurance Portability and Accountability Act of 1996)?

- Does the organization obtain revenue from collecting, using, or reselling electronic data?

- Is the business of the organization heavily dependent on confidential intellectual property (e.g., a software company with confidential source codes)?
- Is the organization responsible for the safety of sensitive electronic data provided to it by third parties (e.g., a service provider for payroll, a law firm, etc.)?

If any of these questions is answered affirmatively, the organization is at a high risk from computer hackers and other information polluters and must take greater security precautions.

There are a myriad of federal and state statutes that protect data and that may be applicable to the organization. Currently, federal statutes mandating affirmative data security protective measures include, but are not limited to, the Children's Online Privacy Protection Act, the Health Insurance Portability and Accountability Act, the Gramm-Leach-Bliley Act, and the Sarbanes-Oxley Act of 2002. Federal statutes prohibiting certain security conduct include, but are not limited to, the Federal Trade Commission Act, the Electronic Communications Privacy Act, and the Computer Fraud and Abuse Act. There are also federal statutes that require particular structuring of systems, including security measures to allow for law enforcement access; these statutes include the Communication Assistance for Law Enforcement Act and the Foreign Intelligence Surveillance Act.

BEST PRACTICE

All organizations should adopt and enforce a written security policy to protect its electronic information.

Security policies provide several benefits to the organization including:

- Provide a standard baseline of security policy for the entire organization.
- Establish a scalable basis for enterprise-wide product deployment.
- Heighten employee awareness of the importance of security.

Any such policy should be developed only after a risk analysis that includes a security vulnerability assessment. For extremely sensitive data, the organization should adopt a need-to-know policy.

Any security policy adopted must be strictly enforced. Strict enforcement requires a continuing education program for employees on data handling, employee confidentiality agreements, a clear procedure for reporting both internal and external attacks, and a qualified and well-trained information technology (IT) security staff. The IT security staff should know when to consult legal counsel for the organization. The organization must also maintain an adequate budget for electronic data security and seek and follow recommendations from outside security consultants.

BEST PRACTICE

If the organization intends to share sensitive information with third parties, including service providers, the organization must assure itself of the strength of the data security systems of such third parties.

If the organization shares sensitive information with third parties, the organization must rely on the third party to protect the data. The dependency of the organization on third parties increases the risk, particularly if the shared information is statutorily protected, since the organization remains responsible for the security of outward data transfers. The more third parties, including service providers, that receive sensitive data from the organization, the greater the risk. Therefore, the organization must assure itself that third parties maintain strong data security.

BEST PRACTICE

The organization should periodically engage outside security consultants to assess the adequacy of its data security system.

The organization should periodically obtain the views of independent security consultants on its data security systems. Use of such consultants helps to establish a due diligence defense against lawsuits for violations of federal or state statutes or common law rights of third parties. Obviously, the recommendations of such outside consultants should be carefully reviewed and implemented where appropriate.

SECURITY THREATS

There are many threats posed to the organization's IT and e-commerce systems, including:

- Internal users may try to gain unauthorized access to the organization's information.
- Hackers on the Internet may try to gain access to sensitive data, alter the organization's Web site, or gain access to financial information about its business or customers for the purpose of fraud.
- Computer viruses may damage the organization's programs, delete or damage its files, and jam resources.

For example, in April 2005, an internal investigation at the LexisNexis division of Reed Elsevier uncovered evidence that as many as 310,000 people may have had their personal information exposed to unauthorized individuals who compromised the security of a massive database of public and private information, including social security and driver's license numbers.[2]

In February 2005, ChoicePoint, Inc., agreed to advise 145,000 potential victims that identity thieves, in a breach of its database, may have gained access to personal information such as social security numbers and credit reports. Since disclosing its security breach, ChoicePoint has been the subject of a U.S. Federal Trade Commission inquiry into its compliance with federal information security laws and lawsuits alleging violations of the federal Fair Credit Reporting Act and California state law. In January 2006, ChoicePoint agreed to pay a $10 million federal fine in connection with the U.S. Federal Trade Commission inquiry, which was the largest civil penalty that agency had ever imposed.[3]

According to the book *Data Security and Privacy Law Combating Cyberthreats,* a few of the cyberattacks against society in general involving identity theft include:

- In 2001, thousands of customers of an American online bank received an e-mail message, purportedly from the bank, indicating that some of their account information had been lost due to an archive problem. The customers were told that, because the bank was "serious about security," it had not kept copies of the information and, therefore, requested that the customer reregister some of the information. A hyperlink was given that purported to be a direct link to the bank's Web site, but it was in fact a "mirror" or "shadow" of the bank's Web site maintained by hackers. Over 250,000 people unwittingly disclosed their information.

- In 2004, a hacker breaking into a University of California computer system accessed the names, addresses, and dates of birth of nearly 1.5 million Californians. The data resided in a database created by a university researcher with the authorization of the State of California but without the consent of the data subjects.[4]

There are a myriad of federal and state laws affecting this area that may be violated by an organization. Some of the more prominent federal laws are the Computer Fraud and Abuse Act, the Stored Communications Act, the Health Care Privacy and the Health Insurance Portability Act of 1996, and the Gramm-Leach-Bliley Act.

BEST IT SECURITY PRACTICES FOR SMALLER COMPANIES

The Committee of Sponsoring Organizations of the Treadway Commission (COSO) provided examples to smaller public companies in October 2005 concerning internal controls.[5] Some of the examples shown in Exhibit 10.1 that are cited in this report should be viewed as best practices for all small organizations, particularly those using packaged software, whether or not those small organizations are public.

Exhibit 10.1   COSO Internal Control Guidance for Small Businesses

Reviewing Logical Security

Management of a software company reviews logical security controls over the financial reporting processes and systems to prevent unauthorized access using the following groupings:

- **Access Controls**—There are formal user account set-up and maintenance procedures to request, establish, issue, suspend, change and delete user accounts. Users are defined as any persons attempting to access a system (e.g. employees, temporary workers, vendors, and contractors).
- **Authentication Controls**—Authentication standards exist that establish the minimum requirements for unique user IDs and passwords, and a finite number of login attempts. Exceptions to the standards are approved by senior management. Unique user IDs afford management the opportunity to log and audit the use of the account and to attribute the use to an individual rather than a group.
- **Privileged Accounts**—Access by system and application administrators (super users) is limited. In a small company there may only be only one employee responsible for information technology security management. Specific attention should be paid to the concentrated powers afforded these employees and controls should be in place to counter potential risks such as segregation of duties issues.
- **Auditing Controls**—Process is in place to periodically review who has access to critical financial data and configuration settings for critical applications and systems. Any violations detected are reported to management.

Using Password Access

A manufacturer of plastic toys set its password standards or critical applications, databases, operating systems, and networks so that passwords:

- Are at least six alphanumeric characters
- Cannot be easily guessed
- Are reset every 90 days
- Are locked out after three consecutive failed login attempts
- Are remembered and cannot be reused for five changes.

Managing Changes to Packaged Software

A manufacturer of plastic toys utilizes the following change management procedures for implementation of a major upgrade to its packaged general ledger software:

- Documents the major change request with a description of the impact of the upgrade, including the impact to the security environment and access controls.
- Documents a back-out plan should the upgrade not perform as expected.
- Develops a plan to test that the edit and validation rules work properly, desired system functions operate properly and produce the desired results, undesired processing results are prevented, and existing technical capabilities continue to work properly.
- Executes, documents, and communicates the results of the tests prior to release into production.
- Maintains a change control log.
- Obtains approval from management and end users of the test results prior to release into production.

Some applications may not support all of the above access controls. In that event management should review what other mitigating access controls exist such as strong network access controls.

Reviewing a Third-Party Vendor

The same manufacturer of plastic toys . . . out sources the hosting and support of the critical financial systems to a third party provider. The company:

- Reviews and approves the third party contract and confirms that the third party has signed a non-disclosure agreement.
- Assigns an individual to manage the relationship.
- Reviews annually a third-party SAS 70 Type II report to identify any deficiencies noted regarding the third party's information technology computer controls. All client consideration noted in the report are addressed by management.

Assessing Spreadsheets

To assess how the company uses spreadsheets, management in a professional services organization groups spreadsheets into the following categories:

- **Operational Spreadsheets**—Used to facilitate tracking and monitoring of workflow to support operational processes, such as a listing of open claims, unpaid invoices, and other information that previously would have been retained in manual, paper file folders. These spreadsheets are used to monitor financial transactions and determine that they are captured accurately and completely.
- **Analytical/Management Information Spreadsheets**—Used to support analytical review and management decision making. They are used to evaluate the reasonableness of financial amounts.
- **Financial Spreadsheets**—Used to directly determine financial statement transaction amounts or balances that are populated into the general ledger and/or financial statements.

The company uses a combination of the following controls to help mitigate the risks inherent in its spreadsheet environment:

- **Change Control**—Maintaining a controlled process for requesting changes to a spreadsheet, making changes, and then testing the spreadsheet and obtaining formal sign-off from an independent individual that changes are functioning as intended.
- **Version Control**—Ensuring only current and approved versions of spreadsheets are used, by creating naming conventions and directory structures.
- **Access Control** (e.g., Create, Read, Update, Delete)—Limiting access at the file level to spreadsheets on a central server and assigning appropriate rights. Spreadsheets also are password protected to restrict access.
- **Input Control**—Performing reconciliations evaluating the completeness and accuracy of data input, which is done either manually or systematically through downloads.
- **Security and Integrity of Data**—Implementing a process that secures data embedded in spreadsheets. This is done by "locking" or protecting cells to prevent inadvertent or intentional changes to standing data. In addition, the spreadsheets themselves are stored in protected directories.
- **Documentation**—Ensuring that the appropriate level of spreadsheet documentation is maintained and kept up-to-date as evidence of the business objective and specific functions of the spreadsheet.

(continued)

Exhibit 10.1   COSO Internal Control Guidance for Small Businesses

- **Development Lifecycle**—Applying a standard software development lifecycle to the development process for more critical and complex spreadsheets covering standard phases: requirements specification, design, building, testing, and maintenance.
- **Back-ups**—Implementing a process to back up spreadsheets on a regular basis so that complete and accurate information is available for financial reporting.
- **Archiving**—Maintaining historical files no longer available for update in a segregated drive and locking them as "read only."
- **Logic Inspection**—Inspecting the logic in critical spreadsheets by someone other than their user or developer, and formally documenting the review.
- **Segregation of Duties/Roles and Procedures**—Defining and implementing roles, authorities, responsibilities, and procedures for functions such as ownership, sign-off, segregation of duties, and usage.
- **Overall Analytics**—Implementing analytics as a detective control to find errors in spreadsheets used for calculations. (However, analytics alone are not a sufficient control to completely address the inherent risk of generating financial amounts using spreadsheets.)

Additional Examples of Effective Ways for Smaller Companies with Custom Software and a More Complex Information Technology Environment to Achieve the Principle

Reviewing Logical Security

Using the same example as above for a company with packaged software, the access, authentication and privileged controls would be the same. A company with custom software or a more-complex information technology environment typically would require more robust auditing controls.

Auditing Controls. Critical applications and systems generate security logs and user activity is monitored and logged. Security violations are reported to senior management. Additionally, a process is in place to periodically review access rights to critical financial data and configuration settings for critical applications and systems.

Setting Parameters for Restricting External Connectivity

The information technology group in a smaller pension fund administrator configures, maintains and monitors its firewall to:

- Limit the number of accounts that are provided to firewall administrative personnel.
- Add a "drop all" rule for packets that do not match all the rules and log such information.

The administrator also configures its routers with the following standards:

- The enable password on the router is kept in a secure encrypted form.
- The number of users who can access routers and enable access only through specific network hosts is limited.
- Limit unnecessary e-directed broadcasts, including:
  - Incoming packets at the router sourced with invalid addresses
  - TCP small services
  - UDP small services
  - All source routing
  - All web services running on routers

- Unnecessary ports on routers are disabled.
- The wireless access point's configuration is set where the SSID is not in broadcast mode and passwords are changed from the default.

Managing Change to Custom Software

Management of a manufacturing company has decided to make significant modifications to its inventory management software. The company has only two developers on staff and will need to rely on those individuals to develop, test and migrate the software to production. Additionally, the company does not have an automated code promotion utility to control versions and migrations to the production environment. In this situation the standard controls relevant to segregation of duties may be obtained though:

- Clear identification and risk analysis of the changes that will be required.
- Assignment of the changes to the developers so that each developer works on only those changes assigned to him/her.
- Having the developer who was not responsible for working on the change execute the testing and migration of the change to production.
- Review by management.

Manual controls may be relied on to manage the code version and migration issues and include:

- Creating a manual log of version of the code copied to the development environment with date and time and manually tracking the version of the code migrated to test and then to production.
- Review of all version control procedures prior to moving the code to production by the individual responsible for the information technology functions, who is independent of the change/migration process.

Source: Committee of Sponsoring Organizations, "Guidance for Smaller Public Companies Reporting on Internal Control over Financial Reporting," October 2005. Reprinted with permission.

IT of Public Companies

Sarbanes-Oxley does not by its terms establish IT corporate governance standards for public companies. Instead, both the Securities and Exchange Commission (SEC) and the Public Company Accounting Oversight Board (PCAOB) have used their authority under Section 404 of that statute to adopt rules relating to IT corporate governance.

In particular, PCAOB Auditing Standard No. 2 has imposed on auditors who are assessing the effectiveness of the company's internal control over financial reporting (pursuant to Section 404 of Sarbanes-Oxley) various requirements relating to IT. Some excerpts from Auditing Standard No. 2 affecting the assessment of IT follow.

Paragraph 50: Some controls (such as company-level controls, described in paragraph 53) might have a pervasive effect on the achievement of many overall objectives of the development, program changes, computer operations, and access to programs and data help ensure that specific controls over the processing of transactions are operating effectively.

Paragraph 69: The auditor should evaluate: . . . The nature and complexity of the systems, including the use of information technology by which the company processes and controls information supporting the assertion.

Paragraph 75: The nature and characteristics of a company's use of information technology in its information system affect the company's internal control over financial reporting . . . .

Paragraph 77: As part of understanding and evaluating the period-end financial reporting process, the auditor should evaluate: . . . The extent of information technology involvement in each period-end financial reporting process element; . . . .

Paragraph 81: While performing a walkthrough, the auditor should evaluate the quality of the evidence obtained and perform walkthrough procedures that produce a level of evidence consistent with the objectives [listed in paragraph 79 of Auditing Standard No. 2]. Rather than reviewing copies of documents and making inquires of a single person at the company, the auditor should follow the process flow of actual transactions using the same documents and information technology that company personnel use and make inquiries of relevant personnel involved in significant aspects of the process or controls . . . . Examples of follow-up inquiries include asking personnel: . . . The degree to which the control relies on the effectiveness of other controls (for example, the control environment or information technology general controls); . . .

The PCAOB has made it clear that it considers IT controls to be extremely important to the determination of the effectiveness of the internal controls over financial reporting. For example, in paragraph 126 in Auditing Standard No. 2, the auditor is not permitted to use the work of others to test controls that detect attempts to override other controls that prevent unauthorized journal entries.

The board of directors of public companies must satisfy itself that the IT systems of the company can comply with PCAOB standards, including the security requirements. Likewise, in view of the four-business-day rule for reporting material contracts and other items on Form 8-K, the internal reporting system must be capable of satisfying SEC reporting requirements.

Other Best Practices

A list of best IT security practices, some of which have been taken from the United Kingdom Web site located at www.dti.gov.uk/bestpractice, follows.

BEST PRACTICE

Utilize security technologies to manage access, and prevent unauthorized access, including, but not limited to:

- Firewalls
- Intrusion detection systems
- Virus and content scanners

(continued)

- Vulnerability assessment
- Patches and hotfixes
- Hardening operating systems and applications
- Training and educating staff to be vigilant of information risks
- Employing basic housekeeping measures, such as regular backups, and disabling logon accounts of people as they leave your company
- Ensuring that password controls are stringent
- Not using passwords that might be guessed by other users; for example, never use personal or company names
- Using network access and permissions to restrict internal access as appropriate

BEST PRACTICE

Maintaining a disaster recovery plan is important to support the organization's business in times of system failure. This includes providing:

- Facilities and services to enable the business to continue to function
- Critical IT applications and infrastructure to support the recovery of critical processes
- Adequate business interruption insurance that is tailored to the failure of your system

BEST PRACTICE

Information technology personnel who reside in different locations (e.g., multinational corporations) should form an IT corporate governance committee to establish uniform content and security rules throughout the organization. The committee should include IT representatives of each of the different locations and the chief corporate governance officer of the organization.

Multinational corporations and other organizations that have IT personnel at different locations must have a uniform method of establishing content and security for the organization. In the absence of an IT corporate governance committee, different practices can develop at different locations. This lack of uniformity will make it difficult to control IT throughout the organization. Therefore, an IT corporate governance committee should be established with representation at different major IT locations throughout the organization to provide uniform IT rules. The chief corporate governance officer of the organization must be included in the

committee in order to insure conformance of IT corporate governance with overall organization corporate governance objectives.

BEST PRACTICE

Form a computer security instant response team (CSERT) trained to handle
attacks on your electronic information systems and other computer security
incidents.

The organization's electronic information systems will, on occasion, be subject to attack by persons attempting to achieve an unauthorized result. A CSERT
trained for instant response to such attacks and other computer security incidents
is necessary to safeguard electronic information.

BEST PRACTICE

Contracts with Internet service providers, outside service providers, application service providers, Web site developers, and other similar providers must
be reviewed by an attorney specializing in intellectual property law.

These contracts are complex and have significant legal risks for the organization. Therefore, these contracts must be reviewed by an attorney specializing in
this area.

BEST PRACTICE

Store backup tapes daily in an off-site facility.

To preserve electronic content and to protect such content from fire, water, and
other types of damage, backup tapes should be stored daily in an off-site facility.

BEST PRACTICES FOR E-MAIL

If the organization connects directly to the Internet (using a dial-in modem,
integrated services digital network [ISDN], or broadband) from a desktop
or laptop machine, it should install personal firewall software. Ensure that
any network connection (such as an e-mail server) has an appropriate firewall installed.

Ensure all e-mail servers have appropriate virus-defense software, and
make sure it is set to check e-mail messages, both incoming and outgoing. It

(continued)

is sensible to use an external virus-scanning service or partner with a separate mail gateway.

Utilize junk mail filters in the organization's software (e.g., Microsoft Outlook) or buy a gateway spam (junk mail) filter product.

Check with the organization's system software vendors if you need to update security software. This is normally done online. Regularly apply appropriate security patches to mail servers.

Regularly update gateway/server virus checkers.

Perform periodic checks on any event logs stored on your systems for anything unusual or suspicious.

ENDNOTES

1. There is a good discussion on IT security on the UK government Web site located at: www.businesslink.gov.uk/bdotg/action/.
2. Jonathan Krim, "LexisNexis Data Breach Bigger Than Estimated," *Washington Post*, April 13, 2005.
3. Arshad Mohammed, "Record Fine for Data Breach, ChoicePoint Case Spotlighted ID Theft," *Washington Post*, January 27, 2006.
4. "Data Security and Privacy Law Combating Cyberthreats" Thomas/West (2002 as supplemented 2005), by Kevin P. Cronin (the lead author's partner) and Ronald N. Weikers.
5. Committee of Sponsoring Organizations of the Treadway Commission, "Guidance for Smaller Public Companies Reporting on Internal Control over Financial Reporting," October 2005.

Part III

The Public Company Audit Committee*

* Portions of Chapters 11 through 16 are reprinted with permission of The Bureau of National Affairs, Inc., Washington, D.C., from Lipman, et al. Corporate Practice Series Portfolio No. 49-4th (2003).

Chapter 11

Who Can Qualify for a Public Company Audit Committee?

Companies whose securities are listed on a national securities exchange (e.g., New York Stock Exchange [NYSE], American Stock Exchange, etc.) or on a national securities association (e.g., the Nasdaq Stock Market [Nasdaq]) must have an independent audit committee. These rules do not currently apply to securities listed on the OTC Bulletin Board or on the so-called Pink Sheets or other similar sheets for debt securities. Some state corporate laws (e.g., Connecticut) may require an independent audit committee.

> **BEST PRACTICE**
>
> The qualifications of the audit committee members should be reviewed annually by an attorney specializing in this area, and personal questionnaires to test qualifications should be submitted annually by each audit committee to such attorney.

To qualify for the audit committee of a company whose securities are listed on a national securities exchange or on the Nasdaq, the director must meet two separate requirements:

- SEC rules adopted pursuant to Sarbanes-Oxley
- Listing rules of the national securities exchange or the Nasdaq Stock Market

The independence rules of the New York Stock Exchange are cited in Appendix D, and the independence rules of the Nasdaq Stock Market are contained in Chapter 8. However, audit committees are also subject to special listing rules imposed by the stock markets as a condition of listing the security for trading; these rules are discussed later in this chapter.

These rules are complicated and require the assistance of an experienced securities lawyer to interpret. Because relationships change over time, it is important to give an annual questionnaire to the audit committee members to make sure that they still qualify. In addition, even if the audit committee member qualifies as independent under the Securities and Exchange Commission (SEC) and other rules, that member may inadvertently disqualify the outside auditor from being independent if there are any relationships with the outside auditor. An annual questionnaire helps to ferret out any such relationships.

SEC RULES

In order to be considered an "independent director" for the audit committee of a company whose stock is registered under Section 12 of the Securities Exchange Act, Sarbanes-Oxley requires that each audit committee member of a listed company be independent. In order to be qualified as independent, under Rule 10A-3 an audit committee member:

- May not accept directly or indirectly any consulting, advisory, or other compensatory fee from the company or any of its subsidiaries, other than (1) in his or her capacity as a director or as a member of the audit committee or any other board committee and (2) fixed amounts of retirement or deferred compensation for prior service not contingent on continuing service
- May not be an affiliated person of the issuer or any of its subsidiaries, other than in his or her capacity as a member of the board[1]

These requirements are in addition to any independence standards maintained by the self-regulatory organizations (SROs), such as the NYSE or Nasdaq.

Advising, Consulting, or Compensatory Fees

Under Rule 10A-3, payments to an audit committee member for service as an officer or employee are prohibited. Moreover, indirect payments are disallowed, including:

- Payments to entities in which the audit committee member is a partner, member, managing director, or executive officer or holds a comparable position that provides accounting, consulting, legal, investment banking, or financial advisory services to the listed company (except for payments to entities in which the audit committee member is a limited partner or nonmanaging member and does not have an active role in providing services to the entity)
- Payments to spouses, minor children, or stepchildren or children or stepchildren who share a home with the audit committee member[2]

The prohibitions on the compensation apply only to current relationships of audit committee members and do not "look back" to periods before a director's appointment to the audit committee. The SEC's final rule has no limitation or restriction on fees paid for services as a member of a board of directors or committees of the board. Dividend payments to an audit committee member who is a shareholder do not automatically disqualify him or her from being considered independent.[3]

Affiliated Person of the Issuer or Any Subsidiary Thereof

The second basic criterion for determining independence is that a member of the audit committee of an issuer may not be an "affiliated person" of the issuer or any subsidiary of the issuer, apart from his or her capacity as a member of the board and any board committee.[4] An affiliated person is defined by the SEC to mean "a person that directly, or indirectly through one or more intermediaries, controls, or is controlled by, or is under common control with, the person specified."[5] The SEC defines the term "control" consistent with other definitions of this term under the Securities Exchange Act as "the possession, direct or indirect, of the power to direct or cause the direction of the management and policies of a person, whether through the ownership of voting securities, by contract or otherwise."[6]

The determination of whether a person falls within the category of an affiliate requires a factual determination based on a consideration of all relevant facts and circumstances. However, the SEC has adopted a "safe harbor" under which a person who is not an executive officer and who does not beneficially own, directly or indirectly, more than 10 percent of any class of voting equity securities of a specified person will be deemed not to control such specified person and therefore will be deemed not to be an affiliate.[7] The ownership prong is based on ownership of any class of voting equity securities, instead of any class of equity securities.

The 10 percent threshold is not an upper ownership limit for nonaffiliate status. Rule 10A-3 specifically provides that the safe harbor does not create a presumption that a person exceeding the 10 percent ownership level controls or is otherwise an affiliate of a specified person. Therefore, a person who cannot rely on the safe harbor but believes that he or she does not control an issuer, could still rely on a facts and circumstances analysis. For instance, under a facts and circumstances analysis of control, a director who is not an executive officer but beneficially owns more than 10 percent of the issuer's voting equity could be determined not to be an affiliate and thus could serve on the audit committee.

Although Rule 10A-3 does not establish an upper limit on share ownership that would automatically disqualify an individual from being deemed "independent," the SEC noted that SROs could propose such limits. The SRO's declined the SEC's invitation to set any upper limit.

Exemptions from Audit Committee Member Independence

The SEC has exempted from the independence requirements particular relationships with respect to audit committee members under Rule 10A-3 for:

1. *New issuers.* Companies coming to market for the first time may face particular difficulty in recruiting members who meet the independence requirements. As a result, the audit committee of a company must have at least one fully independent member at the time of an issuer's initial listing, a majority of independent members within 90 days after the effective date of the issuer's initial registration statement, and a fully independent committee within one year after such effective date.[8]
2. *Overlapping board relationships.* Rule 10A-3 exempts from the "affiliated person" requirement an audit committee member who sits on the board of directors of a listed issuer and any affiliate so long as, except for being a director on each such board of directors, the member otherwise meets the independence requirements for each entity, including the receipt of only ordinary-course compensation for serving as a member of the board of directors, audit committee, or any other board committee of each such entity.[9]

3. *Dual holding companies.* Recognizing that certain foreign private issuers operate under a dual holding company structure, Rule 10A-3 provides an exemption:

1. Where a listed issuer is one of two dual holding companies, those companies may designate one audit committee for both companies so long as each member of the audit committee is a member of the board of directors of at least one of such dual holding companies.

2. Dual holding companies will not be deemed to be affiliates of each other by virtue of their dual holding company arrangements with each other, including where directors of one dual holding company are also directors of the other dual holding company, or where directors of one or both dual holding companies are also directors of the businesses jointly controlled, directly or indirectly, by the dual holding companies (and in each case receive only ordinary-course compensation for serving as a member of the board of directors, audit committee or any other board committee of the dual holding companies or any entity that is jointly controlled, directly or indirectly, by the dual holding companies).[10]

Disclosure of Audit Committee Financial Expert

SEC rules require the disclosure in an annual report on Form 10-K or Form 10-KSB (annual report for small business issuers) or the proxy statement whether the company has at least one "audit committee financial expert" (as defined later) serving on its audit committee, and if so, the name of such expert and whether the audit committee financial expert is independent of management.[11] If the company does not have an audit committee financial expert, the rule requires the company to disclose this fact and explain why it does not have an audit committee financial expert. If the company's board of directors determines that several members of the audit committee qualify as audit committee financial experts, the board may, but it is not required to, disclose the names of all audit committee financial experts and state whether they are independent of management.

The rule defines the term an "audit committee financial expert" as a person who has these attributes:

- An understanding of generally accepted accounting principles and financial statements
- The ability to assess the general application of such principles in connection with the accounting for estimates, accruals, and reserves
- Experience preparing, auditing, analyzing, or evaluating financial statements that present a breadth and level of complexity of accounting issues that are generally comparable to the breadth and complexity of issues that can reasonably be expected to be raised by the company's financial statements, or experience actively supervising one or more persons engaged in such activities
- An understanding of internal controls and procedures for financial reporting
- An understanding of audit committee functions

An audit committee financial expert must have acquired such attributes through:

- Education and experience as a principal financial officer, principal accounting officer, controller, public accountant, or auditor, or experience in one or more positions that involve the performance of similar functions
- Experience actively supervising a principal financial officer, principal accounting officer, controller, public accountant, auditor, or person performing similar functions
- Experience overseeing or assessing the performance of companies or public accountants with respect to the preparation, auditing, or evaluation of financial statements
- Other relevant experience[12]

The SEC believes that the board of directors in its entirety, as the most broad-based body within the company, is best-equipped to make the decision as to who qualifies as an audit committee financial expert. In determining whether a potential audit committee financial expert has all of the requisite attributes, the SEC recommends that the board of directors evaluate the totality of an individual's education and experience and consider all available facts and circumstances, including, but not limited to, these qualitative factors identified by the SEC:

- The level of the person's accounting or financial education, including whether the person has earned an advanced degree in finance or accounting
- Whether the person is a certified public accountant, or the equivalent, in good standing, and the length of time that the person actively has practiced as a certified public accountant or the equivalent
- Whether the person is certified or otherwise identified as having accounting or financial experience by a recognized private body that establishes and administers standards in respect of such expertise, whether that person is in good standing with the recognized private body, and the length of time that the person has been actively certified or identified as having this expertise
- Whether the person has served as a principal financial officer, controller, or principal accounting officer of a company that, at the time the person held such position, was required to file reports pursuant to Section 13(a) or 15(d) of the Securities Exchange Act of 1934, as amended (SEC Reports), and if so, for how long
- The person's specific duties while serving as a public accountant, auditor, principal financial officer, controller, principal accounting officer, or position involving the performance of similar functions
- The person's level of familiarity and experience with all applicable laws and regulations regarding the preparation of financial statements that must be included in the SEC Reports
- The level and amount of the person's direct experience reviewing, preparing, auditing, or analyzing financial statements that must be included in the SEC Reports

- The person's past or current membership on one or more audit committees of companies that, at the time the person held such membership, were required to file the SEC Reports
- The person's level of familiarity and experience with the use and analysis of financial statements of public companies
- Whether the person has any other relevant qualifications or experience that would assist him or her in understanding and evaluating the company's financial statements and other financial information and to make knowledgeable and thorough inquiries whether:
  - The financial statements fairly present the financial condition, results of operations, and cash flows of the company in accordance with generally accepted accounting principles
  - The financial statements and other financial information, taken together, fairly present the financial condition, results of operations, and cash flows of the company

The SEC intends that the board of directors would use the preceding list as guidance rather than a mechanical checklist in assessing whether a person qualifies as an audit committee financial expert. The fact that a person previously has served on an audit committee does not, by itself, justify the board of directors in "grandfathering" that person as an audit committee financial expert under the definition. Similarly, the fact that a person has experience as a public accountant, auditor, principal financial officer, controller, or principal accounting officer or experience in a similar position does not, by itself, justify the board of directors in deeming the person to be an audit committee financial expert. In addition to determining that a person possesses an appropriate degree of knowledge and experience, the board must ensure that it names an audit committee financial expert who embodies the highest standards of personal and professional integrity. In this regard, a board should consider any disciplinary actions to which a potential expert is, or has been, subject in determining whether that person would be a suitable audit committee financial expert.

The SEC believes that an audit committee financial expert chosen by the board of directors should have these characteristics:

- A thorough understanding of the audit committee's oversight role
- Expertise in accounting matters as well as understanding of financial statements
- The ability to ask the right questions to determine whether the company's financial statements are complete and accurate

In order for an audit committee financial expert to be considered "independent," he or she should meet the definition of independence stated in the applicable listing standards of the national securities exchange (e.g., New York Stock Exchange, American Stock Exchange, etc.) or Nasdaq.

The SEC's definition of an "audit committee financial expert" is very broad and includes many individuals who would not necessarily be considered a financial expert from an outsider's viewpoint. The board of directors is given very broad discretion by the SEC to determine who is a financial expert. For example, a person whose entire experience was with private companies in some financial role can arguably qualify if his/her experience included a breadth and level of complexity of accounting issues that are generally comparable to the breadth and complexity of issues that can reasonably be expected to be raised by the company's financial statements, or experience actively supervising one or more persons engaged in such activities.

SEC SAFE HARBOR

The SEC included specific "safe harbor" provisions in its rule clarifying that the designation of a person as an audit committee financial expert will not impose on such person any duties, obligations, or liability that are greater than the duties, obligations, and liability imposed on such person as a regular member of the audit committee and board of directors. However, the Delaware courts impose greater state law fiduciary duties on directors who are "experts" than on other directors who do not possess expertise. Accordingly, the SEC's "safe harbor" is not very safe.

STOCK MARKET LISTING RULES

The listing rules for national securities exchanges and the Nasdaq Stock Market generally require at least three independent directors for the audit committee (with limited exceptions). Each member of the audit committee must possess some level of financial sophistication. For example, the NYSE listing rules require (among other things) that "each member of the audit committee must be financially literate, as such qualification is interpreted by the listed company's board in its business judgment, or must become financially literate within a reasonable period of time after his or her appointment to the audit committee."[13] The Nasdaq listing rules require (among other things) that "each member of the audit committee not have participated in the preparation of the financial statements of the company or any current subsidiary of the company at any time during the past three years; and . . . be able to read and understand fundamental financial statements, including a company's balance sheet, income statement, and cash flow statement."[14]

The SEC rule on audit committee financial experts merely requires the disclosure of whether or not there is such an expert on the audit committee. It is intended to embarrass public companies into putting such an expert on the audit committee.

In contrast, in order to qualify for listing, the listing rules for national securities exchanges require a person with financial expertise to be on the audit committee. However, they do not use the same criteria as the SEC. For example, the NYSE rule provides:

> In addition, at least one member of the audit committee must have accounting or related financial management expertise, as the listed company's board interprets such qualification in its business judgment. While the Exchange does not require that a listed company's audit committee include a person who satisfies the definition of audit committee financial expert set out in Item 401(h) of Regulation S-K,

a board may presume that such a person has accounting or related financial management expertise.[15]

Likewise, the Nasdaq listing rule provides:

Additionally, each issuer must certify that it has, and will continue to have, at least one member of the audit committee who has past employment experience in finance or accounting, requisite professional certification in accounting, or any other comparable experience or background which results in the individual's financial sophistication, including being or having been a chief executive officer, chief financial officer or other senior officer with financial oversight responsibilities.[16]

It is theoretically possible for an individual to satisfy the listing requirements but not qualify as an "audit committee financial expert" for SEC purposes. However, that has not occurred because of the broad discretion given to the board of directors to designate an individual as an "audit committee financial expert."

ACADEMIC STUDY

Once all minimum SEC and stock market listing requirements have been satisfied, the board of directors should consider what other qualifications members of the audit committee should possess.

Professor Roman L. Weil, who coauthored a study on audit committee financial literacy, believes that being a former audit partner in a "Big Four" accounting firm is the best possible background for an audit committee member of a public company board.[17] Weil is the Duane Rath Professor of Accounting at the University of Chicago. Other experts believe that a more diverse background for audit committee members, including being a former chief executive officer (CEO) or chief financial officer (CFO) of a similar company, should be considered.

BEST PRACTICE

At least one member, and preferably more than one member, of a public company audit committee should have had significant experience as an audit partner in a major accounting firm.

ENDNOTES

1. See Securities Act Release No. 33-8220, Subpart II(A)(1).
2. See id. at Subpart II(A)(2).
3. See id.
4. See Securities Act Release No. 33-8220, Subpart II(A)(3).
5. See Exchange Act Rule 10A-3(e)(1)(i).
6. See, e.g., Exchange Act Rule 12b-2.
7. See Securities Act Release No. 33-8220, Subpart II(A)(3).

8. See Securities Act Release No. 33-8220, Subpart II(A)(4).

9. Id., at Subpart II(A)(5).

10. Id.

11. See Securities Act Release No. 33-8177.

12. Id.

13. New York Stock Exchange, Final NYSE Corporate Governance Rules (November 3, 2004), 11. www.nyse.com/pdfs/Section 303A_final_rules.pdf.

14. The Nasdaq Stock Market, Inc., Corporate Governance Rules 4200, 4200A, 4350, 4350A, 4351, and 4360, and Associated Interpretive Material, www.nasdaq.com/about/CorporateGovernance.pdf.

15. See Note 13.

16. See Note 14.

17. Weil et al., "Audit Committee Financial Literacy: A Work in Progress," March 11, 2005, http://papers.ssrn.com/sol3/papers.cfm?abstract_id=680281.

Chapter 12

Public Company Audit Committee: Personal Liability of Audit Committee Members

---

BEST PRACTICE

To protect against personal liability of audit committee members:

- Audit committee members must establish a "due diligence" defense to personal liability
- The public company must have a nondisclaimable director and officer liability policy, in which coverage cannot be affected by bankruptcy of the public company and coverage amounts are sufficient to protect the audit committee members

---

This chapter discusses some of the special duties of public company audit committee members under federal law and as a result of obligations imposed on them by their own charters. However, it is important to first understand director and officer liability insurance available to all board members, including members of the audit committee. Like other members of the board, audit committee members are also liable if they breach their fiduciary duties under state law, as discussed in Chapter 2. That discussion will not be repeated.

The increased public focus on audit committees significantly increases the risk of lawsuits (including both regulatory claims by Securities and Exchange Commission [SEC] seeking statutory fines, penalties and remedial measures, and private lawsuits seeking monetary damages), SEC injunctive actions, administrative cease and desist orders, and, in appropriate cases, criminal prosecution against audit committee members.[1] These risks are in addition to the risks resulting in possible breaches by audit committee members of their state law fiduciary duties described in Chapter 2.

Arguments can be made that neither the Sarbanes-Oxley Act of 2002 (Sarbanes-Oxley) nor the SEC implementing rules significantly actually increase the personal risk of audit committee members, who previously were signing Form 10-K reports containing audited financial statements. The members of the audit committee as such are not required to sign any SEC filings, except that Form 10-K requires the signature of the majority of the members of the board of directors, regardless of their membership on the audit committee. However, these arguments, even if technically accurate, miss the point.

Given the current regulatory and media environment, there simply is a much greater likelihood today that civil and criminal actions will in fact be brought against audit committee members than ever before. Sarbanes-Oxley has merely focused a public spotlight on the audit committee. This spotlight, in turn, will cause government enforcers and private litigants to focus on the role of the audit committee any time there is a public revelation of abusive accounting practices, particularly where these abusive practices caused significant investor losses. Any time there is a financial fiasco, the role of members of the audit committee will be examined under the microscope with the advantage of 20/20 hindsight.

Thus, whether the Sarbanes-Oxley Act actually will result in additional individual liability for audit comments members or not, there currently is a much higher risk of government and private litigation actions against them than even before. Indeed, this risk has already been manifested by numerous high-profile government and private action that have captured the attention of the financial media.

Moreover, the public outrage over corporate corruption has not gone unnoticed by the judiciary, which has expressed equal outrage. For instance, on February 18, 2003, Senior Judge Warren Ferguson of the 9th U.S. Circuit Court of Appeals stated, "[I]n this era of corporate scandal, when insiders manipulate the market with the complicity of lawyers and accountants, we are cautious to raise the bar of the [Private Securities Litigation Reform Act of 1995] any higher than that which is required under its mandates."[2]

Audit committee members should be particularly concerned about the November 18, 2002, decision of the U.S. District Court for the District of Massachusetts entitled *In re Lernout and Hauspie Securities Litigation.*[3] The court in *Lernout* imposed control person liability under Section 15 of the Securities Act of 1933 (1933 Act) and Section 20(a) of the Securities Exchange Act of 1934 (1934 Act) on audit committee members in connection with a massive financial fraud case while at the same time dismissing similar allegations against directors who were not audit committee members.[4] The *Lernout* case is discussed later in this chapter.

Audit committees that are concerned about satisfying their duties and about attempting to reduce the risk of personal liability should seriously consider engaging an experienced and special audit committee counsel to advise them. If an independent counsel is engaged, then the counsel should be experienced in advising other audit committees and securities law and regulation, with an adequate accounting background. The audit committee should also consider whether any counsel chosen should have to satisfy the same strict independence tests (if any) that apply to audit committee members themselves.

DIRECTOR AND OFFICER LIABILITY INSURANCE

All members of the board and particularly the members of the audit committee must have director and officer (D&O) liability coverage for themselves personally that is not disclaimable by the insurance company for misstatements contained in the policy application of which the director was not aware.

At least four risks should be of particular concern:

1. Is there sufficient coverage?
2. Is there coverage if the company is in bankruptcy?
3. Is there coverage if the financial statements of the company submitted with the insurance application were false and misleading?
4. Is the insurer that issues the policy financially able to honor the policy?

A D&O insurance policy typically consists of three parts:

1. Side A coverage for directors and officers personally
2. Side B coverage for the corporation to the extent the organization is required to indemnify directors and officers under its by-laws
3. Side C coverage for the organization's own liability

Audit committee members should insist on Side A coverage, with coverage limits that are not tied to the limits of Side B or Side C. If a bankruptcy petition is filed with respect to the corporation, and there is no Side A coverage, a question arises as to whether the audit committee members may still draw down on the policy to fund legal defense cost or to pay claims. Several bankruptcy courts have raised the issue that director drawdowns on a D&O policy may be depleting an asset of the bankrupt estate of the corporation and, therefore, the bankruptcy court could enjoin the director drawdowns. Even the existence of a single combined coverage limit for both Side A and Side B (corporate reimbursement coverage) may result in delays in obtaining coverage for legal fees and expenses incurred by the director until bankruptcy court approval is obtained.

Nondisclaimable Policies

If the D&O insurance application submitted by management is materially false, the D&O insurer may elect to disclaim coverage. Indeed, on February 25, 2005, *The Wall Street Journal* reported that Chubb had brought an action to rescind D&O coverage for directors and officers of Nortel.[5] Some D&O policies are being written to protect innocent independent directors from misstatements made by management in the D&O insurance application. These policies are relatively new, but serious consideration should be given to this form of D&O coverage.

Coverage Amounts

There is no single answer as to how much coverage a director should have. Much of it depends on the coverage costs, which can vary from year to year.

One key issue in determining the amount of coverage is the value of the public float, that is, the market value of all publicly held securities. The theory is that this is the maximum amount for which directors may be liable since, arguably, the insiders may not have rights against the directors for material misstatements or omissions. While this statement is not necessarily true, the public float does provide a rule of thumb measurement.

Most companies cannot afford coverage equal to the value of the public float or do not wish to pay for such coverage. Another method of measuring coverage amounts is using the average weekly trading volume of the stock and attempting to guess at the maximum the stock will decline in value if there is an announcement of a restatement of the financial statements. For example, if a stock is trading at $20 and may go down to $10 in the event of a restatement of the financial statements, you would multiply $10 by the estimate of the average weekly trading volume between the time the financial statement error would have occurred and until the time the restatement correcting the error was announced.

The amount of the coverage should, in any event, be sufficient to be of interest to a plaintiff's lawyer in a shareholder class action.

Personal D&O Coverage

Other policies can be obtained to cover those liabilities not normally covered in D&O policies. These include securities acts liability insurance, individual director's policies, and nonprofit and charitable organization policies. A recent D&O insurance product of Chubb Insurance Company is personal director's liability insurance, which protects specific assets of the director and the director's spouse if the board of directors' D&O policy or the indemnification obligation of the company proves uncollectible.

In the legal settlement with certain WorldCom directors, the directors were forced to pay a percentage of their personal assets to the plaintiffs.[6] A personal director's liability policy, paid for by the director, may have reimbursed those directors for the payment of their personal assets.

Care must be taken in choosing the D&O insurer to be certain that it will have the financial resources necessary to honor the policy provisions. The cheapest policy is not necessarily the best if it is written by a financially weak insurer. The liquidation of Reliance Insurance Company, which resulted in the disclaiming of a number of D&O liability policies, makes it very clear that great care must be taken to obtain a financially sound insurance company.

CONTROL PERSON LIABILITY

Control persons of a corporation have potential personal liability under Section 15 of the 1933 Act and Section 20(a) of the 1934 Act for corporate acts violating those laws. Is being on the audit committee an indication of a control relationship with the corporation?

Section 15 of the 1933 Act reads:

Every person who, by or through stock ownership, agency, or otherwise, or who, pursuant to or in connection with an agreement or understanding with one or more other persons by or through stock ownership, agency, or otherwise, controls any person liable under Section 11, or 12, shall also be liable jointly and severally with and to the same extent as such controlled person to any person to whom such controlled person is liable, unless the controlling person had no knowledge of or reasonable ground to believe in the existence of the facts by reason of which the liability of the controlled person is alleged to exist.

Section 20(a) of the 1934 Act reads:

Every person who, directly or indirectly, controls any person liable under any provision of this title or of any rule or regulation thereunder shall also be liable jointly
and severally with and to the same extent as such controlled person to any person to
whom such controlled person is liable, unless the controlling person acted in good
faith and did not directly or indirectly induce the act or acts constituting the violation
or cause of action.

Some courts have viewed audit committee members as "control persons"
under the federal securities laws and have required the audit committee member
to prove their good faith and due diligence in order to avoid personal liability. The
key to avoiding personal liability for an audit committee member is to establish a
"due diligence" defense by showing that the audit committee member acted in
good faith and exercised due diligence with respect to his or her responsibilities.
In the event of a financial fraud, it is likely that the audit committee member will
have the burden of proving his or her own good faith and due diligence.

The *Lernout* Case[7]

Lernout involved a class action containing securities fraud claims against an outside
board of directors, including the audit committee, of a bankrupt speech recognition
software corporation, Lernout & Hauspie Speech Products, N.V. (L & H).[8] The proposed class action alleged "that the Audit Committee was asleep at the switch, recklessly
so, and failed to catch the massive fraud by L & H's Senior Officers and auditors." The
chairman of the audit committee allegedly signed a Form S-3 Registration Statement
filed by L & H on August 25, 2000, that publicly incorporated an allegedly fraudulent
1999 Form 10-K Report filed on June 20, 2000, which had been signed by all three
members of the audit committee.

The court in *Lernout* stated that the listed allegations made by the plaintiffs establish
a strong inference of scienter based on recklessness against the members of the audit
committee at least with respect to the fourth-quarter financials in 1999 and the annual
report for 1999. By the Summer of 2000, the defendant Vandendriessche (the chair of
the audit committee), and the remaining audit committee members, knew (among other
things):

- L & H had failed to implement a system of internal audit controls, as KPMG had been
  persistently recommending since May 1998.
- L & H failed to hire an internal auditor until June 2000 despite the audit committee's
  own commitment in August 1999 to get back to the directors with a recommendation.
- The audit committee promised the board of directors that it would meet prior to each
  quarterly financial report to review it and continued to sign off on financial statements
  in 2000 despite the continuing lack of internal controls and various red flags . . . .
- The SEC was investigating L & H accounting practices in January 2000.
- L & H management was issuing financial information in press releases without the
  advance approval of the audit committee.

- In reports to the audit committee, KPMG continually noted issues concerning cash collection from the [new customers allegedly created by *Lernout*] and revenues recognized from Korea, and in a letter dated August 18, 1999, KPMG had reported that at least nine transactions in the second quarter of 1999 were questionable.
- In a confidential letter, KPMG reported on November 17, 1999, to Vandendriessche, the chair of the audit committee, that it did not consider its "limited review of the third quarter financial statements completed, because of outstanding revenue recognition issues in Korea and cash collection issues from the LDC's."
- In a different letter from KPMG to Dammekins dated November 17, 1999, which was communicated to Vandendriessche, KPMG advised that it could not sign the audit opinion for the December 31, 1999 audit unless issues relating to outstanding receivables, revenues, and Korean contracts were resolved.[9]

The court held that the signatures on the Form S-3 Registration Statement and the Form 10-K Report satisfied the requirement that the audit committee members "make" a fraudulent statement for purposes of Section 10(b) of the 1934 Act.[10] More important, the court went on to also hold that the three audit committee members were also control persons under Section 20(a) of the 1934 Act.[11] In refusing to dismiss the control person allegations against the audit committee members, but dismissing these same allegations against nonaudit committee members, the court stated:

> Signatures are one factor supporting a control allegation, but plaintiffs must show signatures plus other indicia of control. See *In re Oxford Health Plans, Inc. Sec. Litig.*, 187 F.R.D. 133, 143 (S.D.N.Y. 1999) (finding that four of the outside directors were control persons based on their director status combined with their equity interests in the corporation and their intimate knowledge of the day-to-day operations of the company); *In re Independent Energy Holdings PLC Sec. Litig.*, 154 F.Supp.2d 741, 772 (S.D.N.Y.2001) (finding director status plus equity interest plus signature on fraudulent prospectus stated sufficient allegation of control); *In re Valujet, Inc. Sec. Litig.* 948 F.Supp. 1472, 1480 (N.D.Ga.1997) (finding outside director who was also founder and signed SEC filing to be control person); *Dequlis v. LXR Biotechnology, Inc.*, 928 F.Supp. 1301, 1315 (S.D.N.Y.1996) (holding that plaintiffs had adequately pled defendants' control and authority by detailing their ability to control the acts of the issuers, their control over the contents of the offering documents as well as their signatures on those documents). In each of these cases, the courts relied both on the special status of the outside director (e.g., audit committee member, equity shareholder) and their involvement with the financial statements of the company in finding the director to be a control person
>
> The distinction lies in the director's ability to control the content of the financial documents. Where the director has some special status within the corporation, such as membership on an Audit Committee, and has the power to exercise content control over financial documents, the director's signature on the SEC filing might suffice for pleading purposes to establish the exercise of control over the contents of the financial statements. Where the defendant's status is merely that of outside director, however, the defendant's signature on the SEC filing does not necessarily constitute an exercise of any power or control over its contents.[12]

The facts in *Lernout* all occurred before the effective date of Sarbanes-Oxley, although the decision was made during the general public outrage over corporate corruption. Before *Lernout* and Sarbanes-Oxley, there were several attempts made to impose control person liability on audit committee members.

(continued)

> Likewise, before *Lernout*, some courts held that audit committee members who signed a company's financial statements were control persons for purposes of Section 20(a) liability because:
>
> > [a]n outside director and audit committee member who is in a position to approve a corporation's financial statements can be presumed to have the power to direct or cause the direction of the management and policies of the corporation, at lease insofar as the "management and policies" referred to relate to ensuring a measure of accuracy in the contents of company reports and SEC registrations that they actually sign.[13]

FORM 10-K SIGNATURE REQUIREMENT

The Form 10-K Report must be signed by a majority of the members of the board of directors, and this majority typically includes members of the audit committee. The SEC has stated that "by signing documents filed with the Commission, board members implicitly indicate that they believe that the filing is accurate and complete."[14]

A number of courts have held that a corporate official, acting with scienter, who signs a documents that is filed with the SEC that contains material misrepresentations, such as a Form 10-K containing false financial statements, "makes" a statement and may be liable as a primary violator under Section 10(b) of the 1934 Act for making a false statement under Section 10(b). This is true whether the director actually participated in the drafting of the document or not.[15]

PROCEDURES ILLUSTRATING DUE CARE

Liability insurance itself is not sufficient to protect directors serving as audit committee members. The insurance policies are often expensive and, as mentioned, do not cover every conceivable potential liability confronting directors. It is therefore essential for audit committee members wishing to reduce the threat of liability to ensure that the committee creates a complete record of its activities and conducts its duties according to identifiable procedures that satisfy its legal obligations.

BEST PRACTICE PROCEDURES

- *Definition of duties.* The audit committee should seek to have the duties that are delegated to it stated with particularity in writing in its charter.
- *Regularly scheduled meetings.* The committee should establish and publish a schedule of meetings. It can accompany this schedule with agendas setting forth the topics to be addressed at each meeting, the timetable to be observed, and the persons scheduled to appear.

(continued)

- *Recordation of activity.* Minutes are normally kept at all meetings of the committee. These can be used not only to document the committee's activity but also as references for future use. Generally, they should state the topics considered, the results of discussions, and the actions recommended. The committee can also institute a filing system with a complete index that catalogs the committee's activities. This not only provides an accessible record of past activity, but also can be of assistance in obtaining and retrieving reports and information that relate to current activity.

- *Establish independent information mechanisms.* One of the apparent mistakes made by the audit committees of Enron and WorldCom was their overdependence on the accuracy and completeness of information supplied by management and the independent auditors. As previously discussed, the audit committee needs independent sources of information to perform its task of monitoring management. This could be supplied in part through a strong internal audit function, with the head of internal audit reporting directly to the audit committee. Some corporations outsource a portion of the internal audit function. The head of internal audit should be hired by the audit committee and have his or her compensation determined by the audit committee. The compensation of the head of internal audit should not contain significant incentives based on financial results.

- *Create a culture of zero fraud tolerance.* The audit committee, together with management, should set a tone within the corporation of zero fraud tolerance. This can be accomplished by codes of ethics and constant reminders of the intolerance of the corporation of illegal or fraudulent conduct. The accessibility of the audit committee for directly reporting fraudulent conduct should be stressed in employee messages.

- *Limiting absences.* Committee members should avoid being absent from meetings. Roll calls should be taken and recorded in the committee's minutes. Directors who are unable to attend most of the meetings, either personally or by telephone, should resign or be replaced.

- *Obtaining advice of independent counsel, auditors, and experts.* Under Sarbanes-Oxley, audit committees have the option of retaining counsel other than the regular corporate counsel. Similarly, audit committees are permitted to engage independent auditors and other experts. Such professional expertise can assist the committee in accomplishing some of its more sophisticated functions.

- *Disclosure of the committee's role.* To eliminate any misconception of the audit committee's role, it might be necessary to explain the scope of its responsibilities. This can be done in full in the annual report or by reference to another document outlining the committee's functions.

(continued)

- *Independent counsel should periodically review audit committee activities.* As previously noted, audit committees should conduct their activities to attempt to establish a "due diligence" defense to control person liability. Periodic review of the activities of the audit committee should be made by independent counsel to determine if a "due diligence" defense has been established.

ENDNOTES

1. See, for example, SEC Press Release 2004-144, announcing action against Roland Fahlin, former member of the supervisory board and audit committee of Royal Ahold.
2. *Employer-Teamster Joint Council Pension Trust Fund v. Am. W. Airlines, Inc.*, 320 F.3d 920, 946 (9th Cir. 2003).
3. *In re Lernout & Hauspie Sec. Litig.*, 286 B.R. 33 (D. Mass. 2002).
4. Id.
5. "Moving the Market: Chubb Asks Court for Relief from Nortel's Accounting Woes," *Wall Street Journal*, February 25, 2005.
6. http://slw.issproxy.com/securities_litigation_blo/2005/01/10_former_world.html.
7. *Lernout*, 286 B.R. at 33.
8. Id.
9. Id. at 37 (emphasis added; citations omitted).
10. Id.
11. *Lernout*, 286 B.R. at 39.
12. Id. at 43–44.
13. *In re Livent Inc. SEC. Litig.*, 148 F. Supp. 2d 331, 373 (S.D.N.Y. 2001); see also *In re Reliance Sec. Litig.*, 135 F. Supp. 2d 480, 518 (D. Del. 2001) (finding that control status was a "genuine issue of material fact" when an outside director "served on subcommitees related to the oversight of [the company's] accounting and reporting practices."); *Jacobs v. Coopers & Lybrand, LLP, Fed. Sec. L. Rep. (CCH)* ¶ 90,443, 1999 WL 101772, *18 (S.D.N.Y. 1999) (stating that "[t]hough his status as a director who allegedly served on the audit committee alone would not raise the inference that Hirsch was a § 20(a) controlling person, the allegation that he signed a fraudulent 10-K form does raise this inference . . .").
14. Audit Committee Disclosure, Exchange Act Release No. 34-41987, 64 Fed. Reg. 55,648, 55,653 (Oct. 14, 1999).
15. *Howard v. Everex Systems, Inc.*, 228 F.3d 1057, 1061 (9th Cir. 2000) (citing *In re JWP Inc., Sec. Litig.*, 928 F. Supp. 12393, 1255-56 (S.D.N.Y. 1996) (holding that a director who signs a fraudulent Form 10-K with scienter can be liable as a primary violator for making a false statement under § 10(b)), and *F.N. Wolf & Co., Inc. v. Estate of Neal*, No. 89 CIV.1223 (CSH), 1991 U.S. Dist. LEXIS 2428, 1991 WL 34186, at *8 (S.D.N.Y. Feb. 25, 1991) (holding that a "director signing a document filed with the SEC . . . 'makes or causes to be made' the statements contained therein" under § 1.8(a) of the 1934 Act)); see also *In re Cabletroff Systems, Incl.*, 311 F.3d 11, 40 (1st Cir. 2002); *In re Reliance Sec. Litig.*, 135 F. Supp. 2d 480, 503 (D. Del. 2001); *In re Indep. Energy Holdings PLC Sec. Litig.*, 154 F. Supp. 2d 741, 767 (S.D.N.Y. 2001), abrogated on other grounds, *In re Initial Public Offering Sec. Litig.*, 241 F. Supp. 2d 281 (S.D.N.Y. 2003); *In re Lernout & Hauspie Sec. Litig.*, 286 B.R. 33, 37 (D. Mass. 2002) (signatures of three members of the Audit Committee on statements filed with the SEC

"satisfy the requirement that defendants make a fraudulent statement" for liability under § 10(b)); *In re Lernout & Hauspie Sec. Litig.*, 230 F. Supp. 2d 152, 163 (D. Mass. 2002) (stating that "[I]t is well established in this Circuit that each defendant may be held responsible for the false and misleading statements contained in the financial statements he signed [under] § 10(b)" citing *Serabian v. Amoskeag Bank Shares, Inc.*, 24 F.3d 357, 367-68 (1st Cir. 1994)). The Ninth Circuit explained that "by placing responsibility on corporate officers to ensure the validity of corporate filings, investors are further protected from misleading information." Howard, 228 F.3d at 1061. Furthermore, "key corporate officers should not be allowed to make important false financial statements knowingly or recklessly, yet still shield themselves from liability to investors simply by failing to be involved in the preparation of those statements. Otherwise the securities laws would be significantly weakened." Id. at 1062.

Chapter 13

Minimum Responsibilities of Public Company Audit Committees

In describing the functions of the audit committee, Warren Buffett stated during a Securities and Exchange Commission (SEC) Roundtable Discussion on Financial Disclosure and Auditor Oversight held on March 4, 2002[1]:

> Their function . . . is to hold the auditor's feet to the fire. And, I suggest . . . the audit committee ask [questions] of the auditors [including]: if the auditor were solely responsible for preparation of the company's financial statements, would they have been prepared in any way differently than the manner selected by management? They should inquire as to both material and non-material differences. If the auditor would have done anything differently than management, then explanations should be made of management's argument and the auditor's response.

In discussing the responsibilities of a public company audit committee, we must distinguish between the minimum responsibilities required by specific statutes or rules or by specific stock market rules from those responsibilities that are needed in order to comply with the general fiduciary duties of audit committee members or to establish a "due diligence" defense to personal liability. Complying with these minimum responsibilities does not necessarily establish a "due diligence" defense for audit committee members under Section 15 of the 1933 Act or Section 20(a) of the 1934 Act. However, it is important to understand these minimum requirements since they represent the least that is expected from public company audit committees.

The minimum responsibilities of public company audit committees consist of the combination of:

- Responsibilities imposed by federal statutes and SEC rules
- Responsibilities imposed by audit committee charters that are, in part, dictated by the listing rules of the stock market on which the company's securities are traded

For example, the New York Stock Exchange (NYSE) and the Nasdaq Stock Market require in their listing rules certain provisions that must be contained in an audit committee charter. No similar listing rules currently exist for public companies traded on the Nasdaq Bulletin Board or the so-called Pink Sheets.

MINIMUM RESPONSIBILITIES IMPOSED
BY FEDERAL STATUTES AND SEC RULES

The minimum responsibilities of public company audit committees imposed by federal statutes and SEC rules are:

- Preapprove all auditing services and all nonauditing services of the auditor, subject to the de minimus exception.
- If the securities of the public company are listed on the national securities exchange (e.g., the NYSE or the American Stock Exchange) or a national securities association (e.g., Nasdaq):
  - Ensure the independence of all audit committee members under applicable SEC and stock market rules.
  - Appoint, compensate, and oversee the work of the registered public accounting firm.
  - Establish procedures for: the receipt, retention, and treatment of complaints received by the issuer regarding accounting, internal accounting controls, or auditing matters; and the confidential, anonymous submission by employees of the issuer of concerns regarding questionable accounting or auditing matters.
- Monitor the independence of the auditor.
- Listen to and discuss all reports given to the audit committee by the registered public accounting firm under SEC Regulation Section 210.2-07[2] and generally accepted auditing standards (relating in part to critical accounting policies and practices and alternative and preferred treatments).
- Listen to and discuss all reports given to the audit committee by management pursuant to SEC Rules 13a-14/15 and 15d-14/15 (relating in part to deficiencies in internal controls and fraud).
- Comply with all applicable stock market rules relating to the duties and responsibilities of audit committees, including, but not limited to, having a written charter that states the audit committee's purpose and states the minimum duties and responsibilities of the audit committee.

The SEC requires that each registrant provide an audit committee report in its proxy statement that discloses whether the audit committee has:

- Reviewed and discussed the audited financial statements with management.
- Discussed with the independent auditors matters required by the Statements on Auditing Standards No. 1.
- Received written communications from the independent auditors that are required by Independence Standards Board Standard No. 1, and discussed with the independent auditors their independence.
- Based on the review of the prior items, recommended to the board of directors that the audited financial statements be included in the company's Form 10-K.

AUDIT COMMITTEE CHARTERS

Audit committee charters contain the functions and responsibilities of the audit committee. Generally, audit committee charters are required to be posted on the Web site of the public company and contained in proxy statements sent to shareholders.

The audit committee must, at a minimum, comply with the duties spelled out in its charter, since the charter is in effect a promise to the shareholders and to the public. Failure to comply with their own charter duties and responsibilities can itself be a basis for personal liability of audit committee members.

The existing rules of the national securities markets (e.g., NYSE and Nasdaq) require audit committee charters to contain specific duties and responsibilities, as discussed next. These listing requirements should, therefore, be viewed as part of the minimum responsibilities of audit committees.

Some audit committee charters go well beyond the minimum requirements for listing and contain flowery and vaguely worded language. Care must be taken to avoid overpromising in an audit committee charter or creating duties the audit committee cannot effectively perform.

New York Stock Exchange Audit Committee Charters

Under the NYSE rules approved by the SEC on November 4, 2003 (and amended on November 3, 2004), the audit committee must have a written charter, and this written charter must contain the minimum responsibilities of audit committees of NYSE listed companies. The portions of the NYSE rules that follow describe what, at minimum, must be in an NYSE charter and contains NYSE commentary as what is expected by these provisions. These requirements may be viewed as "best practices" for all audit committees, whether the company's securities are traded on the NYSE or not.

(c) The audit committee must have a written charter that addresses:

(i) the committee's purpose—which, at minimum, must be to:

(A) assist board oversight of (1) the integrity of the listed company's financial statements, (2) the listed company's compliance with legal and regulatory requirements, (3) the independent auditor's qualifications and independence, and (4) the performance of the listed company's internal audit function and independent auditors; and

(B) prepare an audit committee report as required by the SEC to be included in the listed company's annual proxy statement;

(ii) an annual performance evaluation of the audit committee; and

(iii) the duties and responsibilities of the audit committee—which, at a minimum, must include those set out in Rule 10A-3(b)(2), (3), (4) and (5) of the Exchange Act, as well as to:

(A) at least annually, obtain and review a report by the independent auditor describing: the firm's internal quality-control procedures; any material issues raised by the most recent internal quality-control review, or peer review, of the firm, or by any inquiry or investigation by governmental or professional authorities, within the preceding five years, respecting one or more independent audits carried out by the firm, and any steps taken to deal with any such issues; and (to assess the auditor's independence) all relationships between the independent auditor and the listed company;

Commentary: After reviewing the foregoing report and the independent auditor's work throughout the year, the audit committee will be in a position to evaluate the auditor's qualifications, performance and independence. This evaluation should include the review and evaluation of the lead partner of the independent auditor. In making its evaluation, the audit committee should take into account the opinions of management and the listed company's internal auditors (or other personnel responsible for the internal audit function). In addition to assuring the regular rotation of the lead audit partner as required by law, the audit committee should further consider whether, in order to assure continuing auditor independence, there should be regular rotation of the audit firm itself. The audit committee should present its conclusions with respect to the independent auditor to the full board.

(B) meet to review and discuss the listed company's annual audited financial statements and quarterly financial statements with management and the independent auditor, including reviewing the company's specific disclosures under "Management's Discussion and Analysis of Financial Condition and Results of Operations";

(C) discuss the listed company's earnings press releases, as well as financial information and earnings guidance provided to analysts and rating agencies;

Commentary: The audit committee's responsibility to discuss earnings releases, as well as financial information and earnings guidance, may be done generally (i.e., discussion of the types of information to be disclosed and the type of presentation to be made). The audit committee need not discuss in advance each earnings release or each instance in which a listed company may provide earnings guidance.

(D) discuss policies with respect to risk assessment and risk management;

Commentary: While it is the job of the CEO and senior management to assess and manage the listed company's exposure to risk, the audit committee must discuss guidelines and policies to govern the process by which this is handled. The audit committee should discuss the listed company's major financial risk exposures and the steps management has taken to monitor and control such exposures. The audit committee is not required to be the sole body responsible for risk assessment and management, but, as stated above, the committee must discuss guidelines and policies to govern the process by which risk assessment and management is undertaken. Many companies, particularly financial companies, manage and assess their risk through mechanisms other than the audit committee. The processes these companies have in place should be reviewed in a general manner by the audit committee, but they need not be replaced by the audit committee.

(E) meet separately, periodically, with management, with internal auditors (or other personnel responsible for the internal audit function) and with independent auditors;

Commentary: To perform its oversight functions most effectively, the audit committee must have the benefit of separate sessions with management, the independent auditors and those responsible for the internal audit function. As noted herein, all listed companies must have an internal audit function. These separate sessions may be more productive than joint sessions in surfacing issues warranting committee attention.

(F) review with the independent auditor any audit problems or difficulties and management's response;

Commentary: The audit committee must regularly review with the independent auditor any difficulties the auditor encountered in the course of the audit work, including any restrictions on the scope of the independent auditor's activities or on access to requested information, and any significant disagreements with management. Among the items the audit committee may want to review with the auditor are: any accounting adjustments that were noted or proposed by the auditor but were "passed" (as immaterial or otherwise); any communications between the audit team and the audit firm's national office respecting auditing or accounting issues presented by the engagement; and any "management" or "internal control" letter issued, or proposed to be issued, by the audit firm to the listed company. The review should also include discussion of the responsibilities, budget and staffing of the listed company's internal audit function.

(G) set clear hiring policies for employees or former employees of the independent auditors; and

Commentary: Employees or former employees of the independent auditor are often valuable additions to corporate management. Such individuals' familiarity with the business, and personal rapport with the employees, may be attractive qualities when filling a key opening. However, the audit committee should set hiring policies taking into account the pressures that may exist for auditors consciously or subconsciously seeking a job with the company they audit.

(H) report regularly to the board of directors.

Commentary: The audit committee should review with the full board any issues that arise with respect to the quality or integrity of the listed company's financial statements, the company's compliance with legal or regulatory requirements, the performance and independence of the company's independent auditors, or the performance of the internal audit function.

General Commentary to Section 303A.07(c): While the fundamental responsibility for the listed company's financial statements and disclosures rests with management and the independent auditor, the audit committee must review: (A) major issues regarding accounting principles and financial statement presentations, including any significant changes in the company's selection or application of accounting principles, and major issues as to the adequacy of the company's internal controls and any special audit steps adopted in light of material control deficiencies; (B) analyses prepared by management and/or the independent auditor setting forth significant financial reporting issues and judgments made in connection with the preparation of the financial statements, including analyses of the effects of alternative GAAP methods on the financial statements; (C) the effect of regulatory and accounting initiatives, as well as off-balance sheet structures, on the financial statements of the listed company; and (D) the type and presentation of information to be included in earnings press releases (paying particular attention to any use of "pro forma," or "adjusted" non-GAAP, information), as well as review any financial information and earnings guidance provided to analysts and rating agencies.

(d) Each listed company must have an internal audit function.

Commentary: Listed companies must maintain an internal audit function to provide management and the audit committee with ongoing assessments of the company's risk management processes and system of internal control. A listed company may choose to outsource this function to a third party service provider other than its independent auditor.

General Commentary to Section 303A.07: To avoid any confusion, note that the audit committee functions specified in Section 303A.07 are the sole responsibility of the audit committee and may not be allocated to a different committee.[3]

Nasdaq Stock Market Audit Committee Rules

Under the Nasdaq Stock Market rules approved by the SEC on November 4, 2003, and effective at various dates thereafter, the audit committee must have a written charter, and this written charter must contain the minimum responsibilities of audit committees of Nasdaq listed companies.

Each issuer must certify that it has adopted a formal written audit committee charter and that the audit committee has reviewed and reassessed the adequacy of the formal written charter on an annual basis. The charter must specify:

(A) the scope of the audit committee's responsibilities, and how it carries out those responsibilities, including structure, processes, and membership requirements;

(B) the audit committee's responsibility for ensuring its receipt from the outside auditors of a formal written statement delineating all relationships between the auditor and the company, consistent with Independence Standards Board Standard 1, and the audit committee's responsibility for actively engaging in a dialogue with the auditor with respect to any disclosed relationships or services that may impact the objectivity and independence of the auditor and for taking, or recommending that the full board take, appropriate action to oversee the independence of the outside auditor;

(C) the committee's purpose of overseeing the accounting and financial reporting processes of the issuer and the audits of the financial statements of the issuer; and

(D) the specific audit committee responsibilities and authority set forth next

The audit committee must have the specific audit committee responsibilities and authority necessary to comply with [the SEC rules discussed previously], concerning responsibilities relating to: (i) registered public accounting firms, (ii) complaints relating to accounting, internal accounting controls or auditing matters, (iii) authority to engage advisors, and (iv) funding as determined by the audit committee. Audit committees for investment companies must also establish procedures for the confidential, anonymous submission of concerns regarding questionable accounting or auditing matters by employees of the investment adviser, administrator, principal underwriter, or any other provider of accounting related services for the investment company, as well as employees of the investment company.[4]

Nasdaq rules (cited in Appendix D) contain certain cure periods and require that the audit committee must approve all related party transactions, unless such transactions were approved by another comparable body of the board of directors.

PRACTICAL TIPS FOR SELECTING AN INDEPENDENT AUDITOR

Public company audit committees that are interested in making their operation more cost-efficient should consider the best practices that follow in selecting an independent auditor.

BEST PRACTICES

- Choose an auditing firm with experience in your industry.

- The major cost of complying with the internal control requirements of Section 404 of Sarbanes-Oxley can be reduced by changing your auditor from a "Big Four" to auditing firms ranked five through ten. Auditing firms five through ten tend to have lower fees for providing Section 404 attestations and take a more practical approach to problems. The Public Company Accounting Oversight Board (PCAOB) has not discovered any significant quality differences between the "Big Four" and these lower-level auditing firms.

- If it is not a political possibility to move away from a "Big Four" auditing firm, consider changing the engagement partner to a person who has less of a check-the-box mentality and a more flexible approach. Do not be afraid of changing to an office of your "Big Four" auditing firm that is not local if that is necessary to secure a more practical engagement partner.

- As noted in Chapter 1, both the SEC and the PCAOB have each issued statements criticizing the approach taken by some auditing firms to compliance with Section 404.

It is hoped that these pronouncements will encourage the major accounting firm to take a more practical and cost-efficient approach to complying with Section 404 of Sarbanes-Oxley and related rules.

Huntingdon Bancshares, Inc.

A summary of the major lessons of Huntington Bancshares, Inc. follows.

- Audit committees must be sensitive to qualitative as well as quantitative materiality.
- If significant management bonuses depend on meeting earnings projections, more intensive auditing should be required by the audit committee before payment of such bonuses.
- A strong and independent internal audit department, reporting directly to the audit committee, with financial as well as operational auditing function, is vital in any organization.

The following description of the case against Huntington Bancshares, Inc. and its officers assumes that the allegations in the SEC Complaint are all true and complete, even though they were neither admitted nor denied by the defendants.

During the relevant time period, Huntington Bancshares, Inc. was a financial holding company with more than $30 billion in assets. Through its subsidiaries, Huntington provided commercial and consumer banking services, mortgage banking, automobile leasing and financing, equipment leasing, and brokerage services. Its most significant subsidiary, The Huntington National Bank, had more than 300 banking offices in five states. Huntington's common stock was traded on the Nasdaq National Market.

Thomas E. Hoaglin had been president and chief executive officer of Huntington since February 15, 2001, and its chairman since August 16, 2001. Michael McMennamin was Huntington's treasurer from November 2000 until February 15, 2005, and its chief financial officer from November 2000 until August 9, 2004. He was Huntington's vice chairman from November 2000 until he retired from the bank and resigned all duties effective March 31, 2005. According to the SEC Complaint, John Van Fleet, who was a licensed CPA until September 2003, was Huntington's corporate controller from August 2001 until August 9, 2004.

The principal officers of Huntington Bancshares, Inc., named in the SEC complaint were Thomas Hoaglin, Michael McMennamin, and John Van Fleet. The SEC complaint filed June 2, 2005 was settled without admitting or denying the allegations in the complaint. Huntington consented to pay a penalty of $7.5 million.[5] In addition, Hoaglin, McMennamin, and Van Fleet agreed to pay disgorgement, prejudgment interest, and penalties in the amounts of $667,609, $415,215, and $51,660, respectively.

According to the SEC's complaint, in 2001 and 2002 Huntington reported inflated earnings in its financial statements, enabling Huntington to meet or exceed Wall Street analyst earnings per share (EPS) expectations and internal EPS targets that determined bonuses for senior management. The misstatements, which were allegedly qualitatively material, included up-front recognition of loan and lease origination fees that were required by accounting rules to be deferred and amortized over the term of the loan or lease; improper capitalization of commission expenses and deferral of pension costs that were required to be recognized in the period incurred; misstated reserves; improper deferral of income; and misclassification of nonoperating income as operating income.

Without the misstatements, Huntington's EPS would allegedly have fallen short of analysts' earnings expectations in 2001 and 2002. The 2002 bonuses for Hoaglin and McMennamin would have been eliminated, and Van Fleet's 2002 bonus would have been reduced. All three individuals attended due diligence meetings at which all but one of the misstatements were discussed, and it was decided—without considering the impact of the misstatements on management bonuses and Huntington's ability to meet analysts' expectations—that none of the items were material.

As a result of its accounting misstatements, Huntington allegedly overstated 2001 operating earnings of $293.5 million by $8.5 million ($.04 per share) and 2002 operating earnings of $328.5 million by $17.1 million ($.08 per share). Had it not been for the accounting misstatements, Huntington's reported operating EPS for 2001 and 2002 would have been $1.13 and $1.27, respectively, short of Wall Street analyst expectations and senior management's EPS bonus targets, instead of the $1.17 operating EPS it actually reported for 2001 and the $1.35 operating EPS reported for 2002.

Qualitative Materiality

The Sarbanes-Oxley Act of 2002 became effective July 30, 2002. On July 26, 2002, Huntington's outside counsel sent a memorandum to Hoaglin, McMennamin, Van Fleet, and other Huntington executives, addressing the certification requirements ordered by the SEC in June 2002.[6] The memorandum lays out the materiality requirements specified by Staff Accounting Board (SAB) No. 99 and states that determining materiality of an accounting misstatement or omission required the bank to consider qualitative factors,

(continued)

including whether the impact of the accounting misstatements or omissions affected executive compensation or hid a failure to meet analyst consensus expectations.

On August 4, 2002, senior executives from Huntington allegedly began a series of "due diligence" meetings in anticipation of the signing and filing of the certifications by Hoaglin and McMennamin, as the bank's CEO and CFO, respectively. McMennamin, Van Fleet, and senior members of Huntington's legal department attended the August 4, 2002 meeting, as did the bank's external audit senior manager and Huntington's outside counsel. The senior executives in attendance were cognizant of the qualitative as well as quantitative standards for determining materiality, as described in the memorandum from outside counsel dated July 26, 2002.

The consensus was that the only possibly relevant SAB 99 qualitative materiality factor was whether the item under consideration concerned a segment or other portion of business that had been identified as playing a significant role in the Bank's operations or profitability as it related to the potential impact of Financial Accounting Standards (FAS) No. 91 on the accounting treatment of loan and lease acquisition fees.

An additional due diligence meeting was held on August 8, 2002, to follow up on the FAS No. 91 issues. The senior managers, executives, and others in attendance, including the bank's outside audit engagement partner, decided that the FAS No. 91 issues, including the issue related to deposit commissions, were not material either individually or in the aggregate.

Lessons of Huntington Bancshares, Inc.

Audit committees must be sensitive to qualitative as well as quantitative materiality issues. The alleged overstatement of Huntingdon's 2001 operating earnings was only 2.89 percent, yet the SEC viewed this as qualitatively material and brought legal action. The alleged overstatement of Huntington's 2002 operating earnings was less than 7 percent and was also found to be qualitatively material.

The SEC is particularly sensitive to misstatements of earnings that enable an executive to achieve a bonus objective or to meet an earnings projection to analysts. If the organization barely meets a bonus objective or an earnings projection, it is a warning sign to the audit committee that should trigger more intensive auditing.

ENDNOTES

1. Noelle Knox, "Buffett Tells Directors to Really Dog Auditors" (*USA Today*: March 4, 2002).
2. www.law.uc.edu/CCL/regS-X/SX2-07.html.
3. New York Stock Exchange, Final NYSE Corporate Governance Rules (cited in Appendix D).
4. The Nasdaq Stock Market, Inc., Corporate Governance Rules 4200, 4200A, 4350, 4350A, 4351, and 4360 and Associated Interpretive Material, www.nasdaq.com/about/CorporateGovernance.pdf.
5. U.S. Securities and Exchange Commission, Litigation Rel. No. 19243 (June 2005), www.sec.gov/litigation/litreleases/lr19243.htm. Click on SEC Complaint in this matter.
6. Securities Exchange Act Release No. 51781 (June 2, 2005).

Chapter 14

Other Public Company Audit Committee Functions

This chapter assumes that, in the case of a public company audit committee, all minimum responsibilities described in Chapter 13 have been satisfied, including compliance with SEC and stock market rules.

It is impossible to list the functions that are common to all audit committees across the diverse corporate community. There is simply no consensus as to the duties that should be performed by audit committees. Each corporation must tailor its audit committee's charter to meet that company's particular needs. The delineation of audit committee functions is a creative process that requires a company to balance a need for defined specific duties against a capability to adapt to various situations that may arise in the course of business operations.

> **BEST PRACTICE**
>
> The obligations set forth in committee charters must be complied with strictly in order to avoid personal liability. Therefore, it is preferable to state only the minimum legal responsibilities in the audit committee charter.

It is obvious that a rigid formula defining powers and duties cannot be imposed on audit committees. If too many tasks are assigned to the committee, however, there is a substantial likelihood that most—if not all—will be performed only superficially. The committee will be more likely to perform a limited number of tasks in a thorough and comprehensive fashion. Initially, it is better to assign the committee only a few tasks but to give it sufficient flexibility so that its role can evolve over time.

> **BEST PRACTICE**
>
> The engagement letter with your auditing firm should contain this agreement by the auditing firm:
>
> > We will promptly notify the Chairman of the Audit Committee and management of any investigation or inspection relating to us that is likely to (a) have a material effect on any of the Company's financial statements previously reported on by us or (b) result in a modification of an audit report issued by us to the Company.

The Public Company Accounting Oversight Board (PCAOB) (established by Sarbanes-Oxley) has the responsibility to monitor the quality of registered auditing firms. Some scathing reports on "Big Four" auditing firms appear on the PCAOB Web site.[1] The PCAOB reports to the Securities and Exchange Commission (SEC) any company whose audited financial statements do not comply with generally accepted accounting principles (GAAP). A number of restatements have been required as a result of PCAOB audits of auditing firms. Therefore, it is important that the audit committee be kept informed of any PCAOB inspections of the auditing firm which may have a material effect on the Company.

WARREN BUFFETT'S QUESTIONS

As previously noted, Warren Buffett has suggested an approach based on audit committees asking auditors four intriguing questions[2]:

1. If the auditor were solely responsible for the company's financial statements, would they have been prepared in any way different than the manner selected by management?
2. If the auditor were an investor, would he have received the information essential to a proper understanding of the company's financial performance during the reporting period?
3. Does the auditor know of any operational facts that caused the company's sales or profit to move significantly from one quarter to the next?
4. Is the company using the same internal audit procedure that would be followed if the auditor himself were CEO?

Warren Buffett recommended that, consistent with these four questions, the audit committee document the responses to these questions in its minutes. The answers to these questions really indicate whether, if the auditor were running the company, the same financial statements and disclosures would have been published and the same internal controls would have been established.

FOUR SIGNIFICANT ISSUES FOR PUBLIC COMPANY AUDIT COMMITTEES

Once all minimum responsibilities have been satisfied, public company audit committees should consider at least four other major issues:

1. *Revenue recognition policies.* The primary cause of accounting restatements has been the failure of public companies to comply with the SEC's revenue recognition standards (Staff Accounting Bulletin Nos. 101 and 104), which are currently an important topic for audit committees.
2. *Review of internal controls.* The adequacy of internal controls should be a key concern for audit committees since these internal controls are essential to the integrity of the financial statements and have been focused on in Section 404 of Sarbanes-Oxley. The auditor's report under Section 404 of Sarbanes-Oxley must be carefully reviewed by the audit committee.

3. *Critical accounting policies and practices and alternative treatments of financial information preferred by the auditors.* Under Section 204 of Sarbanes-Oxley and SEC Regulation 210.2-07, the registered public accounting firm is required to report to the audit committee on (among other things) all critical accounting policies and practices and all alternative treatments of financial information preferred by the registered public accounting firm. This report and its ramifications must be carefully reviewed by the audit committee.

4. *Any current hot accounting topic.* These include accounting for derivatives, pension accounting, restructuring charges, acquisition accounting, cookie jar reserves, and the like.

COMPLIANCE WITH GAAP IS NOT ENOUGH

Technical compliance of the financial statements with GAAP does not fully satisfy the obligations of the public company. It is the SEC's position that financial statements must "fairly represent" the financial position of the company.

This position derives from a 1969 criminal case (*U.S. v. Simon, Kaiser and Fishman*) against three accountants associated with a predecessor of PriceWaterhouseCoopers in which these accountants were convicted of conspiring to knowingly draw up and certify a false and misleading corporate financial statement and of using the mails to distribute it.[3] (The accountants were ultimately pardoned by President Nixon.) The accountants had eight expert independent accountants, with impressive credentials, testify generally that their treatment of the loan to an insider complied with GAAP. Nevertheless, the United States Court of Appeals for the Second Circuit upheld a jury instruction that required the jury to determine whether the financial statements as a whole "fairly presented" the financial position of the public company and that proof of compliance with GAAP was "evidence which may be very persuasive but not necessarily conclusive." Moreover, the SEC has taken the position that items that are quantitatively immaterial under GAAP can nevertheless be qualitatively material. (See the discussion of Huntington Bancshares, Inc. in Chapter 13.)

SEVEN PRIMARY FUNCTIONS

Audit committees generally perform seven primary functions. The amount of time devoted to each will vary according to the size and complexity of the company.

1. Preapproval of all audit and nonaudit services of the independent auditor
2. Review of overall audit plan
3. Review and evaluation of financial statements
4. Review of external audit
5. Review of internal audit
6. Review of internal accounting controls
7. Conducting independent investigations of material financial or legal misconduct from whistleblowers and others

The failure of the audit committee to preapprove audit and nonaudit services of the independent auditor can (subject to a de minimis exception) destroy the independence of the outside auditor. This issue is discussed in more detail in Chapter 16.

Independent audit committees should insist on controlling internal investigations of financial or legal misconduct, whether those complaints come from whistleblowers, external or internal auditors, or otherwise. Too often whistleblower complaints are given short shrift by management and superficial investigations are conducted. (See the sad story of Cornell University Medical School in Chapter 2.) Independent counsel should be used for the investigation by the audit committee if there is any potential for the involvement of top management or if the allegations (if true) might be embarrassing to the Company.

INTERNAL ACCOUNTING CONTROLS

Internal accounting controls have become increasingly significant since enactment of the Foreign Corrupt Practices Act of 1977, which provides that public companies "make and keep books, records and accounts, which, in reasonable detail, accurately and fairly reflect the transactions and dispositions of the assets of the issuer" and "devise and maintain a system of internal accounting controls."

It is appropriate that the audit committee be responsible for ensuring that the company has an adequate and effective system that complies with the purposes of the act, namely, that there are "reasonable assurances" that accurate financial information is provided, that corporate assets are protected, and that payments are made pursuant to management authority. These are basically the board of directors' responsibilities, which are delegated to the audit committee.

Section 404 of Sarbanes-Oxley requires the SEC to adopt rules requiring the annual reports of public companies to contain an internal control report prepared by management, which:

- States the responsibility of management for establishing and maintaining an adequate internal control structure and procedures for financial reporting
- Contains an assessment, as of the end of the most recent fiscal year of the issuer, of the effectiveness of the internal control structure and procedures of the issuer for financial reporting

Under Section 404 of Sarbanes-Oxley, each registered public accounting firm that prepares or issues the audit report for the public company must attest to, and report on, the assessment made by management of the company, in accordance with the standards for attestation engagements issued or adopted by the PCAOB.

The audit committee must initially obtain written descriptions of internal controls generally and, in particular, of the control system currently existing in the company. These may be obtained from management, the auditors, and counsel. Basically, the audit committee will seek to ascertain that the company has adopted a well-organized, systematic approach for evaluating the adequacy and effectiveness of its internal accounting controls.

Instruction 1 of Item 308 of SEC Regulation S-K provides that the company must maintain "evidential matter, including documentation, to provide reasonable support for management's assessment of the effectiveness of the registrant's internal control over financial reporting." This evidential matter should be reviewed by the audit committee.

When conducting its internal controls monitoring function, the audit committee necessarily must consult with the external auditors in addition to the company's controller and the internal auditors. Ordinarily, the external auditors are charged with reviewing the company's system of internal accounting controls, and the audit committee is the principal communication line to the board of directors.

The committee will generally coordinate the efforts of the internal and external auditors and discuss the scope of the reviews prior to their commencement. Of necessity, the audit committee's review is a "businessman's" review, and its members must rely on the accounting experts. However, the audit committee, having a broader business perception, might well aid materially the review efforts of the external auditors. If any weaknesses or deficiencies are detected, the audit committee can obtain suggestions and recommendations for rectifying them from the external auditors. Also, the committee might inquire into the auditors' observations regarding the diligence with which management has attempted to identify weaknesses, the urgency with which management has responded, and the sufficiency of the corrective steps that management has initiated.

BEST PRACTICE

If the auditors discover a material weakness in internal controls, the audit committee should engage the auditor in future years to determine whether the previously reported material weakness continues to exist.

Auditor's reports under Section 404 of Sarbanes-Oxley may indicate a weakness in internal controls in a given year. The audit committee, as part of its oversight process, should engage the auditor in future years to determine whether the previously reported material weakness continues to exist. In July 2005 the PCAOB adopted Auditing Standard No. 4, subject to SEC approval (which was received in 2006), which provides directions to the auditor who has been so engaged by the audit committee.

OTHER FUNCTIONS

Seven additional functions should be undertaken by all public company audit committees in addition to their minimum responsibilities and primary functions. Some of these functions are mandated by listing requirements whereas others are not. These functions should be viewed as "best practices" for audit committees, even though these functions may not be mandated by law or listing requirements.

Review of Financial Press Releases, Proposed Guidance to Securities Analysts, Reports to Shareholders, and Quarterly Filings

The NYSE listing requirements (adopted November 4, 2003, as amended November 3, 2004; cited in Appendix D) require audit committees to assess earnings press releases as well as financial information and earnings guidance provided to analysts and rating agencies. However, the Nasdaq listing requirements (adopted November 4, 2003; cited in Appendix D) do not require this review, and such review is not currently required for public companies other than NYSE listed companies.

Financial press releases containing earnings results are typically issued after the end of each fiscal quarter and after completion of fiscal year operations. The audit committee should generally review these releases before issuance as part of its oversight role under Sarbanes-Oxley. Because of time pressures, it may be necessary to have only the chair of the audit committee complete the review.

It is typical for public companies to give earnings review (and sometimes earnings guidance) to securities analysts at teleconferences and Web cast meetings to which the public is invited to avoid Regulation FD violations (a regulation designed to avoid selective disclosure of financial information). This proposed guidance to securities analysts should receive the same advanced scrutiny as financial press releases.

Quarterly reports to shareholders and other interim financial reports and disclosures, and quarterly filings with the SEC on Form 10-Q, must also be scrutinized by the audit committee. The explanations for earnings variations should be subjected to intensive questioning by audit committee members.

Establish and Monitor Codes of Conduct to Foster a Culture of Honesty and Ethics

Section 406 of Sarbanes-Oxley and related SEC rules requires disclosure on Form 8-K within five business days, or disclosure on the company's Internet Web site within such five business days, of the company's amendment or waiver of the financial officers' code of ethics. Therefore, the audit committee should either monitor the code of ethics or coordinate with a nominating/corporate governance committee that does monitor the code of ethics.

The committee may also consider whether it is preferable to require all personnel to furnish an annual statement of compliance, including a question on whether the signer is aware of any violations of the code. Such statements can be reviewed directly by the committee or by its designee.

Of course, if it were determined that the audit committee was overburdened and could not undertake the additional work, another committee (such as the nominating/corporate governance committee) could monitor compliance with the code of conduct.

Review of Conflicts of Interest

Conflicts of interest should receive attention because of their potential legal and economic ramifications, and also because of the adverse publicity they generate.

The audit committee or nominating/corporate governance committee can be an effective force in investigating conflicts of interest and in establishing procedures for their prevention and detection. Additionally, the committee can monitor compliance with the procedures once they are established.

In reviewing conflicts of interest that affect the financial statements, the committee can consult the financial officers of the company and the external auditors. If it does not have its own staff, the audit committee might seek the aid of the internal auditors.

If the conflict of interest involves financial or senior officers (as in Enron), special procedures must be developed to closely monitor the conflict, using independent counsel, outside auditors, and internal auditors who report directly to the audit committee and whose compensation is determined solely by the audit committee.

Review of Perquisites

Management perquisites have received frequent and sustained attention as a consequence of a general loss of public confidence in publicly held companies. Audit committees should consider working with the compensation committee in reviewing the disclosure and abuse of management perquisites, since they bring different perspectives to this subject.

When reviewing management perquisites, the audit committee should first determine the types of corporate benefits that are being received and then examine the manner in which control procedures prevent or detect their use for personal purposes. If there are no specific control procedures for the personal use of corporate benefits or for the reporting of transactions between management and third persons with whom the company engages in business, the audit committee should recommend their adoption and should participate in formulating them.

Care must be taken to determine that perquisites do not violate the broad prohibitions on direct or indirect extensions of credit or personal loans to directors or executive officers contained in Section 402 of Sarbanes-Oxley.

The committee can enlist the internal auditors to assist in the review and monitoring process. In addition, the external auditors should be asked to state their opinion of the company's control procedures and to outline any suggestions for improvement.

The SEC has proposed rules requiring much greater detailed disclosure regarding management compensation.

Review of Sensitive Payments

Audit committees often conduct special investigations into allegations of illegal or other sensitive payments or similar misuse of corporate funds. Many of these special reviews are conducted voluntarily; others are required as a result of consent decrees entered into to settle litigation with the SEC.

The audit committee should retain outside legal special counsel to assist in these investigations. Similarly, special auditors may be engaged if the committee does not have an audit staff. These precautions are necessary because management, corporate counsel, the internal auditors, or the external auditors might be implicated or may have been derelict in uncovering or exposing the misuse of funds.

Section 301 of Sarbanes-Oxley requires companies whose securities are listed on a national securities exchange or on a national securities association to authorize the audit committee to engage independent counsel and other advisors, as it deems necessary to carry out its duties, and to fund such advisors.

The audit committee should investigate the following items (among others) if there is reasonable suspicion of sensitive payments:

- Checks payable to cash
- Documents supporting reimbursements or employee expenses that are apparently excessive
- Billing and payment procedures (with particular attention to unusual payment terms), overbilling, completeness of supporting documents, and whether the authorization for payment was proper
- Expense accounts, including travel and entertainment
- Consulting and agency agreements

With respect to questionable or possibly illegal payments, a review should focus on, among other things, whether:

- The payments were legal in the state or country where such expenditures were made.
- The motivation for the payments was a desire to advance the interests of the company rather than self-dealing or advancing the payer's interests within the company.
- A recurrence is likely.

Review of Settlements and Claims

The audit committee can be authorized to act on behalf of the entire board in reviewing:

- Proposed settlements of lawsuits
- Claims against the company
- Decisions to file suit

It is preferable that a committee that acts in this capacity be composed of disinterested, outside directors who were not affiliated with the company at the time of the alleged wrongs and who are not named as defendants in the litigation.

The committee, exercising its good faith business judgment, can determine whether it is in the best interest of the company to pursue the proposed courses of action. This is true even if the suit commenced is a derivative action naming a majority of the directors as defendants and injury to the company is possible as a result of the alleged illegality.

With respect to all litigation, the committee should consider whether substantial problems will be created by litigating, as well as the costs of the suit, the disruption of management activities, and the efficacy of the claim.

Prepare Performance Reports

The audit committee can be given the duty of preparing reports on the performance of management, the external auditors, and the internal auditors. Additionally, if it has sufficient resources, the committee can prepare similar reports on the efficacy of the internal control and operational control systems.

Since reviews of this nature can be prohibitively time-consuming, it is appropriate for the committee to engage outsiders to perform the evaluations. Written reports can be provided setting forth the methodology and findings as well as recommendations for action, no action, or improvements.

SEC Disclosure Rules for Public Company Audit Committees

The SEC has established disclosure rules for audit committees of public companies.[4] These rules require, among other things, that the audit committee set forth in an audit committee report that the audit committee has "recommended" that the audited financial statements be included in the company's Form 10-K report. The report must also name each member of the audit committee.

Self-Evaluation

Audit committees of NYSE companies are required to evaluate their own operation annually. There is no similar requirement for Nasdaq companies.

BEST PRACTICE

All audit committees should evaluate their own operations annually.

ENDOTES

1. "Board Releases Reports on 2003 Limited Inspections of Big Four Accounting Firms," Public Company Accounting Oversight Board, August 26, 2004, www.pcaobus.org/news_and_events/news/2004/08-26.aspx.
2. Noelle Knox, "Buffett Tells Directors to Really Dog Auditors" (*USA Today*: March 4, 2002), www.usatoday.com/money/finance/2002-03-05-accounting-roundtable.htm.
3. *U.S. v. Simon*, 425 F.2d 796 (CANY 1969).
4. SEC Release No. 34-42266 (December 22, 1999).

Chapter 15

30 Best Practice Considerations for the Public Company Audit Committee

Sarbanes-Oxley has effectively transferred certain powers from the chief executive officer (CEO) and chief financial officer (CFO) to the audit committee of the public company board of directors. Some audit committees have been slow to recognize this power shift while other audit committees have embraced it but seek guidance. The corporate landscape has changed, and audit committees must undertake tasks and exercise powers that previously resided with CEOs and CFOs. Those audit committees that do not recognize this power shift will ultimately discover that their company's stock is punished by the strong lobby for good corporate governance, and the reelection of audit committee members as directors is jeopardized.

It is also important that public company audit committees do not permit Sarbanes-Oxley to drive a wedge between themselves and management. It is possible to perform the oversight function of the audit committee without damaging relationships with management that are essential to the collaborative effort necessary to achieve financial success for the company.

The composition of the company's board and audit committee and how the directors fulfill their responsibilities related to the financial reporting process are key aspects of the company's internal controls.[1] A weak audit committee may itself be a sign of a material weakness in internal controls.

In order to develop "best practices" for audit committees, we present 30 policy and procedural issues that should be considered by all audit committees in light of Sarbanes-Oxley and the related corporate scandals. These 30 policy and procedural issues should be read in conjunction with Chapters 13 and 14, which describe the specific functions and responsibilities of audit committees.

WHAT SOURCES OF INFORMATION DO AUDIT COMMITTEE MEMBERS REQUIRE TO FULFILL THEIR OVERSIGHT ROLE?

BEST PRACTICES

In addition to the outside auditors, the chief executive officer, and the chief financial officer, the audit committee should consider interviewing at least once a year these persons:

- Controller and assistant controller (e.g., ask if there are any accounting policies or procedures with which they are uncomfortable)
- Head of sales (e.g., ask if there are any side deals with any customers, channel stuffing, so-called round-trip sales; ask if they are using best practices listed in Chapter 3, etc.)
- Tax manager (e.g., ask if there are any aggressive tax strategies being pursued by the company, best practices, etc.)
- Internal auditor
- Inside counsel and outside counsel
- Head of disclosure committee
- Corporate governance officer
- Head of Human Resources (ask if they are using best practices listed in Chapter 3)
- Head of information technology, corporate development, purchasing (e.g., ask if they are using best practices listed in this book)

An audit committee cannot act on unrevealed information. Audit committees are limited by the information they obtain. Yet it is the audit committee that can dictate the sources of information it needs to perform its oversight function.

Audit committees cannot operate properly without having information from diverse sources, both from within and from outside the company. Although all the facts are not clear, it appears that the audit committees of the boards of Enron and WorldCom relied primarily, if not exclusively, on information provided to them by the members of the management team over which they were required to exercise oversight as well as on information provided to them by the outside auditor.

Each of the persons named previously should be interviewed separately and not in the presence of superiors within the company; prosecutors have known for many years that subordinates do not talk freely when their bosses are present.

DOES THE AUDIT COMMITTEE PLACE A LIMIT ON AN AUDITOR'S NONAUDIT SERVICES?

BEST PRACTICE

Nonaudit services performed by the auditor should not exceed 100 percent of aggregate of audit services and audit-related services.

The relationship of audit fees to the sum of audit, audit-related services, and tax services has become important to the good governance lobby. For example, Institutional Shareholder Services (ISS) has stated that it will recommend voting against auditors and withholding votes from members of audit committees, if fees for nonaudit services exceed the aggregate of audit fees, audit-related fees, and "permissible" tax fees.[2] Further, under ISS mathematical guidelines, "permissible" tax fees do not include certain tax services, such as formulating tax strategies and tax shelters to minimize the company's taxes.[3]

The pressure to maintain a reasonable ratio of nonaudit services has allegedly led some auditors to fudge what is considered "audit-related" services.

According to *The Wall Street Journal*, Ernst & Young allegedly classified as "audit-related" fees janitorial inspections of health services facilities of HealthSouth Corp., which inspections included "seeing if magazines in waiting rooms were orderly, toilets and ceilings were free of stains and trash receptacles all had liners."[4]

WHAT SAFEGUARDS SHOULD THE AUDIT COMMITTEE REQUIRE TO INSURE AUDITOR INDEPENDENCE?

BEST PRACTICES

- The engagement letter from the auditor should contain a representation that the auditor is and will remain independent (as defined by SEC and PCAOB rules) throughout the audit engagement.

- Conduct a robust discussion with the auditor of his or her independence at least once a year.

- After each assignment of nonaudit work to the auditor, the auditor should be required to represent to the audit committee that the nonaudit service does not impair his or her independence. (An exception may be made for routine nonaudit services, such as tax return preparation.)

- Care must be taken before hiring former employees of the auditing firm as company employees to be certain that the new employee will not impair the auditor's independence. The human resources department should be required to notify the audit committee prior to any such hires. (See Chapter 3.)

If the auditors are not independent, both the Company as well as the auditors violate the Securities Exchange Act of 1934 (the "1934 Act").[5] The auditor independence rules are detailed and extensive and are discussed more fully in Chapter 16. To insure auditor independence, the audit committee should adopt these policies.

The robust discussion with the auditor concerning independence should include any relationships with management that might impair the objectivity of the auditor. For example, it was reported that KPMG LLP, the auditor for First Union Corp., received referrals from First Union Corp. of wealthy banking clients and First Union Corp. was in turn paid referral fees by KPMG LLP. Some have questioned whether this type of relationship could compromise the impartiality of the auditor.[6]

SHOULD THE AUDITOR BE USED FOR TAX PLANNING SERVICES?

> **BEST PRACTICE**
>
> Do not use the auditor for tax planning and tax preparation services.

Although tax planning services do not impair the independence of auditors, audit committees should consider whether using the auditor for tax planning services is in the best interest of the company. The audit committee should consider four issues:

- The auditor is prohibited by the auditor independence rules from providing an expert opinion or other expert services for an audit client, or acting as an audit client's legal representative, for the purpose of advocating an audit client's interests in litigation or in a regulatory or administrative proceeding or investigation.[7]

    The effect of this prohibition is that the auditor is unable to assist the company in advocating the company's tax position before the Internal Revenue Service, since the Internal Revenue Service inquiry might be viewed as a "regulatory or administrative proceeding or investigation."[8] Although the auditor is permitted to be a fact witness in such proceedings or investigations, his or her inability to advocate the company's tax position handicaps the company in the defense of its tax planning.

- If the auditor advises the company to take an aggressive position on its tax return, a conflict of interest may result.

    The auditor is required to audit the company's tax reserve and, under the auditor independence rules, cannot audit its own work.[9] There is difficulty in determining what is an aggressive tax position or a tax shelter (see next question) as distinguished from routine tax planning.

- The auditor does not have the advantage of the attorney-client privilege or the work product doctrine that would otherwise shield its services and work papers from discovery by the Internal Revenue Service.[10]

- CalPERS is reportedly withholding its votes for the election of audit committee members if the auditor provides nonaudit services, other than preparation of tax returns and SEC compliance documents.[11]

Some audit committees have decided to use an accounting firm separate from their auditor for their tax planning and tax preparation work. This separation avoids all but the third problem mentioned, namely the absence of any attorney-client privilege or work-product doctrine. Audit committees should consider using a law firm for company tax planning, in order to preserve the attorney-client privilege and work-product doctrine, and using a separate accounting firm for tax preparation work.

On July 26, 2005, the Public Company Accounting Oversight Board ("PCAOB") adopted a rule, subject to SEC approval, that treats a registered public accounting firm as not independent from an audit client if the firm provides services related to marketing, planning, or opining in favor of the tax treatment of a transaction that is a confidential transaction (generally transactions offered to a taxpayer under conditions of confidentiality designed to protect the advisor's tax strategy and for which taxpayer paid a fee).[12] In addition, the rule would treat a registered public accounting firm as not independent if the firm provides services related to marketing, planning, or opining in favor of a tax treatment on a transaction that is based on an aggressive interpretation of applicable tax laws and regulations, including listed transactions as defined by U.S. Treasury Department regulations.

SHOULD THE AUDIT COMMITTEE PERMIT TAX SHELTERS TO BE SOLD BY NONAUDIT PARTNERS OF THE AUDITING FIRM?

BEST PRACTICE

If you elect to use the auditor for tax planning services, do not purchase tax shelters or aggressive novel tax strategies from the auditor.

The Commission on Public Trust and Private Enterprise has concluded as a "best practice" that an accounting firm should not be providing "novel and debatable tax strategies and products that involve income tax shelters and extensive off-shore partnerships or affiliates" to audit clients.[13]

The SEC, in its adopting release, which it called the auditor independence rules,[14] cited the Commission on Public Trust and Private Enterprise conclusion on best practices and stated:

> In addition, audit committees also should scrutinize carefully the retention of an accountant in a transaction initially recommended by the accountant, the sole business purpose of which may be tax avoidance and the tax treatment of which may be not supported in the Internal Revenue Code and related regulations.[15]

If the tax strategy recommended by the auditor significantly changes the reported earnings per share, the independence of the auditor who audits the tax reserve is seriously in question, since the auditor is arguably auditing his or her own work. The preliminary note to SEC regulation Section 210.2-01 (the auditor independence rule) considers these four factors in determining in the first instance whether a relationship or the provision of a service satisfies the general independence standards:

(a) Creates a mutual or conflicting interest between the accountant and the audit client;

(b) Places the accountant in the position of auditing his or her own work;

(c) Results in the accountant acting as management or an employee of the audit client; or

(d) Places the accountant in a position of being an advocate for the audit client.[16]

There is a valid argument that the auditor's independence is impaired under clause (b) if a novel tax strategy recommended by the auditor significantly increases earnings per share. Another valid argument is that the auditor has a mutual interest under clause (a) in justifying and supporting the recommended tax strategy. The auditor would also be precluded from becoming an advocate for the audit client under clause (d), at least with respect to advocating the correctness of that tax strategy in litigation, or in regulatory or administrative proceedings or investigations.

Aggressive or novel strategies will also violate the PCAOB rules adopted on July 26, 2005, subject to SEC approval.

SHOULD THE AUDIT COMMITTEE PERMIT MEMBERS OF THE AUDIT TEAM (EXCLUDING PARTNERS) TO RECEIVE COMPENSATION FOR SELLING NONAUDIT SERVICES TO THE COMPANY?

BEST PRACTICE

Audit committees should not permit members of the audit team to be compensated for selling nonaudit services.

The SEC's auditor independence rules do not prohibit nonpartner members of the audit team from receiving compensation for selling nonaudit services to the company.[17] However, the SEC has made it clear in the next passage that it expects audit committees to consider this issue in the preapproval process for nonaudit services:

> The rules that we are adopting mitigate the concerns that an audit partner might be viewed as compromising audit judgments in order not to jeopardize the potential for selling non-audit services. These rules do not specifically address the provision of compensation to other audit engagement team members for directly selling non-audit services. We believe that, however, the other audit engagement team members will perform in a fashion that is consistent with the direction and tone set by the

audit partners. *Nonetheless, as it pre-approves non-audit services an audit committee may wish to consider whether, in the company's particular circumstances, compensating a senior staff member on the audit engagement team based on his or her success in selling the service to the company compromises that individual's or the firm's independence.*[18]

HOW CONSERVATIVE SHOULD THE AUDIT COMMITTEE BE IN DETERMINING ACCOUNTING POLICIES AND PROCEDURES?

BEST PRACTICE

The audit committee must determine on a case-by-case basis whether any of the accounting treatments preferred by the registered public accounting firm should be adopted by the company and what the overall effect would be of such adoption. If the audit committee decides not to adopt a recommendation of the registered accounting firm, the reasons for the rejection should be carefully documented by the audit committee, with the assistance of counsel.

The audit committee is responsible for understanding the accounting policies and procedures of the company and ultimately determining their appropriateness. Section 204 of Sarbanes-Oxley amended 10A of the 1934 Act to require that the registered public accounting firm that performs for any issuer any audit required by that law must timely report to the audit committee:

1. All critical accounting policies and practices to be used
2. All alternative treatments of financial information within generally accepted accounting principles that have been discussed with management officials of the issuer, ramifications of the use of such alternative disclosures and treatments, and the treatment preferred by the registered public accounting firm
3. Other material written communications between the registered public accounting firm and the management of the issuer, such as any management letter or schedule of unadjusted differences[19]

SEC Regulation Section 210.2-07 specifically requires that each registered public accounting firm that performs for an audit client that is an issuer (as defined in Section 10A(f) of the 1934 Act), subject to certain minor exceptions, any audit required by the securities laws must report to the audit committee, prior to the filing of such audit report with the SEC, these four items:

1. All critical accounting policies and practices to be used.
2. All alternative treatments with generally accepted accounting principles (GAAP) for policies and practices related to material items that have been discussed with management of the issues or registered, including:
   * Ramifications of the use of such alternative disclosures and treatments
   * The treatment preferred by the registered public accounting firm

3. Other material written communications between the registered public accounting firm and the management of the issuer or registered investment company, such as any management letter or schedule of unadjusted differences.

4. If the audit client is an investment company, all nonaudit services provided to any entity in an investment company complex, as defined in paragraph (f)(14) of this section, that were not preapproved by the registered investment company's audit committee pursuant to paragraph (c)(7) of this section.[20]

The SEC has made it clear that it expects that these communications would be documented by the audit committee as well as by the auditor.[21] The SEC also contemplates that

> communications regarding specific transactions should identify, at a minimum, the underlying facts, financial statement accounts impacted, and applicability of existing corporate accounting policies to the transaction. In addition, if the accounting treatment proposed does not comply with existing corporate accounting policies, or if any existing corporate accounting policy is not applicable, then an explanation of why the existing policy was not appropriate or applicable and the basis for the selection of the alternative policy should be discussed. Regardless of whether the accounting policy selected preexists or is new, the entire range of alternatives available under GAAP that were discussed by management and the accountants should be communicated along with the reasons for not selecting those alternatives. If the accounting treatment selected is not, in the accountant's view, the preferred method, we expect that the reasons why the accountant's preferred method was not selected by management also will be discussed.[22]

WHAT OTHER INFORMATION SHOULD THE AUDIT COMMITTEE EXPECT TO RECEIVE FROM THE AUDITORS?

BEST PRACTICE

Audit committees should carefully consider all information disclosed to them. Any disclosure to the audit committee by either the auditors or management of fraud that involves management or by other employees who play a significant role in financial reporting should generate an immediate investigation by the audit committee and corrective action.

According to the final SEC release on the auditor independence rules, auditors are required by generally accepted auditing standards (GAAS) to communicate certain matters to the audit committee.[23] In particular, GAAS require that the accountant should determine that the audit committee is informed about matters such as:

- Auditor's responsibility under GAAS
- Significant accounting policies
- Methods used to account for significant unusual transactions

- Effects of significant accounting policies in controversial or emerging areas for which there is a lack of authoritative guidance or consensus
- Process used by management in formulating particularly sensitive accounting estimates and the basis for the auditor's conclusions regarding the reasonableness of those estimates
- Material audit adjustments proposed and immaterial adjustments not recorded by management
- Auditor's judgments about the quality of the company's accounting principles
- Auditor's responsibility for other information in documents containing audited financial statements
- Auditor's views about significant matters that were the subject of consultation between management and other accountants
- Major issues discussed with management prior to retention
- Difficulties with management encountered in performing the audit
- Disagreements with management over the application of accounting principles, the basis for management's accounting estimates, and the disclosures in the financial statements[24]

The audit committee should carefully consider the information provided by the auditor in assessing its own responsibilities.

In addition, under Rules 13a-14 and Rules 15d-14, the officers who execute certifications to be filed as exhibits to periodic reports (e.g. Forms 10-Q and 10-K) must certify that they have disclosed to both the audit committee as well as the auditors:

1. All significant deficiencies and material weaknesses in the design or operation of internal control over financial reporting which are reasonably likely to adversely affect the registrant's ability to record, process, summarize, and report financial information
2. Any fraud, whether material or not, that involves management or other employees who have a significant role in the registrant's internal control over financial reporting

SHOULD THE AUDIT COMMITTEE REQUIRE THAT THE INDEPENDENT AUDITOR PROVIDE THE AUDIT COMMITTEE WITH ANY INCONSISTENT DOCUMENTS RETAINED BY THE AUDITOR?

SEC regulation Section 210.2-06(c) (adopted pursuant to Section 802 of the Sarbanes-Oxley Act) requires an accountant who concludes an audit or review of an issuer's financial statement to which Section 10A(a) of the 1934 Act applies to retain records relevant to the audit or review, including records that are inconsistent with the auditor's final conclusions, for a period of seven years.[25]

The SEC's final rule quoting from Statement of Auditing Standards No. 22, *Planning and Supervision,* states in part:

> The auditor with final responsibility for the audit and assistants should be aware of the procedures to be followed when differences of opinion concerning accounting

and auditing issues exist among firm personnel involved in the audit. Such procedures should enable an assistant to document his disagreement with the conclusions reached if, after appropriate consultation, he believes it necessary to disassociate himself from the resolution of the matter. In this situation, the basis for the final resolution should also be documented.[26]

As an example of inconsistent records, the SEC's final rule gave this:

> Another example would be documentation relating to an auditor's communications with an issuer's audit committee about alternative disclosures and accounting methods used by the issuer that are not the disclosures or accounting preferred by the auditor.[27]

BEST PRACTICE

Since the accountants are required to retain audit or review records for a seven-year period, it is important that the audit committee be aware of any such documentation retained by the accountant, particularly any record that is inconsistent with the auditor's final conclusion. If the accountants have chosen a particular record to be retained under this provision, a prudent audit committee should not only be made aware of such retention by the accountant but should be certain that its records reflect adequate deliberation concerning why the accounting treatment was not ultimately adopted.

HOW SHOULD THE INTERNAL AUDITOR BE COMPENSATED?

BEST PRACTICE

The compensation of the head of the internal audit should be established by the audit committee, in consultation with management without excessive reliance on compensation driven by accounting results.

An internal audit function can significantly assist the audit committee in performing its oversight responsibilities. In WorldCom, the internal auditor was the whistleblower. As noted in Chapter 5, the internal auditor should provide the audit committee with another source of information about the internal affairs of the company independent of management and the outside auditor.

Serious consideration should be given to structuring the compensation of the head of the internal audit to avoid excessive reliance on compensation driven by accounting results. To properly maintain the watchdog function of the internal auditor, he or she should not receive significant incentives based on profitability.

Some companies would prefer to outsource all or part of the internal audit function. Under these circumstances, the audit committee should control not only the selection and retention of the outside internal auditor, but also the compensation arrangements.

SHOULD THE AUDIT COMMITTEE REQUIRE THE MANDATORY ROTATION OF AUDITING FIRMS?

BEST PRACTICE

Audit committees ought to consider and balance the pros and cons of changing auditing firms, particularly at the point at which there is mandatory rotation of audit partners.

Section 207 of Sarbanes-Oxley directs the Comptroller General of the United States to conduct a study and review of the potential effects of the mandatory rotation of firms.[28] The SEC does not require the mandatory rotation of auditing firms and instead only requires the rotation of the lead and concurring audit partners, partners such as relationship partners who serve the client at the issuer or parent level (except a partner who consults regarding technical or industry specific issues), and the lead partner on subsidiaries of the issuer whose assets or revenues constitute 20 percent or more of the consolidated assets or revenues of the issuer.[29] Partner rotation is generally required for the lead partner after more than five consecutive years and for the other partners after more than seven consecutive years.[30]

Audit committees may determine that mandatory rotation of auditing firms is more desirable than merely rotating certain partners. Newly rotated partners of the same auditing firm would naturally tend to be supportive of the accounting judgments made by their predecessors and would tend to avoid changing them for fear of legal liability to the auditing firm.

However, the mandatory rotation of auditing firms would cause a loss of background information and knowledge concerning the company that would otherwise generally be retained even after the rotation of auditing firm partners. In addition, mandatory rotation of auditing firms could significantly increase audit costs.

SHOULD THE AUDIT COMMITTEE SEEK SECOND OPINIONS FROM ACCOUNTING FIRMS?

BEST PRACTICE

Accounting issues may arise from time to time that are so sensitive that the audit committee should obtain a second opinion.

Under Section 301 of Sarbanes-Oxley, audit committees of companies whose securities are listed on national securities exchanges or national securities associations are required to have the authority to engage independent counsel and "other advisors," as they determine necessary to carry out their duties, and the company is required to fund the payment to such advisors.[31]

Audit committees should not be hesitant to exercise this authority, despite occasional assertions by some auditing firms that this constitutes opinion shopping.

Typically the "Big Four" accounting firms would not object to a smaller accounting firm being used to provide a second opinion, particularly smaller accounting firms that employ former members of the SEC accounting staff.

SHOULD THE AUDIT COMMITTEE REQUIRE MORE INTENSIVE OR EXTENSIVE AUDITS PRIOR TO CERTAIN EVENTS OR UNDER CERTAIN WARNING CONDITIONS?

Numerous warning events may suggest to the audit committee that a more intensive or extensive audit should be conducted. In some cases, the audit should be conducted by the internal auditor or the internal auditor should be used to supplement the work of the independent auditor. These events include:

Management Sale of Stock

BEST PRACTICE

Audit committees should carefully consider whether more intensive and extensive audits are required on the eve of insider sales of significant amounts of stock. If this policy is adopted, the audit committee should adopt a policy requiring written notice of insider sales several months before the actual date of such sale so as to arrange the necessary audits.

The temptation to inflate earnings is greatest prior to the intended sale of stock of the company by management. The HealthSouth's scandal amply illustrates this tendency.[32]

Conflict of Interest Situations

BEST PRACTICE

In rare situations in which the audit committee elects to approve a conflict of interest, an ongoing independent monitoring mechanism must be established by the audit committee. This mechanism may include more intensive or extensive audits by the independent auditor, possibly supplemented by oversight by the internal auditor. The results of both the independent auditor and the internal auditor oversight should be reported directly to the audit committee.

The Enron audit committee approved off-balance sheet special purpose entities that clearly created a conflict of interest between certain members of management and the company. Yet, based on the currently available facts, the Enron audit committee did not create oversight mechanisms to verify that the representations made by management to the audit committee, which induced approval of the conflict of interest, were in fact being followed.

Short Sellers

BEST PRACTICE

If short sellers take a significant position in the company stock, the audit committee should investigate whether the short sellers know something they do not.

Short sellers sell borrowed shares in hope of replacing them with cheaper shares bought later. They are arguably the only players in the market who do not have a vested interest in seeing stock prices rise.

Short sellers took a significant position in both the stock of Enron and Tyco, allegedly because they spotted accounting abuses before the auditors of these companies. If short sellers take a significant position in your company's stock, try to find out whether they know something that the auditors have not discovered.

Other Warning Events

Other warning events may include:

- The company never fails to meet an earnings projection.
- The chief executive officer or chief financial officer are under personal financial pressure, which may stem from a divorce, a lavish lifestyle, gambling habits, or otherwise.

BEST PRACTICE

If there are other warning events, the audit committee should authorize the auditor to conduct more intensive and extensive audits. Since almost no company consistently meets earnings projections, audit committees may wish to use a certified fraud examiner to supplement the auditor.

DOES THE AUDIT COMMITTEE REQUIRE SHAREHOLDER APPROVAL OF ITS SELECTION OF THE AUDITING FIRM?

BEST PRACTICE

There is no agreement as to whether shareholder approval should be required for the auditing firm.

There is very little benefit in submitting the selection of the auditing firm to a shareholder vote. Outweighing the benefit of obtaining a confirmatory vote from the shareholders is the issue of whether adequate disclosure has been made to the shareholders of the various lawsuits and claims against the auditing firm by other public companies, their shareholders and regulatory agencies. If adequate disclosure has not been made, a question could well be raised as to whether the shareholder vote was obtained after full disclosure. The SEC rules are less than clear on what additional disclosures concerning audit firms are necessary to be made in proxy statements to avoid having the proxy statement contain false or misleading information.

Moreover, since Sarbanes-Oxley imposes upon the audit committee the duty to select the auditors,[33] a confirmatory vote by shareholders provides very little, if any, legal protection for the selection made by the audit committee. Finally, seeking a shareholder vote to approve the auditor's selection can stir up significant opposition among institutional investors who are unhappy with the selection made by the audit committee.[34]

SHOULD THE INDEPENDENT AUDITORS BE PERMITTED TO PERFORM PERSONAL TAX WORK FOR MANAGEMENT (E.G., SPRINT)?[35]

BEST PRACTICE

The auditor should not be permitted to perform personal tax work for management. Potential conflicts of interest can arise that can be harmful to all parties (e.g., Sprint).

On July 26, 2005, the PCAOB adopted a rule, subject to SEC approval, that would treat a registered public accounting firm as not independent if the firm provides tax services to certain members of management who serve in financial reporting oversight roles at an audit client or to immediate family members of such persons.

SHOULD THE AUDIT COMMITTEE PREVENT MANAGEMENT FROM MAKING EARNINGS PROJECTIONS OR MANAGING OPERATIONS TO SATISFY ANALYST PROJECTIONS?

BEST PRACTICE

Do not make earnings projections.

Public earnings projections by management sometimes create undue pressures on management to satisfy the projections in order to maintain credibility with securities analysts. These pressures can lead to attempts by management to engage in "channel stuffing" or to otherwise "cook the books." An example of this can be found in Chapter 13 in the case of Huntington Bancshares, Inc.

Similarly, even if management does not publicly make an earnings projection, some managements attempt to create internal goals based on the projections made by securities analysts. The purpose of these internal goals is to attempt to satisfy the analysts' projections and thereby avoid a drop in the stock price. An example of this can be found in the SEC Complaint against the former CEO and CFO of Bristol-Myers Squibb Company, which was filed on August 22, 2005, in which they were alleged to use channel stuffing and cookie jar reserves to satisfy internal projections based on the projections of securities analysts.

Audit committees must consider whether making public earnings projections or managing to satisfy analysts' earnings projections should be prohibited. The argument for prohibiting these practices is that they tend to lead to management financial fraud by creating undue pressure on management. The argument against such a blanket prohibition is that it does not take into account the particular circumstances of each company and, therefore, should be utilized only on a case-by-case basis. Even with a blanket prohibition on these practices, there will still be incentives for management to attempt to satisfy the projections of securities analysts in order to maintain a high share price.

WHAT COMPANY INFORMATION SHOULD BE REVIEWED BY THE AUDIT COMMITTEE BEFORE BEING DISTRIBUTED TO THE PUBLIC OR GIVEN TO ANALYSTS?

BEST PRACTICE

Any financial information that is submitted by management to the public or to financial analysts, such as press releases, earnings guidance, or otherwise, should be reviewed by the audit committee, or at least one audit committee member, before being released.

This requires at least one audit committee member to be available for consultation with management at all times, since it is typical that earnings releases and guidance are issued during compressed time periods. In the absence of such prior review, the audit committee risks the embarrassment of having to correct previously released financial information, and the company risks the possibility of private lawsuits or regulatory enforcement action for having issued false or misleading information.

SHOULD THE AUDIT COMMITTEE DECIDE ALL ISSUES AS A WHOLE?

BEST PRACTICE

Delegate broad authority to the audit committee chair, but require the chair to keep the other members advised.

Although it is preferable to have all issues decided by the audit committee as a whole, it may not always be practical to do so because of the compressed time periods in which decisions must be made. Therefore, audit committees should consider delegating one or more functions to the chair of the audit committee or possibly another member, particularly if quick decisions are required.

Certain areas lend themselves to divisions of functions among different members of the audit committee. For example, one member of the audit committee could become an expert on auditor independence issues, and that person could help resolve any such issues without a meeting of the entire audit committee, at least in situations in which a meeting of the whole committee is not possible. Since auditor-independence issues are not only complicated but can have dire consequences to the company, it is preferable to ultimately have all of the audit committee members play a role in such decisions.[36]

HOW DOES THE AUDIT COMMITTEE HANDLE ANONYMOUS COMPLAINTS FROM EMPLOYEES?

BEST PRACTICE

At a minimum, the audit committee should require the company to adopt a written policy, distributed to all employees, that contains the name and address of the person on the audit committee (typically the chair) to whom complaints should be directed and provides a procedure for the submission of anonymous complaints concerning questionable accounting or auditing matters. The audit committee is also required to provide procedures for the "receipt, retention, and treatment" of such complaints.

Section 301 of Sarbanes-Oxley requires the SEC, by rule, to direct the national securities exchanges and the national securities associations to prohibit the listing of any security of an issuer that is not in compliance with, among other items, a requirement that:

(4) . . . Each audit committee shall establish procedures for—

(A) the receipt, retention, and treatment of complaints received by the issuer regarding accounting, internal accounting controls, or auditing matters: and

(B) the confidential anonymous submission by employees of the issuer of concerns regarding questionable accounting or auditing matters.[37]

At a minimum, the audit committee should require the company to adopt a written policy, distributed to all employees, which contains the name and address of the person on the audit committee, typically the chair, to whom complaints should be directed and providing a procedure for the submission of anonymous complaints concerning questionable accounting or auditing matters. The audit committee is also required to provide procedures for the "receipt, retention, and treatment" of such complaints.[38]

Except for obviously frivolous complaints, the audit committee should require an investigation of such complaints by counsel. If the complaint is serious or there is a possibility of the involvement of management, outside counsel should be retained. If there is a possibility that regular outside counsel could have a conflict of interest (e.g. top management may be involved), independent outside counsel should be selected to perform the necessary investigation. At a minimum, a formal report should be required from counsel and retained as part of the audit committee records, subject to the attorney-client privilege and potentially the work product doctrine.

SHOULD LEGAL SERVICES FOR THE AUDIT COMMITTEE BE PROVIDED BY INDEPENDENT COUNSEL?

BEST PRACTICE

Use independent counsel for all important audit committee investigations.

The selection of counsel for the audit committee depends on the issue to be determined. Inside counsel, provided they have the necessary expertise, may well be sufficient for certain routine matters or matters that do not involve management. However, in all other circumstances, outside counsel who have the necessary expertise should be utilized. As noted, if the matter involves top management, independent counsel should be strongly considered as opposed to outside regular counsel.

SHOULD THE AUDIT COMMITTEE ALSO ACT AS A QUALIFIED LEGAL COMPLIANCE COMMITTEE?

BEST PRACTICE

The audit committee or another appointed committee of the board of directors should become a qualified legal compliance committee.

It has been reported that Institutional Shareholder Services, in preparing its corporate governance ratings, may in the future ask whether the company has a so-called Qualified Legal Compliance Committee ("QLCC"). The author suspects that director and officer liability insurers may also consider this issue in the future.

The SEC has adopted a standard of professional conduct which requires that attorneys appearing and practicing before the SEC must report evidence of a material violation of securities laws, a breach of fiduciary duty, or similar violation up the ladder within the company.[39] If a company has a QLCC, an attorney can report evidence of a material violation of securities laws or a breach of fiduciary duty or similar violation to the QLCC and has no duty to assess the response, if any, made by such committee.[40] In the absence of a QLCC, the attorney must report the material violation to the chief legal officer of the company (or equivalent) and thereafter assess the appropriateness of the response made by the company to the attorney's report; if an appropriate response is not made within a reasonable time, the attorney must report the evidence of material violation to the audit committee, if there is one, and, if there is no audit committee, to a committee composed of persons who are not employed, directly or indirectly, by the company. In the absence of both an audit committee and a nonemployed director committee, the violation should be reported to the full board of directors.[41]

A QLCC is defined in Section 205.2(k) of the SEC's Standards of Professional Conduct for Attorneys Appearing and Practicing Before the Commission in the Representation of an Issuer in this way:

A committee and an issuer (which also may be an audit or other committee of the issuer) that:

(1) Consists of at least one member of the issuer's audit committee (or, if the issuer has no audit committee, one member from an equivalent committee of independent directors) and two or more members of the issuer's board of directors who are not employed, directly or indirectly, by the issuer and who are not, in the case of a registered investment company, "interested persons" as defined in Section 2(a)(19) of the Investment company Act of 1940 (15 U.S.C. § 80a 2(a)(19));

(2) Has adopted written procedures for the confidential receipt, retention, and consideration of any report of evidence of a material violation under §205.3;

(3) Has been duly established by the issuer's board of directors, with the authority and responsibility:

(i) To inform the issuer's chief legal officer and chief executive officer (or the equivalents thereof) of any report of evidence of a material violation (except in the circumstances described in §205.3(b)(4));

(ii) To determine whether an investigation is necessary regarding any report of evidence of a material violation by the issuer, its officers, directors, employees or agents and, if it determines an investigation is necessary or appropriate, to:

(A) Notify the audit committee or the full board of directors;

(B) Initiate an investigation, which may be conducted either by the chief legal officer (or the equivalent thereof) or by outside attorneys;

(C) Retain such additional expert personnel as the committee deems necessary; and

(iii) At the conclusion of any such investigation, to:

(A) Recommend, by majority vote, that the issuer implement an appropriate response to evidence of a material violation; and

(B) Inform the chief legal officer and the chief executive officer (or the equivalents thereof) and the board of directors of the results of any such investigation under this Section and the appropriate remedial measures to be adopted; and

(4) Has the authority and responsibility, acting by majority vote, to take all other appropriate action, including the authority to notify the Commission in the event that the issuer fails in any material respect to implement an appropriate response that the qualified legal compliance committee has recommended the issuer to take."[42]

The major advantage of having the audit committee also become a QLCC is the SEC's position that service on such a committee would not increase the liability of any board member. The SEC made this statement in its release adopting the requirement for up-the-ladder reporting by attorneys:

> The Commission does not know how widespread adoption of the QLCC alternative will be, but encourages issuers to do so as a means of effective corporate governance. In any event, the Commission does not intend service on a QLCC to increase the liability of any member of a board of directors under state law and, indeed, expressly finds that it would be inconsistent with the public interest for a court to so conclude.[43]

Since audit committees will typically handle internal investigations of financially related issues, the audit committee that elects to become a QLCC will obtain the additional protection of the SEC's strong statement on liability just quoted, in addition to a possible enhancement of the Institutional Shareholder Services's future corporate governance rating system. Another advantage of the audit committee becoming a QLCC is to avoid imposing on an attorney who reports material violations a requirement to assess the "appropriateness" of the response and whether the response was made within a reasonable time. The imposition of such a requirement may well increase the legal fees incurred by the company from the reporting attorney and, more important, avoids having the reporting attorney second-guess the appropriateness of the response.

SHOULD THE AUDIT COMMITTEE REQUIRE THE USE OF DISCLOSURE COMMITTEES AND CERTIFICATIONS BY THE DISCLOSURE COMMITTEE?

BEST PRACTICE

Many companies have required that the disclosure committee issue a subcertification to the chief executive officers and the chief financial officers as a backup to their certifications under Section 302 and Section 906 of Sarbanes-Oxley. The audit committee should obtain similar subcertifications

(continued)

> from the disclosure committee, if one has been formed, to further document the files of the audit committee. If no disclosure committee has been formed, the audit committee should require the use of disclosure committees as recommended by the SEC.

In connection with the requirement in Section 302 of Sarbanes-Oxley for certifications in annual and quarterly reports by the principal executive officers and principal financial officers, the SEC has recommended that a company create a committee (the "disclosure committee") with responsibility for considering the materiality of information and determining disclosure obligations under the 1934 Act.[44] The disclosure committee would report to senior management, including the principal executive and financial officers, who bear express responsibility for designing, establishing, maintaining, reviewing, and evaluating the issuer's disclosure controls and procedures.[45] According to the SEC, the disclosure committee could include the principal accounting officer (or the controller), the general counsel or other senior legal official with responsibility for disclosure matters who reports to the general counsel, the principal risk management officer, the chief investor relations officer (or an officer with equivalent responsibilities), and such other officers or employees, including individuals associated with the issuer's business units, as the company deems appropriate.[46]

SHOULD THE AUDIT COMMITTEE RECEIVE GREATER COMPENSATION THAN OTHER BOARD MEMBERS?

BEST PRACTICE

Audit committee members should receive more compensation than other board members since they must spend a greater amount of time performing their duties than other board members. However, there is no agreement as to whether they should receive a higher retainer or hourly rate for their services than other board members because of their greater personal risk.

Audit committees will normally meet more frequently than other committees and typically will have longer meetings. Many companies compensate directors by a fixed retainer and a per-meeting fee. Therefore, some have argued that audit committee members will receive more compensation than other directors without changing the overall director compensation program.

However, this argument overlooks the greater responsibility and greater potential for personal liability of audit committee members. As noted in Chapter 12, in the event of a financial fraud, audit committee members will likely be determined to be control persons for purposes of Section 15 of the 1933 Act and Section 20(a) of the 1934 Act, particularly if they have personally signed a filing with the SEC containing the fraudulent financial statements.[47] Although audit committees are entitled to a "due diligence defense" under Section 15 of the 1933 Act[48] and Section 20(a) of the 1934 Act,[49] the burden will be on the audit committee member to establish this defense. Moreover, under the doctrine of differential liability, directors who are not audit committee members may have legal rights of contribution and indemnity against audit committee members who fail to perform their assigned responsibilities.[50]

In view of the additional risks assumed by audit committee members, a reasonable argument can be made for greater compensation per meeting for audit committee members because of the greater risk than for other directors. The argument against this position is that it creates two classes of directors and therefore may undermine the collegiality of the board.

HOW OFTEN SHOULD THE AUDIT COMMITTEE MEET?

BEST PRACTICE

The audit committee should meet at least four times a year and preferably more often.

The meetings should correspond to the timing of the quarterly and annual financial press releases and should be scheduled sufficiently in advance of the preparation of these press releases to permit time for a robust discussion and comments. Although it is preferable to meet in person, one or more members of the audit committee could be present on a conference telephone call, provided they are given adequate notice of the telephone call and are furnished with all of the relevant material in advance of the meeting.

Whether the meetings are held in person or through conference telephone call or otherwise, it is important to prepare minutes of these meetings and retain such minutes with the records of the audit committee.

BEST PRACTICE

At least one meeting a year of the audit committee should be an in-person meeting of all members of the audit committee at which relevant information is obtained from all layers of management and the auditors. (See the first question in this chapter.) This meeting typically should be held shortly before or shortly after the completion of the fiscal year.

Additional meetings should be scheduled as needed during the year or as may be required by extraordinary events, such as significant mergers and acquisitions, plant closings and other discontinued operations, and so on.

IN WHAT DETAIL SHOULD MINUTES
OF THE AUDIT COMMITTEE BE KEPT?

BEST PRACTICE

In general, the audit committee minutes should be prepared by an attorney on the assumption that the audit committee members will be personally liable for false financial information released by the company under Section 15 of the 1933 Act or under Section 20(a) of the 1934 Act and the minutes will be used to help establish the "due diligence" defense under these sections.

The level of detail of the minutes of the audit committee meeting requires legal judgment. Excessive detail provides plaintiffs' lawyers with a treasure trove of material to ask questions of audit committee members at depositions and at trial of shareholder class actions and, therefore, should generally be avoided. In general, the topics covered by the audit committee and the persons attending, advising, or interviewed should be recited in the minutes.

Whoever prepares the minutes should assume that they would be subpoenaed in the future in some lawsuit or regulatory action. Therefore, the minutes should be prepared in a manner that reflects well on the activities of the audit committee, their competency, and diligence.

If a lawsuit or regulatory action has already been brought or is threatened to be brought or is likely to be brought, special care must be taken in preparing the minutes of the audit committee meetings at which the issue that is or will be the subject of the lawsuit or regulatory action is discussed. Under these circumstances, counsel may well advise the audit committee to have more circumspect minutes that recite topics, methodology, and conclusions generally—particularly if privileged communications occur. Conversely, there are circumstances when it is advisable to have fulsome minutes of the discussion of the issue that is or will be the subject of the lawsuit or regulatory action. The purpose of having fulsome minutes in these circumstances is to assist, through written as opposed to testimony evidence, in proving to the court or regulatory agency that the audit committee is on top of the issue and is handling the issue in a manner that reflects well on the competency and diligence of the audit committee.

WHO SHOULD ACT AS SECRETARY FOR KEEPING
MINUTES OF THE AUDIT COMMITTEE MEETINGS?

BEST PRACTICE

It is preferable to have an independent counsel, who is not a member of the audit committee, prepare the minutes of the audit committee meeting.

The minutes of the audit committee can be prepared by a member of the audit committee or by an attorney for the audit committee. It is a distraction to require any member of the audit committee (even an attorney member) to take minutes at the same time he or she is trying to concentrate on the substance of the meeting.

The attorney who takes the minutes of the audit committee meetings may be inside counsel, outside regular counsel, or independent counsel. Whichever attorney is selected should be completely familiar with audit committee liability issues. If the subject of the meeting involves top management of the company, inside counsel should not be used, and if the topic of the meeting is very sensitive, independent counsel for the audit committee should be required.

If a private lawsuit regulatory matter is threatened or pending, then it is advisable to consult outside litigation counsel.

SHOULD AUDIT COMMITTEE MEMBERS MAKE AND RETAIN PERSONAL NOTES OF THE AUDIT COMMITTEE MEETINGS?

BEST PRACTICE

Audit committee members should provide their personal notes of the meeting (including all copies) to independent counsel for the audit committee who could then consider whether it is appropriate to maintain or destroy these notes.

Most audit committee members will want to retain personal notes of the meeting to keep track of the consistency of the specific information provided, especially if the official minutes will reflect only general topics covered. However, these personal notes are subject to subpoena and other discovery in the event of a lawsuit or regulatory action. Therefore, great care must be exercised in preparing personal notes of the meetings to avoid making damaging remarks.

The handling of personal notes is a difficult question and has conflicting answers depending on whether a lawsuit or regulatory action is pending, threatened, or likely. The best practice is to provide personal notes to independent counsel to decide whether to maintain or destroy these notes. In some cases, independent counsel may elect to retain the personal notes of audit committee members in counsel's own files between meetings and then distribute them at the next meeting.

SHOULD THE AUDIT COMMITTEE LIMIT THE PERCENTAGE OF COMPENSATION OF CEO AND CFO DRIVEN BY ACCOUNTING RESULTS, OR IS THIS A COMPENSATION COMMITTEE ISSUE?

BEST PRACTICE

Limit the percentage of compensation of the CEO and top officers that is driven solely by accounting results.

The higher the percentage of compensation that is driven by accounting results, the greater the temptation to fudge these results. Although it is probably not desirable or even possible to eliminate all forms of incentive compensation, serious consideration should be given to the proportion between incentive compensation, to the extent driven by accounting results, and fixed compensation. One can argue that even fixed compensation is in part driven by accounting results since increases in yearly fixed compensation are usually based in part on accounting results from prior periods.

A University of Maryland study scrutinized 71 companies that the SEC prosecuted for allegedly engaging in accounting regularities between 1992 and 1999. The study found that, on average, a chief executive of a violating company owned options valued at more than three times his salary and bonus. The violating companies also typically made numerous acquisitions and were run by relatively young men.[51]

Typically the compensation of the top officers is established by the compensation committee and not the audit committee. However, it is important for these two committees to work together to produce a balanced compensation program.

WHEN AND HOW SHOULD AUDIT COMMITTEE INVESTIGATIONS BE CONDUCTED?

BEST PRACTICE

Investigations should be conducted by audit committees rather than management if there is any possibility of the involvement of top management or the matter may be embarrassing to the company. In general, it is preferable to use independent counsel to conduct an investigation. See Chapter 2 for more information.

From time to time, potentially suspicious information will reach audit committees which will suggest that an internal investigation is appropriate. In making judgments as to whether information is suspicious or not, audit committees ought to follow the "20/20 hindsight rule." If as a matter of hindsight a reasonable person might judge the information as suspicious, then the audit committee should investigate, in order to avoid being criticized for ignoring an "obvious" warning sign.

There is a tendency for audit committees to request financial personnel, such as the chief financial officer, to take charge of internal investigations if it is not obvious that top management is involved. In general, this is a mistake for two reasons:

1. Information gathered by financial personnel, such as a chief financial officer, is not privileged under most circumstances[52] and is fully available for discovery in subsequent shareholder litigation or in regulatory proceedings.
2. In the early stages of an investigation, there can be no assurance that top management is not in fact involved.

The better course for the audit committee is to have the investigation conducted by an attorney who reports directly to the audit committee, thereby attempting to preserve the attorney-client privilege and the work product doctrine, preferably independent counsel.

WHAT ROLE SHOULD THE AUDIT COMMITTEE PLAY IN DEVELOPING AND MONITORING THE LAW-COMPLIANCE CULTURE WITHIN THE COMPANY?

BEST PRACTICE

The chair of the audit committee or other appropriate board committee must play a significant role in helping to develop a law-compliance culture.

Enron had an extensive and award-winning code of ethics and corporate governance structure. Indeed, there was no scarcity of grandiose ethics policies among most of the companies suffering from corporate scandals. The problem was failure to follow these policies and to develop an ethical, law-compliance culture within the company (see Chapter 4.)

Management's primary function is to increase shareholder value and to create incentives to employees for accomplishing this goal and disincentives to employees who fail. Management must also be encouraged to equally develop an employee culture that emphasizes law compliance.

The audit committee/corporate governance committee is uniquely situated to help foster the law-compliance culture within the company, although there is no legal requirement to do so in Sarbanes-Oxley. However, the U.S. Sentencing Commission Guidelines place the onus on the board of directors to create and monitor a law-compliance culture (see Chapter 4). This may require the audit committee/ corporate governance committee to create more interface with employees below the chief executive officer and chief financial officer position. Occasionally having the chair of the audit committee present at employee meetings to explain the role of the audit committee helps foster a law compliance culture within the company.

ENDNOTES

1. See SEC Release No. 33-8238 (June 5, 2003) at note 50, which in turn quotes from the report of the Committee of Sponsoring Organizations of the Treadway Commission (COSO) entitled "Internal Control-Integrated Framework" (1992) at 130.
2. See Will Boye, ISS Announces Changes to Voting Policies, January 17, 2002, www.issproxy.com/articles/archived/archived2asp.
3. "Strengthening the Commission's Requirements Regarding Auditor Independence," Exchange Act Release No. 33-8,183, 68 Fed. Reg. 6,006, 6,016-17 (February 5, 2003).
4. Jonathan Weil, "Proxy Document Says Company Performed Janitorial Inspections Misclassified as Audit-Related," *Wall Street Journal*, June 11, 1993.
5. 15 U.S.C. Section 78j-1. See also Chapter 16.

6. See "Did Ties That Bind Also Blind KPMG," *Wall Street Journal*, June 18, 2003.
7. Qualifications of Accountants, 17 C.F.R. § 210.2-01(c)(4)(x).
8. Id.
9. Id. at "Preliminary Note 2."
10. See *United States v. Arthur Young & Co.*, 465 U.S. 805, 815 (1984). In that case the U.S. Supreme Court held that the work-product doctrine did not prevent the disclosure of tax accrual work papers of Arthur Young & Co., to the IRS, which had issued an administrative summons to that accounting firm in connection with an investigation of Amerada Hess Corp. See id. Although accountants have an accountant-client privilege under the Internal Revenue Service Restructuring and Reform Act of 1989 and the laws of over 20 states, the accountant-client privilege does not apply to criminal proceedings and is much more limited than the attorney-client privilege. See Alicia K. Corcoran, "Note: The Accountant-Client Privilege: A Prescription for Confidentiality or Just a Placebo?" 34 *New England Law Review* 697 (2000); Frederick D. Lipman and Joseph T. Gulant, *SEC Proposes New Limits on Auditor Tax Services*, Tax Notes, 373 (January 20, 2003).
11. The CorporateCounsel.net, at: www.thecorporatecounsel.net/home.asp, on The CorporateCounsel.net. Blog page by Broc Romanek, June 5, 2003, at www.thecorporate-counsel.net/blog/index.html.
12. PCAOB Release No. 2005-014 July 26, 2005 PCAOB Rulemaking Docket Matter No. 017.
13. See The Conference Board Commission on Public Trust and Private Enterprise, Findings and Recommendations 37 (2003), *available at* www.conference-board.org/pdf_free/SR-03-04-ES.pdf.
14. Strengthening the Commission's Requirements Regarding Auditor Independence, Exchange Act Release No. 33-8,183, 68 Fed. Reg. 6,006 (February 5, 2003).
15. 68 Fed. Reg. at 6,017.
16. Qualifications of Accountants, 17 C.F.R. § 210.2-01, "Preliminary Note 2."
17. 68 Fed. Reg. at 6,024.
18. Id. at 6,025 (emphasis added).
19. 15 U.S.C. § 78j-1(k).
20. 17 C.F.R. § 210.2-07(a).
21. 68 Fed. Reg. at 6027.
22. Id. at 6029.
23. Id. at 6027.
24. Id. at 6027 n. 194 citing AU § 380, "Communication with Audit Committees," and explaining that "[t]here are additional GAAS requirements related to auditor communications that are not included in this rule, such as the auditor's responsibilities under GAAS, the auditor's responsibilities related to documents containing audited financial statements, and disagreements with management, consultations with other accountants, major issues discussed with management prior to retention, and difficulties encountered in performing the audit, to the extent that those matters do not relate to accounting policies and practices."
25. 17 C.F.R. § 210.2-06(a).
26. Retention of Records Relevant to Audits and Reviews, Exchange Act Release No. 33-8,180, 68 Fed. Reg. 4,862, 4,865 (January 30, 2003) (citing SAS 22, (as amended by SAS 47, 48, and 77)).
27. Id. at 4865.
28. 15 U.S.C. § 7232(a).
29. See Strengthening the Commission's Requirements Regarding Auditor Independence, Exchange Act Release No. 33-8,183, 68 Fed. Reg. 6,006, 6,018-19 (February 5, 2003).

30. 68 Fed. Reg. at 6,021.
31. 15 U.S.C. § 78j-1(m)(5).
32. Deborah Solomon, "HealthSouth Faked Profits, SEC Charges," *Wall Street Journal*, March 20, 2003 (reporting that Mr. Scrushy, chief executive officer of HealthSouth, refused to abandon HealthSouth's earnings manipulation scheme by saying "[n]ot until I sell my stock.").
33. 15 U.S.C. § 78j-1(m)(2).
34. See Rebecca Blumenstein, "Advisor Urges Clients to Reject Sprint's Auditor," *Wall Street Journal*, April 30, 2003 (Institutional Shareholder Services recommended to pension and mutual-fund managers that they vote against Sprint Corp.'s ratification of its auditor, Ernst & Young LLP).
35. Id.
36. www.sec.gov/rules/final/33-7919.htm.
37. 15 U.S.C. § 78j-1(m)(4).
38. Id.
39. Standards of Professional Conduct for Attorneys, 17 C.F.R. § 205.3(b).
40. Id. § 205.3(c).
41. Id. § 205.3(b)(3).
42. Id. § 205.2(k).
43. Implementation Standards of Professional Conduct for Attorneys, Exchange Act Release No. 33-8,185, 68 Fed. Reg. 6,296, 6,305 (Feb. 6, 2003).
44. Certification of Disclosure in Companies' Quarterly and Annual Reports, Exchange Act Release No. 33-8,124, 67 Fed. Reg. 57,276, 57,280 (September 9, 2002).
45. Id.
46. Id. at n. 60.
47. See Chapter 12.
48. See U.S.C.S. § 77o.
49. Id. § 77t.
50. See Chapter 12.
51. See "Study Blames Accounting Fraud on Takeover Fever, Officer's Age," Joanne S. Lublin, *Wall Street Journal*, July 3, 2003, C4.
52. Some courts have adopted a so-called self-evaluative privilege, but this has not been universal. *See, e.g., Bredice v. Doctor's Hosps. Inc.*, 14 Fed. R. Serv. 2d (Callaghan) 759 (D.D.C. 1970); *see also* Robert J. Bush, "Stimulating Corporate Self-Regulation—The Corporate Self-Evaluative Privilege: Paradigmatic Preferentialism or Pragmatic Panacea," 87 *Northwestern University Law Review* 597 (1993).

Chapter 16

Who Is an Independent Auditor?

The independence rules for auditors are set by state boards of accountancy, state certified public accountants' societies, and federal and state agencies, including the Securities and Exchange Commission (SEC), the Government Accountability Office, and the U.S. Department of Labor. In addition, the Public Company Accounting Oversight Board (PCAOB) has set independence standards for registered public accounting firms. (See Chapter 15.)

Audit committees of all organizations that provide audited financial statements should be concerned about the independence of the auditing firm. An audit by a nonindependent auditing firm lacks credibility to its readers, which may include banks, other financial institutions, investors, and, in the case of not-for profit organizations, potential donors. Moreover, in the event of a sale of the assets or stock of a private company that claims to have audited financial statements, the seller will typically have to warrant and represent to the buyer that the auditing firm was independent.

BEST PRACTICE

All organizations that provide audited financial statements should obtain a written representation from the auditing firm as to their independence under all relevant rules.

This chapter focuses primarily on the SEC's auditor independence rules applicable to public companies, keeping in mind that other independence rules can also be relevant to a particular audit.

PUBLIC COMPANY AUDIT COMMITTEES

Some audit committee members of public companies believe that auditor independence is primarily a problem for the auditor. Nothing can be further from the truth. These serious consequences may affect a public company that does not have an "independent" auditor:

- The company may be publicly embarrassed in the trading markets.
- Because the company's Form 10-K report does not satisfy the auditor independence requirements of the Securities Exchange Act of 1934 (the "1934

Act"), therefore the company has violated the requirements of Section 13 or Section 15(d) of that Act.

- The certifications by the chief executive officer and the chief financial officer under Sections 302 and 906 of Sarbanes-Oxley are incorrect.
- The company may incur liability for SEC enforcement actions.
- The company may incur liability for private shareholder actions, particularly if the stock price falls after the public announcement of nonindependence.
- The company loses its eligibility for short-form registration statements (e.g., Forms S-3 and S-8 Registration Statements under the Securities Act of 1933 (the "1933 Act")).
- Directors and officers lose their eligibility to make sales under Rule 144 of the 1933 Act.

Unfortunately, the SEC independence rules do not contain an exception for inadvertent conduct that impairs the auditor's independence unless all of the requirements of a very limited exception are satisfied. It is not clear that this exception would apply to the inadvertent failure of the audit committee to preapprove an audit or nonaudit service. Therefore, it is extremely important that the audit committee always preapprove such services except in the very limited situation in which such preapproval is not required.

BEST PRACTICE

One member of the audit committee should be charged with monitoring the independence of the independent auditor.

SEC INDEPENDENCE RULES

SEC Regulation Section 210.2-01 contains both a general standard (see Chapter 15) and nonexclusive per se disqualifications of auditor independence. Because the per se disqualifications are nonexclusive, it is important that audit committees understand that merely because some auditor activity is not listed as a per se disqualification does not mean that it will not adversely affect independence.

The general standard is explained by the SEC as follows:

> Section 210.2-01(b) sets forth the general standard of auditor independence. Paragraphs (c)(1) to (c)(5) reflect the application of the general standard to particular circumstances. The rule does not purport to, and the Commission could not, consider all circumstances that raise independence concerns, and these are subject to the general standard in Sec. 210.2-01(b). *In considering this standard, the Commission looks in the first instance to whether a relationship or the provision of a service: creates a mutual or conflicting interest between the accountant and the audit client; places the accountant in the position of auditing his or her own work; results in the accountant acting as management or an employee of the audit client; or places the accountant in a position of being an advocate for the audit client.* [Emphasis added.]

These factors are general guidance only and their application may depend on particular facts and circumstances. For that reason, Sec. 210.2-01 provides that, in determining whether an accountant is independent, the Commission will consider all relevant facts and circumstances. For the same reason, registrants and accountants are encouraged to consult with the Commission's Office of the Chief Accountant before entering into relationships, including relationships involving the provision of services, that are not explicitly described in the rule . . . .

In light of the extensive nature of these rules and the fact that the SEC was operating under an extremely tight timetable required by the Sarbanes-Oxley Act (the Act) in adopting them, it is likely that a number of interpretive issues will arise as public companies and their auditors attempt to comply with the new requirements.

PER SE PROHIBITED NONAUDIT SERVICES

Sarbanes-Oxley lists certain nonaudit services that, if provided by an accounting firm to an audit client, would automatically impair the firm's independence. Subject to certain exceptions, these prohibited services are:

- Bookkeeping or other services related to the accounting records or financial statements of the audit client
- Financial information systems design and implementation
- Appraisal or valuation services, fairness opinions, or contribution-in-kind reports
- Actuarial services
- Internal audit outsourcing services
- Management functions
- Human resources
- Broker or dealer, investment advisor, or investment banking services
- Legal services
- Expert services

The SEC rules on independence, as amended in 2003, contain a laundry list of other relationships that will impair the independence of the auditor. These include:

- Financial relationship (investment, loans, etc.)
- Employment relationships
- Business relationships
- Contingent fees
- Partner rotation
- Compensation

The subsections that follow discuss employment relationships through compensation in more detail.

BEST PRACTICE

In view of the complexity of the SEC's independence rules, audit committees should annually obtain a written representation from the auditing firm as to the independence of the auditing firm and an agreement to properly notify the audit committee in writing of any impairment of its independence.

Employment Relationships

Prior to the 2003 amendments, the SEC's rules stated that an accounting firm would not be independent if a former partner, principal, shareholder, or professional employee of an accounting firm accepts employment with a client if he or she has a continuing financial interest in the accounting firm or is in a position to influence the firm's operations or financial policies. The 2003 amendments added to these restrictions by providing that an accounting firm is not independent if the lead partner, the concurring partner, or any other member of the audit engagement team who provided more than 10 hours of audit, review, or attest services for the issuer accepts a position with the issuer in a "financial reporting oversight role" within the one-year period preceding the commencement of audit procedures for the year that included employment by the issuer of the former member of the audit engagement team. The 2003 amendments include exceptions for emergency or unusual circumstances, which the SEC anticipates being invoked very rarely, and conflicts that are created through mergers.

Investment companies must take different employment conflict rules into account. Generally, employment in a financial reporting oversight role with any entity in an investment company complex can preclude independence.

Business Relationships

According to the SEC rule, a "business relationship" will destroy independence of the auditing firm. The SEC rule states:

> An accountant is not independent if, at any point during the audit and professional engagement period, the accounting firm or any *covered person in the firm* has any direct or material indirect business relationship with an *audit client*, or with persons associated with the audit client in a decision-making capacity, such as an audit client's officers, directors, or substantial stockholders. The relationships described in this paragraph do not include a relationship in which the accounting firm or covered person in the firm provides professional services to an audit client or is a consumer in the ordinary course of business. [Emphasis added.]

The term "audit client" means the entity whose financial statements or other information is being audited, reviewed, or attested and any affiliates of the audit client (subject to certain exceptions) and would normally include as "affiliates" directors and executive officers of the company as well as other associated persons of the audit client.

The term "covered person in the firm" is broadly defined to include these partners, principals, shareholders, and employees of an accounting firm:

- The "audit engagement team"
- The "chain of command"
- Any other partner, principal, shareholder, or managerial employee of the accounting firm who has provided 10 or more hours of nonaudit services to the audit client for the period beginning on the date such services are provided and ending on the date the accounting firm signs the report on the financial statements for the fiscal year during which those services are provided, or who expects to provide 10 or more hours of nonaudit services to the audit client on a recurring basis
- Any other partner, principal, or shareholder from an "office" of the accounting firm in which the lead audit engagement partner primarily practices in connection with the audit.

A direct business relationship with the auditing firm or a "covered person in the firm" does not have to be material in order to violate this rule. It is only "indirect business relationships" that are subject to a materiality test.

Some auditing firms have interpreted this no-business-relationship rule very strictly. For example, a shared book royalty between the auditing firm and a director of the public company had to be terminated, even though the royalty was an immaterial amount. Other business relationships that would be prohibited would include a joint venture with a director of a public company and referral relationships.

BEST PRACTICE

A questionnaire should be distributed annually to directors, officers, and other personnel in a financial reporting position to ferret out any business relationships with the auditing firm or a "covered person in the firm."

Contingent Fees

The SEC rules provide that an accountant is not independent if, at any point during the audit and professional engagement period, the accountant provides any service or product to an audit client for a contingent fee or a commission, or receives a contingent fee or commission from an audit client.

The term "contingent fee" means (except as stated) any fee established for the sale of a product or the performance of any service pursuant to an arrangement in which no fee will be charged unless a specified finding or result is attained, or in which the amount of the fee is otherwise dependent on the finding or result of such product or service. Solely for this purpose, a fee is not a "contingent fee" if it is fixed by courts or other public authorities, or, in tax matters, is determined based on the results of judicial proceedings or the findings of governmental agencies. This last exception for tax matters has been strictly construed by the SEC.

BEST PRACTICE

If an auditor claims that a particular fee is not a contingent fee because it falls within the exceptions just listed, require the auditor to obtain a no-action letter from the SEC.

Partner Rotation

The SEC rules provide that the lead and concurring partner on an audit must rotate after five years. In addition, they are subject to a five-year "time-out" period after rotation during which they may not provide audit services to the company. Other significant audit partners are subject to a seven-year rotation requirement with a two-year time-out period. Accounting firms with 10 or fewer partners and 5 or fewer public company audit clients are exempt from these restrictions.

The partner rotation rules have different effective dates depending on the roles of the audit partners. Lead partners are subject to the rotation requirements of the first day of the issuer's fiscal year beginning after May 6, 2003; their five-year service period includes time served as a lead partner prior to May 6, 2003. Concurring partners are subject to the rotation requirements on the first day of the issuer's fiscal year beginning after May 6, 2004; their five-year service period includes any time served in the capacity of a concurring partner prior to May 6, 2003. Other audit partners and all partners with foreign accounting firms are subject to the rotation period on the first day of the issuer's fiscal year beginning after May 6, 2003; their service period does not, however, include any time served prior to May 6, 2003.

For investment companies, the 2003 amendments do not permit audit partners to rotate between investment companies in the same complex in order to satisfy their rotation obligations.

Compensation

The SEC rules provide that an accountant is not independent if, at any point during the audit and professional engagement period, any audit partner earns or receives compensation based on that partner procuring engagements with the audit client to provide any services other than audit, review, or attest services. This provision does not apply to specialty partners. Accounting firms with 10 or fewer partners and 5 or fewer public company audit clients are exempt from these restrictions.

Permitted Nonaudit Service—Tax Services

Accountants are able to provide tax compliance, tax planning, and tax advice to audit clients, subject to audit committee preapproval requirements. Merely labeling a prohibited service as a "tax service," however, will not eliminate its potential to impair independence. Moreover, there are circumstances in which providing certain tax services to an audit client would impair the independence of an accountant, such as representing an audit client in tax court or other situations involving public advocacy. In addition, the SEC indicated in the 2003 amendments that it may be inappropriate to retain an accountant to audit a transaction initially recommended by the accountant when the sole business purpose of the transaction is tax avoidance and the tax treatment of the transaction may not be supported in the Internal Revenue Code and regulations. Additional PCAOB restrictions on tax services were adopted on July 26, 2005, and were discussed in Chapter 15.

Audit Committee Preapproval of Services Provided by Auditor

BEST PRACTICE

Audit committees must establish strict preapproval policies for any audit or nonaudit services from the auditing firm for which preapprovals are sufficiently specific and detailed so that management is not given discretion as to their scope of the preapproval.

The SEC rules require that the audit committee preapprove all audit and nonaudit services provided by the auditor as a condition of auditor independence. In this regard, the engagement must either be:

- Specifically preapproved by the audit committee
- Entered into pursuant to policies and procedures established by the audit committee, provided they are detailed as to the particular service, the audit committee is informed on a timely basis of each engagement, and the policies and procedures do not delegate the audit committee's responsibilities to management.

A de minimis exception waives the preapproval requirements for nonaudit services provided that all such services:

- Do not aggregate to more than 5 percent of total revenues paid by the audit client to its accountant in the fiscal year when services are provided
- Were not recognized as nonaudit services at the time of the engagement
- Are promptly brought to the attention of the audit committee and approved prior to the completion of the audit by the audit committee or one or more designated representatives

An investment company's audit committee is required to preapprove services to be provided directly to the investment company and to other entities in the investment company complex where the nature of the services have a direct impact on the operations or financial reporting of the investment company.

On August 13, 2003, the Office of Chief Accountant issued a release of answers to "Frequently Asked Questions" ("August 13, 2003, FAQ Release") that made it clear that broad preapprovals for nonaudit services to be performed by the auditor would not be acceptable[1]:

Question 3

Q: The Commission's rules require the audit committee to pre-approve all services provided by the independent auditor. In doing so, the audit committee can pre-approve services using pre-approval policies and procedures. Can the audit committee use monetary limits as the basis for establishing its pre-approval policies and procedures?

A: The Commission's rules include three requirements that must be followed in the audit committee's use of pre-approval through policies and procedures. First, the policies and procedures must be detailed as to the particular services to be provided. Second, the audit committee must be informed about each service. Third, the policies and procedures cannot result in the delegation of the audit committee's authority to management. Pre-approval policies and procedures that do not comply with all three of these requirements are in contravention of the Commission's rules. Therefore, monetary limits cannot be the only basis for the pre-approval policies and procedures. The establishment of monetary limits would not, alone, constitute policies that are detailed as to the particular services to be provided and would not, alone, ensure that the audit committee would be informed about each service.

Question 4

Q: Can the audit committee's pre-approval policies and procedures provide for broad, categorical approvals (e.g., tax compliance services)?

A: No. The Commission's rules require that the pre-approval policies be detailed as to the particular services to be provided. Use of broad, categorical approvals would not meet the requirement that the policies must be detailed as to the particular services to be provided.

Question 5

Q: How detailed do the pre-approval policies need to be?

A: The determination of the appropriate level of detail for the pre-approval policies will differ depending upon the facts and circumstances of the issuer. However, a key requirement is that the policies cannot result in a delegation of the audit committee's responsibility to management. As such, if a member of management is called upon to make a judgment as to whether a proposed service fits within the pre-approved services, then the pre-approval policy would not be sufficiently detailed as to the particular services to be provided. Similarly, pre-approval policies must be designed to ensure that the audit committee knows precisely what services it is being asked to pre-approve so that it can make a well-reasoned assessment of the impact of the service on the auditor's independence. For example, if the audit committee is presented with a schedule or cover sheet describing services to be pre-approved, that schedule or cover sheet must be accompanied by detailed back-up documentation regarding the specific services to be provided.[2]

Audit Partner

The SEC rules define the term "audit partner" for purposes of the requirements for partner rotation and partner compensation, which were previously discussed. An audit partner is a partner who is a member of the audit engagement team who has responsibility for decision making on significant auditing, accounting, and reporting matters that affect the financial statements or who maintains regular contact with management and the audit committee. The term "audit partner" includes the lead and concurring partners as well as partners who serve the client at the issuer or parent level, and the lead partner on subsidiaries of the issuer whose assets or revenues constitute 20 percent or more of the consolidated assets or revenues of the issuer. It does not include specialty partners who consult with those on the audit engagement team regarding technical or industry-specific issues, such as partners assigned to national offices.

AUDITOR COMMUNICATION WITH AUDIT COMMITTEE BEST PRACTICE

Audit committees should schedule meetings at which the auditor can make all legally required disclosures to the audit committee sufficiently in advance of the filing of the audit report with the SEC so that they can make any necessary changes, and should carefully discuss alternative accounting treatments related to material items contained in the financial statements that are disclosed to them by the auditors.

As noted in Chapter 15, the SEC rules require the accounting firm to report to the audit committee, prior to the filing of its audit report with the SEC (among other things)[3]:

- All critical accounting policies and practices to be used
- All alternative accounting treatments within generally accepted accounting principles (GAAP) for policies and practices related to material items that have been discussed with management of the issuer or registered investment company, including the ramifications of the use of such alternative disclosures and treatments and the treatment preferred by the registered public accounting firm
- Other material written communications between the registered public accounting firm and the management of the issuer or registered investment company, such as any management letter or schedule of unadjusted differences

Audit committees must schedule meetings with the auditors sufficiently in advance of filing the audited financial statements with the SEC so that they have time to consider all of the disclosures legally required to be made by the auditor to them, and to make any appropriate changes. Audit committees must allow themselves sufficient time to discuss alternative accounting treatments disclosed by the auditors.

DISCLOSURES TO INVESTORS OF SERVICES PROVIDED BY THE AUDITOR

Public companies are now required to provide, in their annual proxy statements, disclosure of these categories of fees paid to the independent accountant for the two most recent fiscal years:

- Audit fees
- Audit-related fees
- Tax fees
- All other fees

Audit fees include fees for services necessary to perform and audit or review in accordance with GAAP and fees for services that generally only the independent accountant reasonably can provide, such as comfort letters, statutory audits, attest services, consents, and assistance with SEC filings. The issuer must describe the services provided other than for audit fees and disclose the percentage of services approved by the audit committee. The disclosures must also include the audit committee's policies and procedures for preapproval of services by the independent accountant as well as the percent of fees paid subject to the de minimis exception.

An investment company must disclose audit and nonaudit fees, with a breakdown by types of services, from services provided directly to the investment company and nonaudit fees from services provided to all other entities in the investment company complex where the services were subject to preapproval by the investment company's audit committee. It must also disclose if the audit committee has considered whether the provision of nonaudit services provided to the investment company's adviser and its related parties that were not subject to the investment company audit committee's preapproval is compatible with maintaining the principal accountant's independence.

The August 13, 2003, FAQ Release attempted to clarify what is included in "audit-related fees"[4]:

Question 7

Q: What fee disclosure category is appropriate for professional fees in connection with an audit of the financial statements of a carve-out entity in anticipation of a subsequent divestiture?

A: The release establishes a new category, "Audit-Related Fees," which enables registrants to present the audit fee relationship with the principal accountant in a more transparent fashion. In general, "Audit-Related Fees" are assurance and related services (e.g., due diligence services) that traditionally are performed by the independent accountant. More specifically, these services would include, among others: employee benefit plan audits, due diligence related to mergers and acquisitions, accounting consultations and audits in connection with acquisitions, internal control reviews, attest services related to financial reporting that are not required by statute or regulation and consultation concerning financial accounting and reporting standards. Fees for the above services would be disclosed under "Audit-Related Fees."

Question 8

Q: Would fees paid to the audit firm for operational audit services be included in "Audit-Related Fees"?

A: No. "Audit-Related Fees" are fees for assurance and related services by the principal accountant that are traditionally performed by the principal accountant and which are "reasonably related to the performance of the audit or review of the registrant's financial statements." Operational audits would not be related to the audit or review of the financial statements and, therefore, the fees for these services should be included in "All Other Fees." As required by the rules, the registrant would need to include a narrative description of the services included in the "All Other Fees" category.

ENDNOTES

1. These FAQs are currently designated as Questions 3 through 5 under the heading "Audit Committee Pre-Approval" on the SEC's Web site (as modified December 14, 2004).
2. August 13, 2003, the Office of Chief Accountant release of answers to "Frequently Asked Questions."
3. SEC Rel. No. 33-8183, effective May 6, 2003 as amended by Rel. No. 33-8518, effective March 8, 2005.
4. These FAQs are currently designated as Questions 7 and 8 under the heading "Fee Disclosures" on the SEC's Web site (as modified December 14, 2004).

Part IV

Private and Not-for-Profit Organizations

Chapter 17

Corporate Governance for Family-Owned and Other Private Businesses

---

BEST PRACTICE

Private companies (including family-owned businesses) can benefit from the use of independent directors or, alternatively, an independent board of advisors.

The best practices listed in Chapters 2 through 10 of this book are applicable to private companies, including family-owned businesses. Small private companies may not be able to attract independent directors to their board because of liability concerns. If this is the case, a board of advisors can be formed to mitigate any liability concerns. The charter of the board of advisors should indicate that the advisors do not have the powers or authority of a board of directors. (See Chapter 2.)

The Sarbanes-Oxley Act of 2002 does not generally apply to family-owned and other private businesses. Therefore, there is no legislative compulsion to have these organizations comply with good corporate governance. However, there are good practical and financial reasons to do so.

All private businesses produce financial statements, and almost all private businesses seek bank and other institutional financing using these financial statements. The principals of private businesses are typically guarantors of these bank loans and, therefore, are personally liable for any covenant or payment defaults. Bank loans typically require a warranty and representation concerning the accuracy of the financial statements provided to the bank and their compliance with generally accepted accounting principles (GAAP). If these financial statements are wrong or do not comply with GAAP, the personal net worth of the principal shareholders may be in jeopardy.

The use of independent directors on the audit committee of a private company creates a perception of good corporate governance, which is helpful in bank relationships and in raising capital from investors. If independent directors are permitted to establish an independent audit committee and have access to an independent external and internal auditor for information, and if the independent director pays attention to the culture of the organization, these activities can pay handsome dividends to the private company. The use of an independent audit committee permits greater assurance as to the accuracy of the financial statements and their compliance with GAAP.

FAMILY-OWNED BUSINESSES

BEST PRACTICE

Establish dispute resolution mechanisms in the charter of family-owned businesses that are effective automatically once the founder dies or retires.

The greatest benefit of good corporate governance is to establish dispute resolution mechanisms for family-owned businesses. Once the founder of the family-owned business passes away or retires, it is not unusual for disputes to occur among his or her children or grandchildren or other relatives in the business. Indeed, sensational litigation between family members is very common. Such litigation is extremely expensive, diverts the time of the management away from the business, and many times results in the sale or failure of the business.

Family-owned businesses are particularly susceptible to disputes because business issues and emotional family issues get intertwined. Sibling rivalry mixes with genuine business disagreements and the results can be disastrous to the business.

Many family-owned businesses do not last beyond the second or third generation because of this heady mixture of emotion and business. The businesses are sold, liquidated, or end up in bankruptcy.

These unfortunate results can be avoided if the founder of the business, while still in control of the business, establishes a dispute resolution mechanism using independent directors to resolve the disputes. An example of a dispute resolution mechanism, upheld by the courts, is described in the Hanover Foods Corporation case.

BEST PRACTICE

Insert dispute resolution provisions into the charter of family business, using independent directors to resolve the dispute after the death of the founder.

Hanover Foods Corporation

Hanover Foods Corporation ("HFC") is a vertically integrated processor of food products located in Hanover, Pennsylvania, with 10 plants in Pennsylvania and plants in Maryland, Delaware, New Jersey, and Guatemala. HFC is involved in the growing, processing, canning, freezing, freeze-drying, packaging, marketing, and distribution of its products under its own trademarks as well as other branded, customer, and private labels.

During the relevant time frame, the Class B common stock of HFC was owned generally by less than 40 members of the Warehime family and was the only voting stock of the company. During this time frame, HFC's Class A common stock was nonvoting and was publicly traded on the Nasdaq Bulletin Board.

Alan Warehime ("Alan"), arguably the founder of both HFC and its sister company, Snyders of Hanover (Snyders Pretzels), had three children, John, Sally, and Michael. As part of his estate planning, Alan established a 10-year voting trust expiring in 1997 to vote a majority of the Class B shares of HFC. Upon Alan's death, John, his oldest son, became the sole voting trustee. The voting trust was created in 1987 and expired in 1997 because that was the maximum period (10 years) then permitted under Pennsylvania law. Michael was given control of Snyders of Hanover, and each of the children was given equity in each of the family-owned businesses.

When Alan died in 1991, John succeeded Alan as sole voting trustee of the Class B common stock of HFC. Disputes arose between Michael and Sally on one hand and John on the other concerning HFC. Until the HFC voting trust expired in 1997, John had all the voting power; it became clear that, once the voting trust expired in 1997, Michael, Sally, and John would be in a free-for-all fight for control, and it was likely that the company would be sold.

Alan had wisely created an independent board of directors for HFC. The HFC independent directors decided to hire their own counsel in 1996 (namely, the author). The independent directors also hired an investment banker and other outside advisors to assist them in evaluating the strategic alternatives for HFC once the voting trust expired.

After extensive deliberations, the independent directors decided to install a dispute resolution mechanism in the articles of incorporation of HFC before the voting trust expired. The dispute resolution mechanism permitted the independent directors, in the event of a dispute among the members of the Warehime family, to cast approximately 80 percent of the votes of all Class B shareholders. This permitted the independent directors to decide most disputes among members of the Warehime family unless the remaining shareholders were overwhelmingly on one side or the other.

The specific dispute resolution mechanism used was to create a special class of voting stock that, for a five-year period, had 35 votes per share in the event of a dispute among members of the family, and could be voted by the independent directors in their capacity as trustees of the HFC 401(k) plan trust. This special class of shares was then contributed to the HFC 401(k) plan trust.

After significant litigation concerning this dispute resolution mechanism, it was upheld by the Pennsylvania Supreme Court in two separate decisions.[1] As a result, HFC today remains an independent company.

Similar dispute resolution mechanisms could be established in other family-owned businesses prior to the death or retirement of the founder, to preserve the family-owned business for the future.

PRIVATELY OWNED BUSINESSES IN VICINITY OF INSOLVENCY

BEST PRACTICE

When the organization is in the "vicinity of insolvency," independent directors should hire their own independent counsel to assist them in performing their potential fiduciary duties to creditors.

In privately owned businesses, it is typical for the principal shareholder or share-holders to sit on the board of directors or, in the case of a limited liability company, the board of managers. As long as the organization is solvent and able to pay its bills, the directors or managers owe their fiduciary duties to the organization and, under Delaware law, to the equity holders. Since the board of directors of a privately held company usually consists of the major equity holders, the duties of the directors are typically to the organization and to themselves, in their capacity as equity holders of the organization. If there are equity holders other than the directors, under Delaware law these directors owe fiduciary duties to all of the equity holders as well as the organization.

However, once the organization begins to have financial problems, a line of cases says that the fiduciary duty of the directors of the private company may be owed to creditors as well as equity holders. Some courts create such a duty to creditors when the private company is in the "vicinity of insolvency." In effect, the creditors are treated like equity holders by the courts when it is unlikely there will be any distribution to the equity holders if the business is liquidated.

It is very helpful to the principal shareholders of a company in the "vicinity of insolvency" to have independent directors on its board. It is typical for a private company to engage in transactions with its principal shareholders; for example, it may lend money to the principal shareholder or set compensation for the principal shareholder that, at least in hindsight, is excessive. If the private company in the "vicinity of insolvency" ultimately winds up in bankruptcy, a trustee in bankruptcy may well sue the principal shareholder for such insider loans or allegedly excessive compensation. Thus, in the event of a bankruptcy, the principal shareholder will not only lose his or her own investment in the company, but could also become personally liable to creditors.

The use of independent directors to approve loans from the private company to the principal shareholder and to approve compensation of the principal shareholder and other insider transactions can significantly assist the principal shareholder in avoiding such personal liability. This is particularly true if the independent directors establish a good record with regard to their decision to approve such insider transactions, including the use of independent consultants to advise them.

Trace International Holdings, Inc.[2]

The case against Marshall S. Cogan, the controlling stockholder of Trace International Holdings, Inc. ("Trace"), a closely held private company, illustrates what can go wrong if the private company does not utilize the services of independent directors to approve insider transactions when the company is in the "vicinity of insolvency."

In May 2003, the United States District Court for the Southern District of New York in *Pereira v. Cogan* directors and officers of Trace, a Delaware corporation, were held personally liable for breach of fiduciary duty. The case was brought by the Trace bankruptcy trustee, for millions of dollars of losses suffered by Trace (and thus by its credi-

(continued)

tors in bankruptcy) as a result of self-dealing (including loans and excessive compensation), by its majority stockholder, chief executive officer, and chairman, Marshall S. Cogan. Judge Sweet noted that Pereira raised "novel" issues of Delaware law, including to what extent a controlling stockholder and founder of a privately held corporation can be held liable for self-dealing and what the obligations of the officers and directors of such corporation are when faced with the possibility that such controlling stockholder (and their boss) is acting solely in his best interests and not those of the corporation. In July 2005 the lower court decision was reversed on a procedural error, namely the failure to provide a jury trial; nevertheless, the case is illustrative of the problems of a private company in the vicinity of insolvency.

The U.S. District Court for the Southern District of New York found that Trace was either insolvent or "in the vicinity of insolvency" from 1995 until 1999, with the consequence that during that period the directors owed a fiduciary duty to Trace's creditors. The court also held that a provision in Trace's certificate of incorporation protecting directors from liability was inapplicable, since that provision did not limit directors' liability in an action by or on behalf of creditors. In any event, the provision did not prevent directors from being sued for a breach of the duty of loyalty, which is owed under Delaware law.

In Trace, the five principal defendants other than Marshall S. Cogan were all officers of Trace; three of them were also Trace directors. The two officers who were not directors (an accountant and Trace's general counsel) were held liable, although not to the same extent as the directors.

Many private companies put their accountant or attorney on the board of directors thinking that they have established an independent board. In general, the court will not treat suppliers of professional or other services to the organization as independent directors for most purposes.

In Trace, these points should be noted:

- None of the defendants (other than Cogan) materially benefited from Cogan's self-dealing.
- Liability was imposed not for what the defendants did but for their inattention to Trace's affairs. Among the many examples of inattention and poor corporate governance mentioned by the court:
  - The last Trace board meeting at which a quorum was recorded and minutes were taken was in September 1995; thereafter, until 1999, the board acted solely by unanimous written consents prepared by in-house counsel or by outside counsel (including three well-known law firms).
  - No process existed for providing financial information to the directors.
  - The general counsel did not advise the board or the officers regarding their respective duties.
  - Trace did not have an audit committee and until 1995 did not have a compensation committee. (A closely held Delaware corporation is not required by law to have either committee). The compensation committee never convened in person.
  - The compensation committee and the directors allowed an automatic renewal clause (for a new 10-year term) in Cogan's employment agreement to take effect without any consideration whatsoever.
  - The compensation committee did not retain a compensation consultant or conduct salary surveys.

(continued)

This case should remind privately held directors and officers that good corporate governance practices are just as important for privately held organizations as for publicly held companies. If a private company goes into bankruptcy, a creditors' committee or a trustee acting on behalf of creditors will examine the board's actions under a microscope and will not hesitate to bring an action against directors and officers to create a fund for creditors. The use of truly independent directors on the board of the private company helps insulate the principal shareholder from any such legal action.

ENDNOTES

1. *Warehime v. Warehime*, 563 Pa 400, 761 A.2d 1138 (2000); *Warehime v. Warehime*, 860 A.2d 41 (Pa. 2004).
2. *Pereira v. Cogan*, 2003 WL 21039976 (S.D.N.Y. May 27, 2003).

Chapter 18

Corporate Governance for Not-for-Profit Organizations

The corporate governance structure of a not-for-profit does not have to replicate all of the requirements for public companies. However, at a minimum, all not-for-profit organizations that produce financial statements should have an audit committee consisting of independent persons, preferably individuals who would satisfy the independence standards of either the Nasdaq Stock Market or the New York Stock Exchange. The best practices listed in Chapters 2 through 10 of this book are equally applicable to not-for-profit organizations and should be read in conjunction with this chapter.

Not-for-profit does not mean nonliability. One large association of not-for-profits reports that director and officer liability claims have doubled during the past five years, fueled by employment-related actions. The average settlement value of director and officer liability suits also doubled to approximately $45,000 and can range up to $1 million.

The basis for not-for-profit director and officer liability actions has not changed much since the late 1990s. Employment-related suits from employees, led primarily by age discrimination, sex discrimination, and wrongful termination, comprise 90 percent of all loss activity. A variety of stakeholder claims filed by donors and benefit recipients for financial mismanagement, antitrust, and membership issues contribute the remaining 10 percent. Recent actions by regulators suggest that government enforcement of foundation and charitable institution rules also contribute to the losses.

A few examples of scandals involving not-for-profit organizations follow. The examples suggest the need for stricter corporate governance.

AHERF

Allegheny Health, Education and Research Foundation (AHERF) was at one time the largest nonprofit healthcare organization in Pennsylvania. From 1987 to 1997, AHERF expanded rapidly, acquiring other not-for-profit healthcare organizations, including several in the Philadelphia metropolitan area: the Medical College of Pennsylvania, United Hospitals, Inc., Hahnemann University Hospital, and the Graduate Health System. The acquired entities became direct or indirect subsidiaries of AHERF.[1] On July 21, 1998, AHERF and four of its subsidiaries filed for protection under Chapter 11 of the U.S. Bankruptcy Code. The $1.3 billion bankruptcy of AHERF was the nation's largest not-for-profit healthcare failure.[2]

AHERF was an umbrella holding company and managed and provided centralized corporate support services for the acquired entities, but did not assume liability for their preexisting debt. The obligation to repay debt within AHERF was placed on collections of one or more of its not-for-profit subsidiaries known as obligated groups. By 1997, AHERF had five obligated groups: Allegheny General Hospital, Allegheny University Medical Centers, Allegheny Hospitals, Centennial, and Allegheny Hospitals, New Jersey, and several subsidiaries collectively known as the Delaware Valley Obligated Group (Delaware Valley). By the time of the bankruptcy in July 1998, AHERF's obligated groups were responsible for repaying at least 13 bond issues, with outstanding debt of more than $900 million.

The individual issues ranged from $12.7 million to $306 million, the latter incurred on behalf of Delaware Valley in a 1996 refinancing of its older bonds. At least $400 million of AHERF bonds were not supported by a letter of credit, bond insurance, or other credit enhancement.

Between December 1996 and February 1998, AHERF and Delaware Valley issued annual financial statements and disclosure reports that materially misrepresented, among other things, AHERF's and Delaware Valley's net income. AHERF, through certain members of its senior management and in violation of GAAP: (1) overstated Delaware Valley's 1996 net income before extraordinary items and change in accounting principles by approximately $40 million (by failing to adjust Delaware Valley's bad debt reserves to reflect uncollectible accounts receivable); (2) overstated Delaware Valley's and its own 1997 net income through the inappropriate transfers of approximately $99.6 million in reserves (that were utilized to address the bad debt reserve shortfall not addressed in 1996 as well as an additional shortfall in 1997); and (3) overstated AHERF's 1997 net income by misclassifying certain restricted trust funds (the Lockhart Trusts).

The misclassification of the restricted funds and the transfers in the disclosure reports resulted in the overstatement of AHERF's consolidated net income for the period ended June 30, 1997, by approximately $114 million and overstated Delaware Valley's net income by approximately $60 million. Significantly, both Delaware Valley and AHERF would have posted substantial net losses for fiscal year 1997 without the fraudulent reporting activity.

Among the corporate governance failures discovered in the bankruptcy were:

- AHERF had a large parent board whose membership varied between 25 and 35 persons (rather than the optimal smaller board recommended in this book), and board meetings were scripted affairs that limited board oversight and participation by board members.

- AHERF had a network of 10 different boards with little overlap in their membership, with the consequence that directors on one board were never certain what was happening elsewhere.

- Board members and officers had conflicts of interest, including five board members who were current or former directors or executives of Mellon Bank (the chief AHERF creditor) and officers who were also officers of hospitals that were debtors of AHERF.

- AHERF's corporate by-laws allowed the chief executive officer (CEO) to move cash between and among operating units without board oversight.

Board members relied solely on the outside independent auditor, which gave AHERF a clean bill of health in its last audit (June 1997), rather than using other mechanisms to discharge the board's oversight function.

THE NATURE CONSERVANCY[3]

In May 2003, a three-part series in the *Washington Post* placed a spotlight on the operations of The Nature Conservancy, the largest philanthropic environmental group in the world. The articles noted that the disclosure of the 2001 compensation of Steven J. McCormick, president and CEO, had not highlighted lucrative components: a signing bonus of $75,000, a living allowance of $75,000, and a home loan for $1.55 million. Some contributors were also upset by the Conservancy's close relationship with business interest and so-called conservation buyer deals. In those deals, the Conservancy sold, at a discount, land that it first encumbered with development restrictions. In several cases, Conservancy insiders bought the land in deals that allowed them to build the homes they wanted. To make the Conservancy whole, the buyers wrote checks as donations—and then took tax deductions.

As a result of this unfavorable publicity, members of the Conservancy were outraged and a stricter corporate governance system was installed.

UNITED WAY OF THE NATIONAL CAPITAL AREA[4]

In 2002, it was revealed that Oral Suer, former CEO of the United Way of the National Capital Area, stole $497,000 from the charity. The revelation produced outrage among contributors. A forensic audit in 2003 confirmed that Suer, who retired at the end of 2001, had loaded up on unreimbursed advances, questionable vacation and sick-leave cash payments, and excess deferred pay. His wrongdoing dated as far back as 1976. Other employees had allegedly cashed personal checks and had the finance department hold them until they had the money to cover them (a short-term loan), took reimbursements for tax liability they incurred for personal use of United Way Care, and so on.

PIPEVINE INC.[5]

In 2004, the United Way of the Bay Area agreed to pay a $13 million settlement to help make up a multimillion-dollar shortfall when PipeVine Inc., the San Francisco donation precession center it founded, was closed.

PipeVine processed more than $100 million in charitable contributions per year and worked with some of the country's largest companies, including Bay Area employers such as Bank of America, Clorox, and ChevronTexaco. In exchange for a fee, PipeVine was supposed to take money raised from corporate workplace campaigns and an Internet fundraising site and route the money to thousands of charities. But when PipeVine closed, it acknowledged that it had misspent millions of dollars on its own operations.

Partly as a result of the PipeVine fiasco, a California law was passed in 2004, which mandated that the board of every charitable corporation required to register with the attorney general that receives annual gross revenues of $2 million must appoint an audit committee. The board must appoint members of the audit committee, which may include nonboard members. The committee members must be independent, meaning they cannot be members of the staff or receive any compensation from the corporation aside from compensation for services as a director, and cannot have a material financial interest in any entity doing business with the corporation. If the corporation has a finance committee, it must be separate from the audit committee. The chair of the audit committee cannot be on the finance committee, and members of the finance committee must constitute less than one-half of the membership of the audit committee. Educational organizations, hospitals, and religious organizations are specifically exempted from application of the statute.

AUDIT COMMITTEES OF NOT-FOR-PROFIT ORGANIZATIONS

As previously mentioned in Chapter 2, all not-for-profit organizations should have an audit committee composed of independent directors. If the not-for-profit organization is not raising debt or equity capital, the audit committee should at least have these minimum functions:

BEST PRACTICES

- Create an internal audit function (which may be outsourced) that is hired and compensated by the audit committee.
- Preapprove all auditing services and all nonauditing services of the auditor, subject to the same de minimus exception as applies to public company audit committees.
- Establish procedures for:
  - The receipt, retention, and treatment of complaints received by the organization regarding accounting, internal accounting controls, or auditing matters.
  - The confidential, anonymous submission by employees of the organization of concerns regarding questionable accounting or auditing matters.
- Treat allegations of material financial or legal misconduct (including whistleblower complaints) seriously, and investigations should be conducted by the independent audit committee, preferably using independent counsel (e.g., to avoid the Cornell University Medical School fiasco dis-

(continued)

---

cussed in Chapter 2) if the allegations (if true) may involve top management or would be embarrassing to the organization or top management.

- Monitor the independence of the auditor.
- Listen to and discuss all reports given to the audit committee by man-
  agement or any internal auditor.
- Create a written charter that states the audit committee's purpose and
  states the minimum duties and responsibilities of the audit committee.
- Prohibit personal loans to directors and executives officers.

In addition, such organizations should at least once a year have a meeting of
the independent directors, without management present.

If the not-for-profit organization is selling debt or equity securities, either publicly or privately, these additional steps should also be taken.

BEST PRACTICES

- Have management certify to the audit committee the financial information
  provided to investors in the debt or equity securities of the organization.
- Rotate the lead audit partner and audit review partners at suitable intervals.
- Have the auditing firm report to the audit committee on critical accounting policies and practices and alternative and preferable treatments.
- Require that one member of the audit committee possess financial
  expertise.

COMPENSATION COMMITTEES OF NOT-FOR-PROFIT ORGANIZATIONS

As discussed in Chapter 6, compensation of executives of tax-exempt organizations has become a major issue in the media and with Congress and state attorneys
general. For example, *The New York Times* of February 11, 2006, disclosed a state
investigation into the finances of the J. Paul Getty Trust in Los Angeles, the nation's third largest private foundation, resulting from a $3 million severance pay-
ment to the director of the Getty Museum and a $250,000 severance payment to
another trust executive. Information about the severance payments came to light
after the trust's president and CEO resigned amid questions about his leadership
and possible abuse of expenses and perquisites.

In 2004, the IRS described its Tax Exempt Compensation Enforcement Project, an aggressive audit and compliance check program in which 2,000 charities
and foundations will be asked about their compensation practices. In 2005, the
IRS's Exempt Organizations Division's new compliance unit sent an estimated
1,250 letters to a wide range of charities and private foundations inquiring about

executive compensation, insider transactions (e.g., loans or sales of property to officers or directors), 990 reporting, and other issues that impact compensation.

To maintain tax-exempt status under Section 501(c)(3), an organization must be both organized *and* operated so that no part of its net earnings inures to the benefit of any private shareholder or individual.[6] In addition, a charity must not be organized and operated for the benefit of private interests, such as designated individuals, founders of the organization or their family members, shareholders, or persons controlled (directly or indirectly) by such interests.[7]

Excessive compensation is one form of private inurement or impermissible private benefit. Whether a particular compensation arrangement is excessive or reasonable is a question of fact, to be determined based on the facts and circumstances of each case. For tax purposes, "reasonableness" is determined according to the standard applicable to business deductions under Section 162 of the Internal Revenue Code (Code), taking into account the aggregate benefits provided to a person and the rate at which deferred compensation accrues.[8] In this context "reasonable" compensation for services is the amount that would ordinarily be paid for like services by like enterprises (whether taxable or tax-exempt) under like circumstances (i.e., reasonable compensation).

The principal enforcement tools available to the IRS are known as Intermediate Sanctions (Section 4958 of the Code) for public charities (organizations described in Section 501(c)(3) or 501(c)(4) of the Code) and the "Self-Dealing Excise Tax" (Section 4941 of the Code), which applies to private foundations. In addition, the IRS can revoke the tax-exempt status of the organization.

Section 4958 imposes taxes on so-called excess benefit transactions with "disqualified persons." Excess benefit transactions refer generally to transactions in which the economic benefit, directly or directly, to the disqualified person exceeds the value of the services or other consideration received by the tax-exempt organization. The additional tax, which is imposed on the disqualified person, can be as much as 25 percent of the excess benefit and can rise to 225 percent of the excess benefit if the transaction is not corrected within the taxable period. Disqualified persons include (among others) persons who are in a position to exercise substantial influence over the affairs of the organization (e.g., CEOs, chief financial officers, etc.) and members of their families (as defined in the Code and the regulations).

In cases where an initial 25 percent tax has been imposed on disqualified persons, a 10 percent tax is imposed by Section 4958 on the organization managers (e.g., directors and officers) who participate in the transaction knowing that it was an excess benefit transaction, unless the participation is not willful and is due to reasonable cause.

BEST PRACTICE

If there is the slightest doubt as to the reasonableness of executive compensation, compensation committees should receive a reasoned written opinion as to the reasonableness of executive compensation from an independent compensation professional.

There is a safe harbor under which participation by an organization manager in a transaction will ordinarily not be subject to the 10 percent tax, even though the transaction is later held to be an excess benefit transaction. Specifically, an organization manager is ordinarily not considered to have knowingly participated in a transaction to the extent that, after full disclosure of the factual situation to an appropriate professional, the organization manager relies on a reasoned written opinion of that professional regarding the elements of the transaction within the professional's expertise.

MAINTAINING TAX-EXEMPT STATUS

BEST PRACTICE

An insider transaction with a tax-exempt organization or any other transaction involving a conflict of interest should not be approved by the board of directors in the absence of a written opinion from an independent and competent third party as to the fairness of the transaction. If a so-called excess benefit transaction has occurred, the board should take prompt action to correct it and to impose safeguards against similar transactions in the future.

State attorneys general are constantly reviewing insider transactions with tax-exempt organizations within their jurisdictions. In addition, the Council on Foundations, which represents more than 2,000 grant-making foundations and corporations, also helps to police its members. For example, it was reported in *The New York Times* of February 11, 2006 that the Council on Foundations was investigating a land deal between the J. Paul Getty Trust and a friend of the trust's president. As noted, Section 4958 of the Code imposes significant taxes on the recipient of excess benefit transactions and potentially on the board of directors.

Any transaction that may involve a conflict of interest should be subject to independent review and scrutiny as to its fairness. The best protection for the board of directors and other organization managers is a written opinion from an independent and competent third party as to the fairness of the transaction.

Such an opinion will protect the tax-exempt status of the organization as well as protect the organization managers from tax assessments under Section 4958 of the Code. In determining whether to continue to recognize the tax-exempt status of an applicable tax-exempt organization that engages in one or more excess benefit transactions, the IRS will consider all relevant facts and circumstances, including:

- The size and scope of the organization's regular exempt activities
- The size and scope of the excess benefit transaction(s) in relation to the organization's regular exempt activities
- Whether the organization has been involved in repeated excess benefit transactions

- Whether the organization has implemented safeguards to prevent future violations

- Whether the excess benefit transaction has been corrected or the organization has made good faith efforts to seek correction from the disqualified persons who benefited from the excess benefit transaction

The last two factors will weigh more strongly in favor of continued tax exemption where the organization discovers the excess benefit transaction and takes corrective action before it is discovered by the IRS.

THE VOLUNTEER PROTECTION ACT OF 1997[9]

Federal law provides certain protection for acts or omissions of directors of not-for-profit boards that is not available to directors of for-profit boards. The Volunteer Protection Act of 1997 (VPA) shields "volunteers" from liability caused by a simple act of negligence, and a "volunteer" serving as a director, officer, or trustee is covered. The term "volunteer" means an individual performing services for a nonprofit organization or a governmental entity who does not receive compensation (other than reasonable reimbursement or allowance for expenses actually incurred) or any other thing of value in lieu of compensation in excess of $500.00 per year. A "nonprofit organization" includes Section 501 (c)(3) organizations and any not-for-profit organization that is organized and conducted for public benefit and operated primarily for charitable, civic, educational, religious, welfare, or health purposes (subject to an exception for hate crime organizations).

There are important exceptions to liability protection, including some of these: willful conduct and gross negligence are not protected; likewise, reckless misconduct or a conscious, flagrant indifference to the rights or safety of an individual are not protected.

However, the VPA still offers some degree of comfort and protection for the individuals serving on not-for-profit boards who exercise care and good judgment and who do not receive more than $500.00 per year in compensation. The law does not protect the entity itself, only volunteers. It also preempts the patchwork of state laws, unless the state provides greater protections. Some states, such as Pennsylvania, have even greater protections.

PANEL ON THE NONPROFIT SECTOR

A final report to the U.S. Congress and the Nonprofit Sector, dated June 2005,[10] issued by the Panel on the Nonprofit Sector, makes these recommendations, among others:

> **Financial Audits and Reviews**—Having financial statements prepared and audited in accordance with generally accepted accounting principles and auditing standards improves the quality of financial information available to governing boards, government officials, and the public. Congress should require charitable organizations with at least $1 million or more in annual revenues to conduct an audit and attach audited financial statements to their Form 990 series returns, and those with annual

revenues between $250,000 and $1 million to have their financial statements reviewed by an independent public accountant.

Executive Compensation—Charitable organizations should be required to disclose more clearly the compensation paid to their chief executive officer and other "disqualified persons" and to the five highest compensated employees. Congress should require officers and other disqualified persons who receive compensation that the IRS alleges is excessive to demonstrate that their compensation is reasonable, and should increase penalties imposed on individuals who receive and managers who approve excessive compensation. Members of boards or other authorized bodies who followed the rebuttable presumption procedures in determining the reasonableness of compensation should not ordinarily be subject to penalties, even if the compensation is later found to be excessive, but penalties should be imposed on board members and managers who approved such compensation if they did not follow those procedures nor otherwise exercised reasonable care in approving the transaction. As a matter of good practice, the full board of charitable organizations should approve any change in the compensation of the CEO annually and in advance and review the organization's full staff compensation program periodically.

Audit Committees—Charitable organizations should include individuals with some financial literacy on their boards of directors in accordance with the laws of their state or as a matter of recommended practice. Every charitable organization that has its financial statements independently audited, whether legally required or not, should consider establishing a separate audit committee of the board. If the board does not have sufficient financial literacy, and if state law permits, it may form an audit committee comprised of non-staff advisors who are not board members.

The board's responsibilities for overseeing the audit process and duties it should either perform itself or delegate to an audit committee include:

- Retaining and terminating the engagement of the independent auditor;
- Reviewing the terms of the auditor's engagement at least every five years;
- Overseeing the performance of the independent audit;
- Conferring with the auditor to ensure that the affairs of the organization are in order;
- Recommending approval of the annual audit report to the full board;
- Overseeing policies and procedures for encouraging whistleblowers to report questionable accounting or auditing matters of the organization;
- Approving any non-audit services performed by the auditing firm;
- Reviewing adoption and implementation of internal financial controls through the audit process; and
- Monitoring the organization's response to potentially illegal or unethical practices within the organization, including but not limited to fraudulent accounting.

Conflict of Interest and Misconduct—As a matter of recommended practice, charitable organizations should adopt and enforce a conflict of interest policy consistent with its state laws and organizational needs. The IRS should require every charitable organization to disclose on its Form 990 series return whether it has such a policy. Charitable organizations should also adopt policies and procedures that encourage and protect individuals who come forward with credible information on illegal practices or violations of adopted policies of the organization. There should be a vigorous sectorwide effort to educate and encourage all charitable organizations, regardless of size, to adopt and enforce policies and procedures to address possible conflicts of interest and to facilitate reporting of suspected malfeasance and misconduct by organization managers.

Recommendations for Charitable Organization Action

1. Every charitable organization, as a matter of recommended practice, should review its board size periodically to determine the most appropriate size to ensure effective governance and to meet the organization's goals and objectives. All boards should establish strong and effective mechanisms to ensure that the board carries out its oversight functions and that board members are aware of their legal and ethical responsibilities in ensuring that the organization is governed properly.
2. A board of directors should ensure, as a matter of recommended practice, that the positions of chief executive officer, board chair, and board treasurer are held by separate individuals. If the board deems it is in the best interests of the charitable organization to have the CEO serve as the board chair, the board should appoint a lead director to handle issues that require a separation of responsibilities.
3. The charitable sector should undertake a vigorous effort to provide information and education to its organizations regarding the roles and responsibilities of board members and the factors that boards should consider in evaluating the appropriate size and structure needed to ensure the most effective and responsible governance.

The recommendations of the Panel on the Nonprofit Sector should be carefully considered by all not-for-profit boards and trustees.

WHISTLEBLOWER POLICIES RECOMMENDED FOR NOT-FOR-PROFITS

Whistleblower policies are a key defense against fraud. According to a 2004 survey by the Association of Certified Fraud Examiners (ACFE), fraud is detected 40 percent of the time by tips.[11] A sample whistleblower policy that is recommended by the ACFE for not-for-profit organizations follows.

Start of Sample Whistleblower Policy

These points should be considered in developing and implementing a whistleblower policy:

- Consider state regulatory requirements, if any, in reporting instances of complaints.
- Determine, if possible, whether the complainant notified any regulatory or other industry and/or watchdog group(s) or press.

ABC ORGANIZATION WHISTLEBLOWER POLICY

The ABC Organization Code of Conduct (hereinafter referred to as the Code) requires directors, other volunteers, and employees to observe high standards of business and personal ethics in the conduct of their duties and responsibilities. Employees and representatives of the organization must practice honesty and integrity in fulfilling their responsibilities and comply with all applicable laws and regulations.

Reporting Responsibility

Each director, volunteer, and employee of ABC Organization has an obligation to report in accordance with this Whistleblower Policy (a) questionable or improper accounting or auditing matters, and (b) violations and suspected violations of ABC Organization's Code (hereinafter collectively referred to as "Concerns").

Authority of Audit Committee

All reported Concerns will be forwarded to the Audit Committee in accordance with the procedures set forth herein. The Audit Committee shall be responsible for investigating, and making appropriate recommendations to the Board of Directors, with respect to all reported Concerns.

No Retaliation

This Whistleblower Policy is intended to encourage and enable directors, volunteers, and employees to raise Concerns within the Organization for investigation and appropriate action. With this goal in mind, no director, volunteer, or employee who, in good faith, reports a Concern shall be subject to retaliation or, in the case of an employee, adverse employment consequences. Moreover, a volunteer or employee who retaliates against someone who has reported a Concern in good faith is subject to discipline up to and including dismissal from the volunteer position or termination of employment.

Reporting Concerns

Employees   Employees should first discuss their Concern with their immediate supervisor. If, after speaking with his or her supervisor, the individual continues to have reasonable grounds to believe the Concern is valid, the individual should report the Concern to the Director of Human Resources. In addition, if the individual is uncomfortable speaking with his or her supervisor, or the supervisor is a subject of the Concern, the individual should report his or her concern directly to the Director of Human Resources. If the Concern was reported verbally to the Director of Human Resources, the reporting individual, with assistance from the Director of Human Resources, shall reduce the Concern to writing. The Director of Human Resources is required to promptly report the Concern to the Chair of Audit Committee, which has specific and exclusive responsibility to investigate all Concerns. If the Director of Human Resources, for any reason, does not promptly forward the Concern to the Audit Committee, the reporting individual should directly report the Concern to the Chair of the Audit Committee. Contact information for the Chair of the Audit Committee may be obtained through the Human Resources Department. Concerns may be also be submitted anonymously. Such anonymous Concerns should be in writing and sent directly to the Chair of the Audit Committee.

Directors and Other Volunteers   Directors and other volunteers should submit Concerns in writing directly to the Chair of the Audit Committee. Contact information for the Chair of the Audit Committee may be obtained from the Chief Financial Officer.

Handling of Reported Violations

The Audit Committee shall address all reported Concerns. The Chair of the Audit Committee shall immediately notify the Audit Committee, the President, the Executive Director, and Chief Operating Officer of any such report. The Chair of the Audit Committee will notify the sender and acknowledge receipt of the Concern within five business days, if possible. It will not be possible to acknowledge receipt of anonymously submitted Concerns.

All reports will be promptly investigated by the Audit Committee, and appropriate corrective action will be recommended to the Board of Directors, if warranted by the investigation. In addition, action taken must include a conclusion and/or follow-up with the complainant for complete closure of the Concern.

The Audit Committee has the authority to retain outside legal counsel, accountants, private investigators, or any other resource deemed necessary to conduct a full and complete investigation of the allegations.

Acting in Good Faith

Anyone reporting a Concern must act in good faith and have reasonable grounds for believing the information disclosed indicates an improper accounting or auditing practice, or a violation of the Codes. The act of making allegations that prove to be unsubstantiated, and that prove to have been made maliciously, recklessly, or with the foreknowledge that the allegations are false, will be viewed as a serious disciplinary offense and may result in discipline, up to and including dismissal from the volunteer position or termination of employment. Such conduct may also give rise to other actions, including civil lawsuits.

Confidentiality

Reports of Concerns, and investigation pertaining thereto, shall be kept confidential to the extent possible, consistent with the need to conduct an adequate investigation.

Disclosure of reports of Concerns to individuals not involved in the investigation will be viewed as a serious disciplinary offense and may result in discipline, up to and including termination of employment. Such conduct may also give rise to other actions, including civil lawsuits. (See Exhibit 18.1.)

Exhibit 18.1 Sample Whistleblower Tracking Report

Instructions for Using This Tool. Before using this tool, the audit committee should review any applicable state or local laws or regulations, and the appropriate rules promulgated by other relevant regulatory bodies, if any.

Sample Whistleblower Tracking Report

Date Submitted	Tracking Number	Description of Concern	Submitted By Employee (E) Constituent (C) Vendor (V) Stakeholder (S) Other (O)	Current Status: R—Resolved UI—Under Investigation D—Dismissed W—Withdrawn P—Pending/ No Action	Actions Taken	
					Date	Comments

ENDNOTES

1. Speech by Stephen Weinstein, "Understanding AHERF: Observations on the Recent Settlements Involving Allegheny Health, Education and Research Foundation," August 1, 2000, www.sec.gov/news/speech/spch406.htm. Much of the material in this section is taken from this speech.
2. Lawton R. Burns, Ph.D and James Joo-Jin Kim, Professor, "The Fall of the House of AHERF: The Allegheny Bankruptcy," *Health Affairs* (January/February 2000), http://hcmg.wharton.upenn.edu/burnsl/.
3. "Senators Question Conservancy's Practices," *Washington Post,* June 8, 2005.
4. "Ex-Chief of Local United Way Sentenced," *Washington Post*, May 15, 2004.
5. "Charity Settles in PipeVine Fiasco," *San Francisco Chronicle*, February 19, 2004.
6. Treas. Reg. Section 1.501(c)(3)-1(c)(2).
7. Treas. Reg. Section 1.501(c)(3)-1(d)(1)(ii).
8. Treas. Reg. Section 53.4958-4(b)(1)(ii)(A).
9. United States Congress (111 Stat. 218).
10. Panel on the Nonprofit Sector Convened by Independent Sector, "Strengthening Transparency Governance Accountability of Charitable Organizations," final report to Congress and the Nonprofit Sector, June 2005. www.nonprofitpanel.org/final/Panel_Final_Report.pdf.
11. "2004 Report to the Nation on Occupational Fraud and Abuse," Association of Certified Fraud Examiners. www.cfenet.com/pdfs/2004/RttN.pdf.

Part V

Appendixes

Summary of Sarbanes-Oxley Act of 2002

On July 30, 2002, the Sarbanes-Oxley Act of 2002 (Sarbanes-Oxley) was signed into law by President George W. Bush. Sarbanes-Oxley is a comprehensive revision of the federal securities laws applicable to public companies. Sarbanes-Oxley establishes an oversight board to regulate the public accounting firms that audit public companies; requires the adoption of new auditor and audit committee independence standards; requires executive officers of public companies to certify the company's Securities and Exchange Commission (SEC) reports; restricts trading by directors and executives during benefit plan blackout periods; increases the liability for violations of the federal securities laws by public companies, their management, and others; and imposes additional obligations on attorneys to report securities law violations and conflicts of interest.

This appendix provides a description of the significant provisions of Sarbanes-Oxley, some of which took effect July 30, 2002, and others of which are subject to the phase-ins or additional rule-making actions by the SEC.

A. PUBLIC COMPANY ACCOUNTING OVERSIGHT BOARD

Sarbanes-Oxley establishes the Public Company Accounting Oversight Board (the "PCAOB") to:

- Register and conduct inspections of public accounting firms that prepare audit reports for a company, the securities of which are registered under Section 12 of the Securities Exchange Act of 1934, as amended (the 1934 Act) or that is required to file reports under Section 15(d) of the 1934 Act or that has filed a registration statement under the Securities Act of 1933, as amended (the 1933 Act), which has not yet become effective (a "public company").
- Oversee the audits of public companies.
- Establish auditing quality control, ethics, independence, and other standards and rules relating to the preparation of audit reports for public companies.
- Investigate, inspect, and enforce compliance relating to registered public accounting firms, associated persons, and the obligations and liabilities of accountants.
- Set a budget and manage the operations of the PCAOB.
- Conduct disciplinary proceedings and impose sanctions for violations of Sarbanes-Oxley.

1. Establishment of the PCAOB

- The PCAOB will be a not-for-profit, private corporate entity and will not be an agency or establishment of the U.S. government.
- The PCAOB will consist of five members.
- The PCAOB may not include more than two certified public accountants. If one of the two PCAOB members who are certified public accountants is the chairperson of the PCAOB, such member may not have been a practicing CPA during the last five years.
- Each PCAOB member must serve in a full-time capacity.
- Each PCAOB member will serve for a five-year term (with a two-term limit).
- The PCAOB will be staggered.

2. Registration with the PCAOB

- Sarbanes-Oxley requires registration with the PCAOB by any public accounting firm that performs or participates in any audit report with respect to any public company.
- Registered public accounting firms must file annual reports with the PCAOB.
- Applications and annual reports of registered public accounting firms will be available for public inspection.
- 180 days after the SEC deems the PCAOB "operational," only registered public accounting firms may perform audits for public companies.

3. Auditing, Quality Control, and Independence Standards and Rules

- The PCAOB will adopt quality control and ethics standards to be used by registered public accounting firms in the preparation and issuance of audit reports.
- Each audit report of a public company must be signed by two partners, one of whom was involved in the audit and the other of whom concurs in the review and approval of the audit and must describe in the audit report the scope of the auditor's internal control structure.
- Registered public accounting firms must retain work papers for at least seven years.

4. Inspections of Registered Public Accounting Firms

- Sarbanes-Oxley requires the PCAOB to conduct inspections to assess compliance with Sarbanes-Oxley by each registered public accounting firm and associated persons of that firm.
- Such inspections will occur annually for registered public accounting firms regularly performing audits for more than 100 public companies and once every three years if the registered public accounting firm regularly performs audits for less than 100 public companies.

5. Investigations and Disciplinary Proceedings

- Sarbanes-Oxley permits the PCAOB to conduct investigations of any act or practice (or omission to act) by a registered public accounting firm or any associated person who violates Sarbanes-Oxley, including the securities laws relating to the preparation and issuance of audit reports and the obligations and liabilities of accountants with respect to them.
- Sarbanes-Oxley also permits the PCAOB to impose disciplinary or remedial sanctions for violations of such act.
- Civil fines can be imposed up to $100,000 for a natural person and $2.0 million for all others and may be more if the PCAOB finds intentional or repeated negligent conduct. In addition, the PCAOB may suspend or revoke registration under Sarbanes-Oxley, or limit a registered public accounting firm's activities.
- Sarbanes-Oxley authorizes the PCAOB to impose sanctions on a registered accounting firm or its supervisory personnel for failure to supervise.

6. Foreign Public Accounting Firms

- Sarbanes-Oxley also applies to: (1) foreign public accounting firms that prepare or furnish an audit report or perform material services on which a registered public accounting firm relies, in issuing its audit report or any opinion contained in the audit report with respect to any public company; and (2) audit work papers prepared by the foreign public accounting firm.

7. SEC Oversight of the PCAOB

- Sarbanes-Oxley grants the SEC general oversight of the PCAOB and the power to review PCAOB actions, including general modification and rescission of PCAOB authority.

8. Accounting Standards

Sarbanes-Oxley amends the 1933 Act to:

- Authorize the SEC to recognize, as "generally accepted" for purposes of the securities laws, any accounting principles established by a standard-setting body.
- Direct the SEC to study and report to Congress on the adoption by the U.S. financial reporting system of a "principles-based" accounting system (as opposed to the current "rules-based" reporting system).

9. Funding

Sarbanes-Oxley provides for PCAOB funding to cover the PCAOB's budget by imposing annual assessments to be paid by public companies. In addition, registered public accounting firms will also pay registration and annual fees.

B. AUDITOR INDEPENDENCE

1. Nonaudit Services

Sarbanes-Oxley amends the 1934 Act, to prohibit a registered public accounting firm (and its associated persons) from performing specified nonaudit services contemporaneously with an audit. These services are:

- Bookkeeping or other services relating to accounting or financial records
- Financial information systems design and implementation
- Appraisal or valuation services, fairness opinions or contribution in-kind reports
- Actuarial services
- Internal audit outsourcing services
- Management functions or human resources
- Broker or dealer, investment advisor, or investment banking services
- Legal services and expert services unrelated to the audit
- Any other service the PCAOB determines is prohibited

Sarbanes-Oxley requires preapproval by the audit committee of the public company for any nonaudit services, other than those just listed. Any such approval must be disclosed in the public company's periodic reports filed with the SEC.

A de minimus exception is provided for nonaudit services that do not exceed in the aggregate 5 percent of the total revenues paid by the public company to the auditor during the fiscal year, so long as such services are approved prior to the completion of the audit and such services were not recognized by the public company to be nonaudit services at the time of the engagement.

2. Audit Partner Rotation and Reports to Audit Committee

Sarbanes-Oxley mandates:

- Audit partner rotation on a five-year basis
- Each registered public accounting firm provide a report to the audit committee of the public company regarding critical accounting policies and practices utilized and the alternative treatment of financial information within generally accepted accounting principles (GAAP) discussed with management of the public company (as well as the ramifications of such treatment) and the treatment preferred by the registered public accounting firm

3. Conflicts of Interest

Sarbanes-Oxley prohibits a registered public accounting firm from performing statutorily mandated audit services for a public company if the public company's senior management officials had been employed by such firm and participated in the audit of that public company during the one-year period preceding the audit initiation date.

4. Study of Mandatory Rotation of Registered Public Accounting Firms

Sarbanes-Oxley requires the comptroller general to conduct a study of the effect of requiring mandatory rotation of registered public accounting firms.

C. ENHANCED CORPORATE GOVERNANCE REQUIREMENTS

1. Audit Committee Requirements

- Sarbanes-Oxley requires the SEC to adopt rules, no later than April 26, 2003, that direct the exchanges and Nasdaq to prohibit the listing of any security of a public company that does not meet these requirements.

- The audit committee of the public company's board of directors shall be directly responsible for the appointment, compensation, and oversight of the work of the company's independent auditors (including the resolution of disagreements between management and the auditors related to financial reporting).

- The independent auditors report directly to the audit committee.

- Each member of the audit committee is independent, which means, subject to any exceptions that the SEC may provide for, that: (i) no audit committee member shall accept consulting advisory or other compensatory fees from the public company; and (ii) no audit committee member shall be an affiliated person of the public company or any subsidiary.

- The audit committee shall establish procedures for: (i) the receipt, retention, and treatment of complaints received by the public company regarding accounting, internal accounting controls, or auditing matters; and (ii) the confidential, anonymous submission by employees of the company of concerns regarding questionable accounting or auditing matters.

- The audit committee has the authority to engage independent counsel and other advisors.

- The public company shall provide funding as determined by the audit committee for payment to the independent auditors and other advisors employed by the audit committee.

The SEC is required to adopt rules, no later than January 26, 2003, requiring each public company to disclose whether or not, and if not the reasons therefore, the audit committee does not have at least one member who is a "financial expert."

In determining the definition of "financial expert," the SEC must take into consideration whether the applicable audit committee member through his or her education and experience as a public accountant, auditor, principal financial officer, controller, or principal accounting officer or similar position has: (i) an understanding of GAAP and financial statements; (ii) experience in the preparation or auditing of financial statements of comparable public companies and the application of such principles in connection with the accounting for estimates, accruals, and reserves; (iii) experience with internal accounting controls; and (iv) an understanding of audit committee functions.

2. Prohibition on Loans to Insiders

Sarbanes-Oxley prohibits any public company from, directly or indirectly, extending or maintaining credit, arranging for the extension of credit, or renewing an extension of credit or a personal loan to any director or executive officer of a public company. Extensions of credit maintained as of July 30, 2002, are grandfathered under Sarbanes-Oxley provided that there is no material modification to any term or renewal on or after July 30, 2002. A limited exception to this prohibition exists for consumer credit and credit card loans made in the public company's ordinary course of business, loans by financial institutions subject to Federal Deposit Insurance Corporation (FDIC) regulations related to insider lending, as well as margin loans by broker/dealers (other than loans to purchase the public company stock).

D. CEO/CFO CERTIFICATIONS

1. Section 302 Certification Requirements

Sarbanes-Oxley requires the SEC to adopt rules no later than August 29, 2002, that would require each of the principal executive officer (CEO) and the principal financial officer (CFO) of every public company to certify in each annual or quarterly report that:

- The officer has reviewed the report.
- Based on the officer's knowledge, the report does not contain any untrue statement of a material act or omit to state a material fact necessary in order to make the statements made, in light of the circumstances under which such statements were made, not misleading.
- Based on such officer's knowledge, the financial information included in the report fairly presents in all material respects the financial condition and results of operations of the company as of, and for, the periods presented in the report.

The certification must also state that the signing officers:

- Are responsible for establishing and maintaining internal controls
- Designed such internal controls to ensure that material information relating to the public company and its consolidated subsidiaries is made known to such officers by others within those entities, particularly during the period in which the periodic reports are being prepared
- Evaluated the effectiveness of the public company's internal controls as of a date within 90 days prior to the report
- Presented in the report their conclusions about the effectiveness of their internal controls based on their evaluation as of that date

The signing officers must also certify that they have:

- Disclosed to the public company's independent auditors and audit committee: (i) all significant deficiencies in the design or operation of internal controls that could adversely affect the company's ability to record, process, summarize, and report financial data and have identified for its public company's auditors any material weaknesses in internal controls; and (ii) any fraud, whether material or not, that involves management or other employees who have a significant role in the public company's internal controls

- Reported whether or not there were significant changes in internal controls or other factors that could significantly affect internal controls subsequent to the date of their evaluation, including any corrective actions taken with regard to significant deficiencies and material weaknesses

2. Independent Auditor Assessment

Sarbanes-Oxley requires independent auditing firms to attest to and report on the assessment made by the public company's management regarding the effectiveness of the public company's internal controls for financial reporting. Attestation rules will be adopted by the PCAOB, as described, at some future date.

3. Section 906 Certification

In addition, effective July 30, 2002, Section 906 of Sarbanes-Oxley requires that the CEOs and CFOs of public companies must each provide a written statement to accompany any periodic report filed with the SEC on or after July 30, 2002, certifying that:

(i) The report fully complies with the requirements of Section 13(a) or 15(d) of the 1934 Act.
(ii) Information contained in the report fairly presents, in all material respects, the financial condition and results of operations of the company.

Any CEO or CFO who provides the Section 906 certification: (i) knowing that the report does not meet those two standards can be fined up to $1.0 million, imprisoned for up to 10 years, or both; or (ii) willfully provides the certification knowing that the report does not meet those two standards can be fined up to $5 million, imprisoned for up to 20 years, or both.

4. Considerations Related to Internal Controls

Given the extensive nature of the certifications required to be filed, consideration should be given to the following, as the SEC is required to adopt rules related to this certification by August 29, 2002:

- Establishment and maintenance of internal controls
- Review and evaluation of existing internal controls to determine whether material information is made known to management prior to filing periodic reports and appropriate adjustments made to such controls to achieve this goal. (The certification requires this evaluation be performed within 90 days of filing.)

- Establishment of a method and/or procedures to disclose to the independent auditors and the audit committee significant deficiencies in controls and any fraud as well as changes in internal controls, including corrective actions taken

E. ENHANCED DISCLOSURE REQUIREMENTS

1. Financial Disclosure Requirements

- Sarbanes-Oxley amends Section 13 of the 1934 Act to require that each report that is filed with the SEC that contains financial statements be prepared in accordance with GAAP and reflect all material correcting adjustments that have been identified by the independent accountants in accordance with GAAP and related SEC rules.
- Sarbanes-Oxley requires the SEC to adopt rules no later than January 26, 2003, that require:

  (i) Each annual and quarterly report filed with the SEC include disclosure regarding all material off-balance sheet transactions, arrangements, obligations (including contingent obligations), and other relationships of the company with unconsolidated entities or persons that may have a material current or future effect on the public company's financial condition, changes in financial condition, results of operations, liquidity, capital expenditures, capital resources, or significant components of revenues or expenses

  (ii) Pro forma financial information included in any periodic or other report filed with the SEC or in any public disclosure, including press releases, be presented in a manner that: (1) does not contain an untrue statement of a material fact or omit to state a material fact necessary in order to make the pro forma financial information, in light of the circumstances under which it is presented, not misleading; and (2) reconciles the pro forma information with the financial condition and results of operations of the public company under GAAP

2. Section 16 Disclosure Requirements

(a) Shortened Time Period for Filing Section 16 Reports   Effective August 29, 2002, directors, officers, and 10 percent beneficial owners of public companies are required to file Form 4 reports to reflect changes in their beneficial ownership, including changes resulting from a security-based swap, no later than two business days following the day on which the transactions occurred. The SEC by rule may provide for exceptions to the two-day requirement. This new accelerated filing requirement will necessitate public companies to require directors and officers to notify the public company and preclear purchases and sales of company securities prior to the execution of the transaction.

(b) Mandated Filing of Section 16 Reports via EDGAR   Effective July 30, 2003, Section 16 reports will be required to be filed via EDGAR (an SEC searchable

database) and posted on the public company's Web site not later than the end of the business day following the filing.

3. Internal Control Report

Sarbanes-Oxley requires the SEC to adopt rules at an unspecified future date that would require public companies to disclose in their annual reports an internal control report that would: (i) state the responsibility of management for establishing and maintaining an adequate internal control structure and procedures for financial reporting; and (ii) contain an assessment, as of the end of the most recent fiscal year of the company, of the effectiveness of the internal control structure and procedures of the company for financial reporting. As previously noted, each registered public accounting firm that prepares or issues the audit report for the issuer must attest to, and report on, the assessment made by management of the effectiveness of the internal control structure and procedure of the company for financial reporting, in accordance with standards for attestation engagements adopted by the PCAOB.

4. Disclosure of Adoption of and Changes in Code of Ethics

Sarbanes-Oxley requires the SEC to adopt rules no later than January 26, 2003 that would require public companies to disclose whether or not, and if not the reasons therefore, the public company has adopted a code of ethics for senior financial officers. Senior financial officers include the public company's principal financial officer, controller, or principal accounting officer or other persons performing similar functions.

The SEC is required to amend its Form 8-K disclosure requirements to provide for the immediate disclosure in a Form 8-K as well as dissemination by electronic means of a public company's change or waiver of the financial officer's code of ethics.

5. Real-Time Disclosure

Each public company is required to disclose on a current basis and in plain English any additional information regarding material changes in such company's financial condition or operations, including any trend and qualitative information as the SEC may require by rules adopted at some unspecified future date.

F. ENHANCED SEC REVIEW OF PUBLIC COMPANY REPORTS

Sarbanes-Oxley requires the SEC to review reports by "publicly traded" companies no less frequently than every three years, the scheduling of which shall take into consideration: (i) public companies that have issued material restatements of financial results; (ii) public companies that experience significant volatility in their stock price as compared to other companies; (iii) public companies with the largest market capitalization; (iv) emerging companies with disparities in price to earning ratios; (v) public companies whose operations significantly affect any material sector of the economy; and (vi) any other facts that the SEC may consider relevant.

G. ATTORNEY RULES OF PROFESSIONAL RESPONSIBILITY

Sarbanes-Oxley requires the SEC to adopt rules by January 26, 2003 that set forth minimum standards of professional conduct for attorneys who practice before the SEC, which would include requiring the attorney to report evidence of material violations of securities law or breaches of fiduciary duty or similar violations by the public company or any of its agents: (i) to the company's CEO or chief legal officer; and (ii) to the audit committee (or similar independent committee) of the board of directors of the public company, or the board of directors if the chief legal officer or CEO does not appropriately respond to the evidence.

H. PROHIBITION ON INSIDER TRADING DURING BENEFIT PLAN BLACKOUT PERIODS

Sarbanes-Oxley prohibits directors and executive officers from purchasing or selling any equity security of the company acquired in connection with his or her employment during any "blackout period." Subject to certain exceptions, a "blackout period" means any period of more than three consecutive business days in which the ability of 50 percent or more of the participants of the company's "individual account plans" to buy or sell equity securities of the company in such plans is temporarily suspended. Sarbanes-Oxley requires that effective January 26, 2003, companies provide notice of such blackout periods to directors and executive officers as well as to the SEC. Profits realized on prohibited trades must be disgorged to the company, and shareholders may bring derivative suits to enforce this penalty.

Additional requirements of Sarbanes-Oxley including amendments to the Employee Retirement Income Security Act (ERISA) and other employee benefits–related changes will be the subject of a separate corporate alert specifically detailing those requirements.

I. CORPORATE AND CRIMINAL FRAUD ACCOUNTABILITY

1. Prohibitions

Sarbanes-Oxley provides for a new act titled "Corporate and Criminal Fraud Accountability Act of 2002" (the CCFA Act), which amends federal criminal law to:

- Prohibit any person from knowingly altering, destroying, mutilating, concealing, covering up, falsifying or making a false entry in any records with the intent to impede, obstruct or influence an investigation in a matter within the jurisdiction of any federal agency or under any federal bankruptcy case.

- Prohibit an auditor from knowingly or willfully failing to maintain for a five-year period all audit or review work papers pertaining to a public company. Although it is a crime not to maintain such work papers for at least five years, Sarbanes-Oxley requires auditors to maintain work papers for seven years.

2. Bankruptcy Law Amendments

The CCFA Act amends the Federal Bankruptcy Code to make nondischargeable in bankruptcy certain debts that result from a violation relating to federal or state securities laws or common law fraud, deceit, or manipulation in connection with the sale or purchase of securities. The amended section of the Bankruptcy Code applies only to individual debtors and not to corporations or partnerships.

Since the securities laws apply to securities of privately held companies as well as publicly held companies, individuals violating the securities laws will be subject to this restriction irrespective of whether the securities are issued by a company that is registered under the 1934 Act. It should be noted that a violation of the securities laws can occur as a result of technical violations of registration provisions, broker dealer regulations, margin rules, and so on, and the language does not appear to be confined to securities fraud rules, even though that is the title of the applicable section of Sarbanes-Oxley.

3. Judicial Code Amendments

The CCFA Act amends the federal judicial code to permit a private right of action for a securities fraud claim to be brought not later than the earlier of: (i) five years after the violation; or (ii) two years after discovery of the facts constituting the violation.

4. Sentencing Guideline Amendments

The CCFA Act directs the United States Sentencing Commission to review and amend federal sentencing guidelines to ensure that the offense levels, existing enhancements, and/or offense characteristics are sufficient to deter and punish violations involving obstruction of justice, criminal fraud, fraud, and other crimes taking into account the number of victims and otherwise are sufficient to deter and punish that activity.

5. Prohibition against Retaliation

The CCFA Act prohibits a public company from discharging or otherwise discriminating against an employee because of any lawful act done by the employee to:

- Assist in an investigation by federal regulators, Congress, or supervisors regarding any conduct that the employee reasonably believes constitutes a violation of securities laws, SEC violations, or securities fraud.
- File or participate in a proceeding relating to fraud against shareholders. This provision became effective upon enactment of the CCFA.

J. WHITE-COLLAR CRIMINAL PENALTY ENHANCEMENTS

1. Attempts and Conspiracies to Commit Criminal Fraud

Sarbanes-Oxley provides that attempts and conspiracies to commit violations of mail fraud statutes will be subject to the same penalties as would apply to the actual violation.

2. Criminal Penalties for Mail and Wire Fraud

Sarbanes-Oxley increases the maximum prison sentence for mail and wire fraud from 5 years to 20 years.

3. Increased Criminal Penalties for ERISA Violations

Sarbanes-Oxley increases criminal penalties for violation of reporting and disclosure requirements under ERISA. Fines or penalties against individuals may now be up to $100,000 or 10 years in prison. Fines against corporations may now be up to $500,000.

4. Sentencing Guidelines

Sarbanes-Oxley directs the U.S. Sentencing Commission, no later than January 26, 2003, to review and, as appropriate, amend the federal sentencing guidelines and related policy statements to implement Sarbanes-Oxley's criminal penalty provisions.

5. Establishment of Fund for the Benefit of Victims of Securities Violations

The SEC was authorized to establish and administer a disgorgement fund for the benefit of victims of securities law violations. If the SEC obtains an order requiring disgorgement against any person, or an agreement related to disgorgement for violating the securities laws or regulations or a civil penalty, the disgorgement or penalty shall become part of the disgorgement fund for the benefit of victims of the violation.

K. CORPORATE FRAUD/ACCOUNTABILITY

1. Alteration of Documents

Sarbanes-Oxley makes the knowing destruction, alteration, concealment, or falsification with the intent to impede, obstruct, or influence official investigations or proceedings punishable by fines and imprisonment of up to 20 years, or both.

2. Improper Influence on Conduct of Audits

Sarbanes-Oxley makes it unlawful for any officer or director of a public company or any other person acting on their behalf to take any action to fraudulently influence, coerce, manipulate, or mislead any independent auditor auditing the company's financial statements for the purpose of rendering the financial statements materially misleading. The SEC is required to adopt final rules for implementing this prohibition not later than April 26, 2003.

3. Forfeiture of Certain Bonuses and Profits

If a public company is required to restate its financial statements due to material noncompliance with any financial reporting requirements imposed by the securities laws, as a result of misconduct, Sarbanes-Oxley requires that the CEO and CFO reimburse the public company for any bonus or other incentive-based compensation received by that person during the 12-month period following the first public issuance or filing with the SEC (whichever first occurs) of the financial document embodying such financial reporting requirement and any profits realized from the sale of securities of the company during that 12-month period.

4. Temporary Freezes of Payments to Officers, Directors, and Other Employees

When it appears likely to the SEC, during the course of a lawful investigation, that a company is about to make extraordinary payments to officers, directors, other employees, or agents, the SEC may petition a federal court for a temporary order requiring that the payments be placed in escrow under court supervision in an interest-bearing account for 45 days. The temporary order may be issued only after notice and opportunity for a hearing, unless the court determines that notice and hearing would be impracticable and contrary to the public interest. The period of time for which funds may be held in escrow may be increased by up to 45 additional days (for a total of 90 days) on order of the court for good cause shown. However, if the company is charged with a securities law violation before the funds are released from escrow, the escrow will continue until the conclusion of any related legal proceedings, subject to court approval.

5. Sentencing Commission Review

Sarbanes-Oxley requires the U.S. Sentencing Commission to review sentencing guidelines applicable to securities and accounting fraud and related offenses and consider promulgation of amendments by January 26, 2003, to provide an enhancement for officers and directors of publicly traded corporations who commit fraud and related offenses under detailed standards.

6. Prohibitions on Securities Law Violators Serving as Officers and Directors

Sarbanes-Oxley authorizes the SEC to prohibit persons who are the subject of a cease and desist order under either the 1933 Act or the 1934 Act from serving as officers or directors of any public company if the person's conduct demonstrates unfitness to serve.

7. Increased Penalties for 1934 Act Violations

Sarbanes-Oxley increased the maximum penalties for individuals who willfully violate any provision of the 1934 Act to $5 million from $1 million and imprisonment of up to 20 years from 10. The maximum penalty for corporate violations was increased to $25 million from $2.5 million.

8. Retaliation against Informants

Current criminal statutes impose criminal penalties on any person who kills or causes bodily injury to witnesses, victims, or informants in official proceedings. Sarbanes-Oxley now imposes penalties on any person, intending to retaliate, by taking any action harmful to any other person, including interference with the lawful employment or livelihood of the person, for providing to a law enforcement officer any truthful information relating to the SEC or possible commission of any federal offense. Penalties for violations of these provisions of Sarbanes-Oxley include imprisonment of up to 10 years.

L. EXTENSION OF STATUTE OF LIMITATIONS FOR PRIVATE ACTIONS

Sarbanes-Oxley extends the statute of limitations for a private right of action that "involves a claim of fraud, deceit, manipulation, or contrivance in contravention of a regulatory requirement concerning the securities laws," as defined in the 1934 Act to the earlier of two years after discovery of facts or five years after the occurrence of the alleged violation (versus the current one-year and three-year rule, respectively). The change applies to all actions that are commenced on or after July 30, 2002. Arguably, the effect of this provision is to extend the statute of limitations for prior acts of securities fraud so long as the suit has not been filed to date.

M. ANALYST CONFLICTS OF INTEREST

Sarbanes-Oxley requires the SEC or, upon the direction of the SEC, the exchanges and Nasdaq to adopt by July 30, 2003, rules designed to address conflicts of interest that arise when securities analysts "recommend" securities.

N. SENSE OF THE U.S. SENATE REGARDING TAX RETURNS

Sarbanes-Oxley states that it is the sense of the U.S. Senate that the federal income tax return of a company, regardless of whether the company is a public company, should be signed by the CEO of such company.

Risk Assessment Chart under Auditing Standard No. 2

This risk assessment chart was provided by Accume and derives from these paragraphs from Auditing Standards No. 2 of the Public Company Accounting Oversight Board (PCAOB):

65. When deciding whether an account is significant, it is important for the auditor to evaluate both quantitative and qualitative factors, including the:

- Size and composition of the account;
- Susceptibility of loss due to errors or fraud;
- Volume of activity, complexity, and homogeneity of the individual transactions processed through the account;
- Nature of the account (for example, suspense accounts generally warrant greater attention);
- Accounting and reporting complexities associated with the account;
- Exposure to losses represented by the account (for example, loss accruals related to a consolidated construction contracting subsidiary);
- Likelihood (or possibility) of significant contingent liabilities arising from the activities represented by the account;
- Existence of related party transactions in the account; and
- Changes from the prior period in account characteristics (for example, new complexities or subjectivity or new types of transactions) . . . .

72. Different types of major classes of transactions have different levels of inherent risk associated with them and require different levels of management supervision and involvement. For this reason, the auditor might further categorize the identified major classes of transactions by transaction type: routine, nonroutine, and estimation.

- Routine transactions are recurring financial activities reflected in the accounting records in the normal course of business (for example, sales, purchases, cash receipts, cash disbursements, payroll).
- Nonroutine transactions are activities that occur only periodically (for example, taking physical inventory, calculating depreciation expense, adjusting for foreign currencies). A distinguishing feature of nonroutine transactions is that data involved are generally not part of the routine flow of transactions.
- Estimation transactions are activities that involve management judgments or assumptions in formulating account balances in the absence of a precise means of measurement (for example, determining the allowance for doubtful accounts, establishing warranty reserves, assessing assets for impairment)."

Risk Rating Legend

No Risk or N/A	0
Low	1
Medium Low	2
Medium	3
Medium High	4
High	5

Relative Risk Score

Low	=	0 to 150
Medium	=	150 to 300
High	=	300 to 500

Qualitative Risk Factors	Estimation	Routine/ Nonroutine	Automatic/ Manual	Accounting/ Reporting Complexity	Fraud Risk	Complexity/ Homogeneity	Nature of Accounts	Potential Contingencies	Related Party Risk	Total Weight
Weights	20	10	10	10	10	10	10	10	10	100
Significant Accounts										
Cash										
Rating	0	3	3	1	4	3	2	1	0	
Relative Risk Score	0	30	30	10	40	30	20	10	0	170
Accounts Receivable										
Rating	0	5	2	4	4	4	5	2	4	
Relative Risk Score	0	50	20	40	40	40	50	20	40	300
Accounts Receivable Reserve										
Rating	4	3	4	3	4	4	4	1	3	
Relative Risk Score	80	30	40	30	40	40	40	10	30	340
Marketable Securities										
Rating	0	4	4	4	4	4	2	1	2	
Relative Risk Score	0	40	40	40	40	40	20	10	20	250
Prepaid Expenses and Other										
Rating	2	2	3	2	2	2	3	0	2	
Relative Risk Score	40	20	30	20	20	20	30	0	20	200
Fixed Assets										
Rating	1	3	4	2	1	1	1	1	1	
Relative Risk Score	20	30	40	20	10	10	10	10	10	170
Goodwill										
Rating	4	5	5	4	1	3	2	1	3	
Relative Risk Score	80	50	50	40	10	30	20	10	30	320

Qualitative Risk Factors	Estimation	Routine/ Nonroutine	Automatic/ Manual	Accounting/ Reporting Complexity	Fraud Risk	Complexity/ Homogeneity	Nature of Accounts	Potential Contingencies	Related Party Risk	Total Weight
Weights	20	10	10	10	10	10	10	10	10	100
Significant Accounts										
Intangibles										
Rating	4	5	5	4	1	3	2	1	3	
Relative Risk Score	80	50	50	40	10	30	20	10	30	320
Other Assets										
Rating	2	3	3	3	1	3	1	1	3	
Relative Risk Score	40	30	30	30	10	30	10	10	30	220
Ownership Interests										
Rating	3	4	3	4	2	3	3	2	3	
Relative Risk Score	60	40	30	40	20	30	30	20	30	300
Notes Receivable										
Rating	4	3	3	1	1	1	1	1	5	
Relative Risk Score	80	30	30	10	10	10	10	10	50	240
Accounts Payable										
Rating	1	3	3	2	3	3	1	3	3	
Relative Risk Score	20	30	30	20	30	30	10	30	30	230
Accrued Liabilities										
Rating	2	3	4	2	3	3	1	4	3	
Relative Risk Score	40	30	40	20	30	30	10	40	30	270
Deferred Revenue										
Rating	4	4	4	5	1	4	3	1	0	
Relative Risk Score	80	40	40	50	10	40	30	10	0	300

(continued)

Qualitative Risk Factors		Estimation	Routine/ Nonroutine	Automatic/ Manual	Accounting/ Reporting Complexity	Fraud Risk	Complexity/ Homogeneity	Nature of Accounts	Potential Contingencies	Related Party Risk	Total Weight
Weights		20	10	10	10	10	10	10	10	10	100
Significant Accounts											
Debt											
	Rating	0	3	3	2	1	2	1	1	2	
	Relative Risk Score	0	30	30	20	10	20	10	10	20	150
Other Liabilities											
	Rating	1	3	3	2	1	2	1	1	2	
	Relative Risk Score	20	30	30	20	10	20	10	10	20	170
Equity											
	Rating	0	1	2	4	1	2	1	0	2	
	Relative Risk Score	0	10	20	40	10	20	10	0	20	130
Revenue—Product											
	Rating	2	5	3	5	3	4	3	3	0	
	Relative Risk Score	40	50	30	50	30	40	30	30	0	300
Revenue—Service											
	Rating	5	4	3	5	1	4	2	1	0	
	Relative Risk Score	100	40	30	50	10	40	20	10	0	300
Cost of Sales—Product											
	Rating	2	5	2	5	3	5	4	2	0	
	Relative Risk Score	40	50	20	50	30	50	40	20	0	300
Cost of Sales—Service											
	Rating	4	4	3	5	1	4	4	1	0	
	Relative Risk Score	80	40	30	50	10	40	40	10	0	300

Risk Rating Legend

No Risk or N/A	0
Low	1
Medium Low	2
Medium	3
Medium High	4
High	5

Relative Risk Score

Low	=	0 to 150
Medium	=	150 to 300
High	=	300 to 500

Qualitative Risk Factors		Estimation	Routine/ Nonroutine	Automatic/ Manual	Accounting/ Reporting Complexity	Fraud Risk	Complexity/ Homogeneity	Nature of Accounts	Potential Contingencies	Related Party Risk	Total Weight
Weights		20	10	10	10	10	10	10	10	10	100
Significant Accounts											
S, G & A	Rating	0	1	2	2	3	1	2	3	2	
	Relative Risk Score	0	10	20	20	30	10	20	30	20	160
Amortization	Rating	1	3	2	3	0	3	1	0	0	
	Relative Risk Score	20	30	20	30	0	30	10	0	0	140
Impairment	Rating	5	5	4	4	0	4	2	0	2	
	Relative Risk Score	100	50	40	40	0	40	20	0	20	310
Impairment—Related Party	Rating	4	4	4	3	1	1	2	0	4	
	Relative Risk Score	80	40	40	30	10	10	20	0	40	270
Interest Expense	Rating	0	1	3	1	0	1	1	0	2	
	Relative Risk Score	0	10	30	10	0	10	10	0	20	90
Interest Income	Rating	0	1	2	1	0	1	1	0	0	
	Relative Risk Score	0	10	20	10	0	10	10	0	0	60

"Uncooking the Books: How Three Unlikely Sleuths Discovered Fraud at WorldCom"[1]

COMPANY'S OWN EMPLOYEES SNIFFED OUT CRYPTIC CLUES AND FOLLOWED HUNCHES—MRS. COOPER SAYS NO TO HER BOSS

BY SUSAN PULLIAM AND DEBORAH SOLOMON

Clinton, Mass.—Sitting in his cubicle at WorldCom Inc. headquarters one afternoon in May, Gene Morse stared at an accounting entry for $500 million in computer expenses. He couldn't find any invoices or documentation to back up the stunning number.

"Oh my God," he muttered to himself. The auditor immediately took his discovery to the boss, Cynthia Cooper, the company's vice president of internal audit. "Keep going," Mr. Morse says she told him.

A series of obscure tips last spring had led Ms. Cooper and Mr. Morse to suspect that their employer was cooking its books. Armed with accounting skills and determination, Ms. Cooper and her team set off on their own to figure out whether their hunch was correct. Often working late at night to avoid detection by their bosses, they combed through hundreds of thousands of accounting entries, crashing the company's computers in the process.

By June 23, they had unearthed $3.8 billion in misallocated expenses and phony accounting entries. It all added up to an accounting fraud, acknowledged by the company, that turned out to be the largest in corporate history. Their discoveries sent WorldCom into bankruptcy, left thousands of their colleagues without jobs and rolled the stock market.

At a time when dishonesty at the top of U.S. companies is dominating public attention, Ms. Cooper and her team are a case of middle managers who took their commitment to financial reporting to extraordinary lengths. As she pursued the

---

[1] Reprinted with permission from *The Wall Street Journal* from an article that appeared on October 30, 2002.

trail of fraud, Ms. Cooper time and again was obstructed by fellow employees, some of whom disapproved of WorldCom's accounting methods but were unwilling to contradict their bosses or thwart the company's goal.

WorldCom is under investigation by the Justice Department and the Securities and Exchange Commission. Scott Sullivan, WorldCom's former chief financial officer and Ms. Cooper's boss, has been indicted. He has denied any wrongdoing. Four other officers have pleaded guilty and are cooperating with prosecutors. Federal investigators are still probing whether Bernard J. Ebbers, the company's former chief executive, knew about the accounting improprieties. Since the initial discoveries, WorldCom's accounting misdeeds have grown to $7 billion.

Behind the tale of accounting chicanery lies the untold detective story of three young internal auditors, who temperamentally didn't fit into WorldCom's well known cowboy culture. Ms. Cooper, 38 years old, headed a department of 24 auditors and support staffers, many of whom viewed her as quiet but strongwilled. She grew up in a modest neighborhood near WorldCom's headquarters and had spent nearly a decade working at the company, rising through its ranks. She declined to be interviewed for this story. Mr. Morse, 41, was known for his ability to use technology to ferret out information. The third member of the team was Glyn Smith, 34, a senior manager under Ms. Cooper. In his spare time he taught Sunday school, took photographs and bicycled. His mom had taught him and Ms. Cooper accounting at Clinton High School.

Frightened that they would be fired if their superiors found out what they were up to, the gumshoes worked in secret. Even so, their initial discreet inquiries were stonewalled. Arthur Andersen, WorldCom's outside auditor, refused to respond to some of Ms. Cooper's questions and told her that the firm had approved some of the accounting methods she questioned. At another critical juncture in the trio's investigation, Mr. Sullivan, then the company's CFO, asked Ms. Cooper to delay her investigation until the following quarter. She refused.

Ms. Cooper's first inkling that something big was amiss at WorldCom came in March 2002. John Stupka, the head of WorldCom's wireless business, paid her a visit. He was angry because he was about to lose $400 million he had specifically set aside in the third quarter of 2001, according to two people familiar with the meeting. His plan had been to use the money to make up for shortfalls if customers didn't pay their bills, a common occurrence in the wireless business. It was a well-accepted accounting device.

But Mr. Sullivan decided instead to take the $400 million away from Mr. Stupka's division and use it to boost WorldCom's income. Mr. Stupka was unhappy because without the money, his unit would likely have to report a large loss in the next quarter.

Mr. Stupka's group already had complained to two Arthur Andersen auditors, Melvin Dick and Kenny Avery. They had sided with Mr. Sullivan, according to federal investigators.

But Mr. Stupka and Ms. Cooper thought the decision smelled funny, although not obviously improper. Under accounting rules, if a company knows it is not going to collect on a debt, it has to set up a reserve to cover it in order to avoid reflecting on its books too high a value for that business. That was exactly what Mr. Stupka had done. Mr. Stupka declined to comment.

Ms. Cooper decided to raise the issue again with Andersen. But when she called the firm, Mr. Avery brushed her off and made it clear that he took orders only from Mr. Sullivan, according to the investigators. Mr. Avery and Mr. Dick declined to comment. Patrick Dorton, a spokesman for Andersen, said his firm thought that the $400 million wireless reserve was not necessary.

"That was like putting a red flag in front of a bull," says Mr. Morse. "She came back to me and said, 'Go dig.' "

Some internal auditors would have left it at that and moved on. After all, both the company's chief financial officer and its outside accountants had signed off on the decision. But that was not Ms. Cooper's style. One favorite pastime among the auditors who reported to her was applying the labels of the Myers-Briggs & Keirsey personality test to their fellow staffers. Ms. Cooper was categorized as an INTJ—introspective, intuitive, a thinker and judgmental. "INTJs," according to the test criteria, are "natural leaders" and "strong-willed," representing less than 1% of the population.

And so Ms. Cooper decided to appeal the decision. As head of auditing, it was her responsibility to bring sensitive issues to the audit committee of WorldCom's board. She brought the reserves question to the attention of the committee's head, Max Bobbitt. At a committee meeting at the company's Washington offices on March 6, she and Mr. Sullivan backed down, according to people familiar with his decision.

The next day he tracked down Ms. Cooper. Unable to reach her immediately, Mr. Sullivan called her husband, a stay-at-home dad to their two daughters, to get her cellphone number. He finally caught up with her at the hair salon. In the future, she was not to interfere in Mr. Stupka's business, Mr. Sullivan warned, according to people familiar with the reserves question.

The confrontations put Ms. Cooper in a sticky position. Mr. Sullivan was her immediate supervisor. Plus, her vague discomfort with the way WorldCom was handling its accounting led her into areas that were not normally her bailiwick. Although her department did a small amount of financial auditing, it primarily performed operational audits, consisting of measuring the performance of World-Com's units and making sure the proper spending controls were in place. The bulk of the company's financial auditing was left to Arthur Andersen. But neither of those things dissuaded Ms. Cooper from following her nose to the root of the ill-defined problem.

A SURPRISE REQUEST

On March 7, a day after Ms. Cooper had visited with the audit committee, the SEC surprised the company with a "Request for Information." While WorldCom's closest competitors, including AT&T Corp., were suffering from a telecom rout and losing money throughout 2001, WorldCom continued to report a profit. That had attracted the attention of regulators at the SEC, who thought WorldCom's numbers looked suspicious.

But investigators had grown frustrated as they combed through public filings looking for evidence of wrongdoing, according to people familiar with the inquiry.

So they asked to see data on everything from sales commissions to communications with analysts.

Concerned about why the SEC was sniffing around, Ms. Cooper directed her group to start collecting information in order to comply with the request.

She also was growing concerned about another looming problem. Andersen was under fire for its role in the Enron case, which soon would lead to the accounting firm's indictment. It was clear that WorldCom would have to retain new outside auditors.

Ms. Cooper set off on an unusual course. Her own department would simply take on a role that no one at WorldCom had assigned it. The troubles at Enron and Andersen were enough to warrant a second look at the company's financials, she explained to Mr. Morse one evening as they walked out to WorldCom's parking lot. Her plan: her department would start doing financial audits, looking at the reliability and integrity of the financial information the company was reporting publicly.

It was a major decision, which would necessitate a lot more work for Ms. Cooper and her staffers. Still, Ms. Cooper took on financial auditing without asking permission from Mr. Sullivan, her boss, according to investigators and a person familiar with Ms. Cooper's decision.

"We could see a strain in her face," recalls her mother, Patsy Ferrell, about that time period. "She didn't look happy. We knew she was working late and some of the other people were working late. We would call and say, 'Can we bring some sandwiches?' and her father would bring them sandwiches."

A CURIOUS E-MAIL FROM AFAR

Several weeks later, Mr. Smith, a manager under Ms. Cooper, received a curious e-mail from Mark Abide, based in Richardson, Texas, who was in charge of keeping the books for the company's property, plants and equipment.

Mr. Abide had attached to his May 21 e-mail a local newspaper article about a former employee in WorldCom's Texas office who had been fired after he raised questions about a minor accounting matter involving capital expenditures. "This is worth looking into from an audit perspective," Mr. Abide wrote. Mr. Smith, who declined to be interviewed, forwarded the e-mail to Ms. Cooper, according to investigators and a lawyer involved in the case.

The e-mail piqued Ms. Cooper's interest. As part of their initial foray into financial auditing, Ms. Cooper and her team had already stumbled on to the issue of capital expenditures, a subject that would prove to be crucial to their quest.

The team had run into an inexplicable $2 billion that the company said in public disclosures had been spent on capital expenditures during the first three quarters of 2001. But they found that the money had never been authorized for capital spending.

Capital costs, such as equipment, property and other major purchases, can be depreciated over long periods of time. In many cases, companies spread those costs over years. Operating costs such as salaries, benefits and rent are subtracted from income on a quarterly basis, and so they have an immediate impact on profits.

Ms. Cooper and her team were beginning to suspect what was up with the mysterious $2 billion entry: It might actually represent operating costs shifted to capital expenditure accounts—a stealthy maneuver that would make the company look vastly more profitable.

When Ms. Cooper and Mr. Smith asked Sanjeev Sethi, a director of financial planning, about the curious adjustment, he told them it was "prepaid capacity," a term they had never heard before. Further inquiries led them to understand that prepaid capacity was a capital expenditure. But when they asked what it meant, Mr. Sethi told them to ask David Myers, the company's controller, according to Mr. Morse and a person familiar with Ms. Cooper's situation. Mr. Sethi did not return phone calls.

Ms. Cooper and Mr. Smith opted instead to call Mr. Abide, who had pointed out a capital expenditures problem in his e-mail. When they asked him about "prepaid capacity," he too answered very cryptically, explaining that those entries had come from Buford Yates, WorldCom's director of general accounting.

While perusing records looking for accounting irregularities later that same day, May 28, Mr. Morse made the big discovery of the $500 million in undocumented computer expenses. They also were logged as a capital expenditure. "This stinks," Mr. Morse recalls thinking to himself. He immediately went to Ms. Cooper to tell her what he'd found. She called a meeting of her department. "I knew it was a horrific thing and she did too, right off the bat," says Mr. Morse.

Several days later, Ms. Cooper and Mr. Smith met to try to make sense of their growing list of clues. Particularly puzzling were the cryptic comments made by Mr. Sethi and Mr. Abide. Finally the two auditors came up with a plan of action to test their sense that when it came to the booking of capital expenditures, something was very wrong at WorldCom. Ms. Cooper would send Mr. Smith an e-mail saying she wanted to know more about prepaid capacity as soon as possible, and asking how much harder they should press Mr. Sethi. They would copy Mr. Myers on the e-mail.

Mr. Myers shot back an e-mail. Mr. Sethi should be working for him and did not have time to devote to Ms. Cooper's inquiries, he wrote. Ms. Cooper had been stonewalled yet again.

A SECRET PLAN

Ms. Cooper and Mr. Smith didn't know it, but they had stumbled onto evidence that some executives were keeping two sets of numbers for the then-$36 billion company, one of them fraudulent.

By 2000, WorldCom had started to rely on aggressive accounting to blue the true picture of its badly sagging business. A vicious price war in the long-distance market had ravaged profit margins in the consumer and business divisions. Mr. Sullivan had tried to respond by moving around reserve, according to his indictment. But by 2001 it wasn't enough to keep the company afloat.

And so Mr. Sullivan began instructing Mr. Myers to take line costs, fees paid to lease portions of other companies' telephone networks, out of operating-expense accounts where they belonged and tuck them into capital accounts, according to Mr. Sullivan's indictment.

It was a definite accounting no-no, but it meant that the costs did not hit the company's bottom line—at least in the version of the books that were publicly scrutinized. Although some staffers objected, the scheme progressed for the next five quarters.

Ms. Cooper, Mr. Smith and Mr. Morse didn't know this. They only knew that accounting entries had been hopscotching inexplicably around WorldCom's balance sheets and that nobody wanted to talk about it. To put all the pieces together, they would need to plumb the depths of WorldCom's computerized accounting systems.

Full access to the computer system was a privilege that normally had to be granted by Mr. Sullivan. But Mr. Morse, a bit of a techie, had recently figured out a way around that problem.

Without explaining what he was up to, Mr. Morse had asked Jerry Lilly, a senior in manager in WorldCom's information technology department, for better access to the company's accounting journal entries. Mr. Lilly was testing a new software program and gave Mr. Morse permission to road test the system, too.

The beauty of the new system, from Mr. Morse's perspective, was that it enabled him to scrutinize the debit and credit sides of transactions. By clicking on a number for an expense on a spreadsheet, he could follow it back to the original journal entry—such as an invoice for a purchase or expense report submitted by an employee, to see how it had been justified.

Sifting through the data for answers to still-vague questions about capital expenditures amounted to a frustrating task, Mr. Morse says. He combed through an account labeled "intercompany accounts receivables," which contained 350,000 transactions per month. But when he downloaded the giant set of data, he slowed down the servers that held the company's accounting data. That prompted the IT staff to begin deleting this requests because they were clogging and crashing the system.

Mr. Morse began working at night, when there was less demand on the servers, to avoid having his work shut down by the IT department. During the day, he retreated to the audit library—a windowless, 12-by-12 room piled with files from previous projects and tucked away in the audit department—to avoid arousing suspicion.

By the first week of June, Mr. Morse had turned up a total of $2 billion questionable accounting entries, he says.

THE SLEUTHS GET NERVOUS

Having found the evidence they were looking for, the sleuths were suddenly faced with how serious the implications of their endeavor really were.

Mr. Morse grew increasingly concerned that others in the company would discover what he had learned and try to destroy the evidence, he says. With his own money, he went out and bought a CD burner and copied all the incriminating data into a CD-Rom. He told no one outside of internal audit what he had found.

Mr. Morse even kept his wife, Lynda, in the dark. Each night, he'd bring home documents he was studying. He instructed his wife not to touch his briefcase. His wife thought the usually gregarious father of three looked drained.

Ms. Cooper had begun confiding in her parents, with whom she was especially close. Without going into detail, she told her mother that she was worried about what her team was finding, and that it was definitely a very big deal, according to a person close to Ms. Cooper.

Meanwhile, Mr. Sullivan began to ask questions about what Ms. Cooper's team was up to. One day the finance chief approached Mr. Morse in the company cafeteria. When Mr. Morse saw him coming, he froze. The auditor had only spoken to Mr. Sullivan twice during his five-year tenure at WorldCom.

"What are you working on?" Mr. Morse later recalled Mr. Sullivan demanding. Mr. Morse looked at his shoes. "International capital expenditures," he says he replied, referring to a separate, and less-threatening auditing project. He quickly walked away.

Days later, on June 11, Ms. Cooper got an unexpected phone call from Mr. Sullivan. He told her that he would have some time later in the day, and invited her to come by and tell him what her department was up to, according to a person familiar with Ms. Cooper's situation.

When confronted, he admitted that he knew the accounting treatment was wrong, according to the memo. Mr. Myers said that he could go back and construct support for the entries but that he wasn't going to do that. Ms. Cooper then asked if there were any accounting standards to support the way the expenses were treated, according to the memo, which was later made public by a Congressional committee.

Mr. Myers answered that there were none. He said that the entries should not have been made, but that once it had started, it was hard to stop.

Mr. Smith asked how Mr. Myers planned to explain it all to the SEC. Mr. Myers replied that he hoped it wouldn't come to that, according to the memo.

An hour or so later, Ms. Cooper returned to her department to brief Mr. Morse and her other auditors, "They have no support," she told them, according to Mr. Morse.

It was clear to Ms. Cooper's team that their findings would be devastating for the company, and the prospect of going before the board with their evidence was sobering. They worried about whether their revelations would result in layoffs and obsessed about whether they were jumping to unwarranted conclusions that their colleagues at WorldCom were committing fraud. Plus, they feared that they would somehow end up being blamed for the mess.

Ms. Cooper's staffers began to notice that she was losing weight. Mr. Morse's wife noticed he was preoccupied and short tempered.

During the third week in June, Mr. Smith called his mother, who was vacationing in Albuquerque, according to a person familiar with the conversation. Without providing specifics, he told her that he was about to take actions at WorldCom that were not going to make people happy. He asked his mother, Ms. Cooper's former high school accounting teacher, to remember him in her prayers and to pray for him to he strong.

Ms. Cooper prepared for several meetings with the audit committee. At one, on June 20, Mr. Sullivan was scheduled to defend himself.

One evening, as Ms. Cooper worked late with accountants from KPMG, she suddenly dropped her head into her arms on the conference-room table. Mr.

Malone of KPMG led her onto a balcony, put his arm around her and showed her the sunset, according to a person familiar with the meeting.

Ms. Cooper, Mr. Smith and Mr. Malone headed to Washington to brief the board's audit committee. At the meeting on Thursday, June 20, Mr. Malone described the transfer of line costs to capital accounts and told the audit committee that, in his view, the transfers didn't comply with generally accepted accounting principles, according to a document WorldCom later submitted to the SEC.

That afternoon, Ms. Cooper, Mr. Smith and another auditor arrived at Mr. Sullivan's office. They talked about pending promotions and other administrative matters, according to lawyers involved in the case.

As the meeting was breaking up, Ms. Cooper turned to Mr. Smith and suggested that he tell Mr. Sullivan what he was working on. It was meant to seem like a casual comment. In fact, the two auditors had planned it out beforehand, so that they could gauge Mr. Sullivan's reaction, according to a person familiar with Ms. Cooper's situation.

Mr. Smith briefly described the audit, without going into the explosive material they already had found.

Mr. Sullivan urged them to delay the audit until after the third quarter, saying there were problems he planned to take care of with a write-down, according to several people familiar with the meeting.

Ms. Cooper replied that no, the audit would continue. Mr. Sullivan didn't respond, and the meeting ended in a stalemate.

Concerned now that Mr. Sullivan might try to cover up the accounting improprieties, Ms. Cooper and Mr. Smith appealed to Mr. Bobbitt, the head of WorldCom's audit committee. Mr. Bobbitt had to travel to Mississippi from his home in Florida for a board meeting scheduled for June 14, so the day before he met with Ms. Cooper and Mr. Smith at a Hampton Inn in Clinton.

The two auditors told Mr. Bobbitt what they had found. He asked Ms. Cooper to contact KPMG, the company's new outside auditors, and brief them on what was happening. Mr. Bobbitt did not raise Ms. Cooper's suspicions at the board meeting the next day, according to a document WorldCom later submitted to the SEC. James Sharpe, Mr. Bobbitt's lawyer, declined to comment.

Farrell Malone, the KPMG partner in charge of the WorldCom account, urged Ms. Cooper to make sure she was right.

On June 17, Ms. Cooper's team began a series of informal confrontations meant to convince themselves that there was no legal explanation for the accounting entries.

That morning, Ms. Cooper and Mr. Smith went to the office of Betty Vinson, director of management reporting, and asked her for documentation to support the capital-expense-accounting entries. Ms. Vinson told the two that she had made many of the entries but did not have any support for them, according to an internal memo prepared by Ms. Cooper and Mr. Smith. Ms. Vinson's lawyer did not return phone calls.

Next they walked a few feet to Mr. Yates' office. He said he was not familiar with the entries and referred Ms. Cooper and Mr. Smith to Mr. Myers.

The duo then paid a call on Mr. Myers.

Mr. Sullivan tried to give an explanation for the accounting adjustments but asked for more time to support the line-cost transfers. The committee gave Mr. Sullivan the weekend to explain himself. He got to work constructing what he called a white paper that argued that the accounting treatments he used were proper, according to the document.

It didn't work. On June 24, the audit committee told Mr. Sullivan and Mr. Myers they would be terminated if they didn't resign before the board meeting the next day. Mr. Sullivan refused and was fired. Mr. Myers resigned.

The next evening, WorldCom stunned Wall Street with an announcement that it had inflated profits by $3.8 billion over the previous five quarters.

Afterward, Ms. Cooper drove to her parents' house, which was near World-Com's headquarters. She sat down at the dining room table without saying anything, says Ms. Ferrell, her mother. "She was deeply, deeply pained. She was grief stricken that it was true and that all these people would feel the consequences of having gone astray," Ms. Ferrell says. "We were all so proud of WorldCom and it's just been the saddest, most tragic thing."

Mr. Morse worked late that night, and his wife phoned after she watched the news. The anchors were calling the company World-Con, she reported. Did he know anything about it?

The SEC on June 26 slapped the company with a civil fraud suit, and trading of WorldCom's stock was halted. Ultimately the company was delisted by the Nasdaq Stock Market.

Mr. Sullivan is preparing to go to trial. "We will demonstrate at the appropriate time that a number of the negative points that WorldCom's internal auditors have recently suggested about Mr. Sullivan are not accurate," says Irvin Nathan, a lawyer for Mr. Sullivan. "The fact is that he was always supportive of internal audit and was instrumental in the promotion of Cynthia Cooper and securing resources, for her staff."

Mr. Myers, Mr. Yates, Ms. Vinson and Troy Normand, the director of legal entity accounting, have all pleaded guilty to securities fraud and a variety of other charges. David Schertler, an attorney for Mr. Yates, says that while his client pleaded guilty, "all the evidence would suggest he was acting under the orders of supervisors."

Ms. Cooper and her team have continued to work at WorldCom's Clinton headquarters and are responding to requests related to the various Investigations of the company. Ms. Cooper, Mr. Smith and Mr. Morse have been interviewed by FBI agents in connection with the Justice Department's investigation.

Some WorldCom employees have told the auditors that they wish they had left the accounting issues alone.

Suggested Corporate Governance Web Site Resources

NEW YORK STOCK EXCHANGE CORPORATE GOVERNANCE RULES

Final rules: www.nyse.com/pdfs/finalcorpgovrules.pdf
303A Rulings: www.nyse.com/pdfs/section303A_final_rules.pdf
Proposed rule changes: www.nyse.com//regulation/construles/1098741855384.html

NASDAQ CORPORATE GOVERNANCE RULES

www.nasdaq.com/about/CorporateGovernance.pdf

SEC RULES

Auditor Independence Rules: www.sec.gov/rules/final/33-7919.htm
Disclosure Rules for Audit Committees: www.sec.gov/rules/final/34-42266.htm
Rule on Auditor Communication with Audit Committee: www.sec.gov/rules/final/
    33-8183.htm

PUBLIC COMPANY ACCOUNTING OVERSIGHT BOARD

www.pcaobus.org/

OTHER SELECTED WEB SITE RESOURCES

ASSOCIATION OF AUDIT COMMITTEE MEMBERS, INC.

www.aacmi.org

BUSINESS ROUNDTABLE

www.businessroundtable.org/

THE CONFERENCE BOARD

www.conference-board.org/

CORPORATE GOVERNANCE NETWORK

www.corpgov.net/

CORPORATE LIBRARY

www.thecorporatelibrary.com/

INSTITUTIONAL SHAREHOLDER SERVICES

www.issproxy.com

THE INTERNATIONAL CORPORATE GOVERNANCE NETWORK

www.icgn.org/

INVESTOR RESPONSIBILITY RESEARCH CENTER

www.irrc.org/

SOCIETY OF CORPORATE SECRETARIES
AND GOVERNANCE PROFESSIONALS

www.ascs.org/

Index

not-for-profit managers, excess benefits, 227
Sales department
    audit confirmations, 41
    bill and hold abuse, 40
    channel stuffing abuse, 40, 47–51, 188
    commissions, 38, 39
    expense reports, internal audit of, 40
    modification of contracts, 39
    return policies, 39, 40
    revenue recognition policies, 39
Sarafoglou, Kyriakie, Dr., 24, 25
Sarbanes-Oxley Act of 2002
    accounting policies and procedures, 180
    advisors, use of, 172, 185
    audit committee independence, 137, 138
    auditing firms, rotation of, 184
    auditors, selection of, 187
    certifications, 192, 193
    complaints, treatment of, 36, 189, 190
    and computer security, 123
    criminal liability, 3
    document preservation, 3, 46, 112, 113
    internal controls, 168, 169
    and IT corporate governance, 129
    nonaudit services prohibited, 203
    and not-for-profit businesses, 3
    personal loans, 20, 21, 171
    and private businesses, 3, 215
    provisions of, 237–250
    requirements of and "impractical" governance, 4, 5
    whistleblower protection. *See* Whistleblower protection
Scandals
    and audit committees, 65
    Cornell University Medical School, 3, 24, 25
    Enron. *See* Enron
    internal audit cost as "scandal insurance," 66
    nonprofits, 3, 223
    and outside auditors, 6
    and personal liability of directors, 6
    prevention of, 3
    and Sarbanes-Oxley, 3
    WorldCom. *See* WorldCom
Securities analysts, 170, 188
Securities and Exchange Commission (SEC)
    accounting policies and procedures, 180, 181
    audit committee
        independence rules, 138–143
        minimum responsibilities, 157
    board committee member rules, 92

compensation of officers' or directors' children, reporting, 37
disclosure committee, 193
disclosure rules
    for audit committees, 173
    for compensation committees, 84, 85
independent auditor, independence rules, 177, 201–211
IT corporate governance, 129, 130
IT general controls, 109
journaling, e-mail retention requirements, 113, 114
Regulation FD, 170
Regulation S-K, 169
rejection of "check-the-box" analysis, 5
retention of documents by auditor, 182, 183
Standards of Professional Conduct for Attorneys, 191, 192
Tyson Foods, Inc., 84
Web sites, 265
Securities Exchange Act of 1934, 201, 202
    auditor independence, 177
    control persons, 193, 194
Security, computer data. *See* Information technology (IT)
Self-evaluation
    audit committees, 173
    committee functions, 11, 12
Settlements, 172
Severance and retirement benefits, 80
Shareholders
    auditing firm, approval of, 186, 187
    communication with, 15
    directors as, 15
    election of directors, 22, 23
    and fiduciary duties of board, 26–27
    and insolvency of organization, 20
    reports to, 170
Small business. *See also* Private businesses
    Form 10-KSB, 140
    IT security practices, 125–129. *See also* Information technology (IT)
Smith v. Van Gorkom, 17, 28–30
Society of Corporate Secretaries and Governance Professionals, 266
Special committees, 96–103
Spitzer, Eliot, 83, 111, 115
State law
    civil and criminal liability, generally, 31
    constituency statutes, 27
    fiduciary duties. *See* Fiduciary duties
Statements of Accounting Standards (SAS)
    No. 22, inconsistencies and document retention, 183
    No. 99, honesty of management, 8